IN THE BEGINNING...

The story of The International Trade Cartel

RICHARD KELLY HOSKINS

Published by

Virginia Publishing Company
P. O. Box 997
Lynchburg, Virginia 24505
Phone 804-384-3261

Printed in the United States of America

First printing 1995

Library of Congress Catalog Card Number: 95-62062

ISBN 1-881867-04-8 15.00

Also by Richard Kelly Hoskins

OUR NORDIC RACE, 1958

ISBN 1-881867-00-5

Add'l printings 1961, 1961, 1962, 1964, 1966, 1975, 1986, 1994

One of the few histories of the White race still in print

76 p. sb

$5/copy plus $2 postage & handling ($5 overseas)

WAR CYCLES/PEACE CYCLES, 1985

ISBN 1-881867-01-3

Add'l printings 1985, 1986, 1991, 1994

History of usury and war. 250 p. sb, 5th printing

$15/copy plus $2 postage & handling ($5 overseas)

VIGILANTES OF CHRISTENDOM, 1990

ISBN 1-881867-02-1

The Story of the Phineas Priesthood, 472 p. H.B.

$20/copy plus $2 postage & handling ($5 overseas)

WOLF & THE SHEEP, 1993

ISBN 1-881867-03-X

The wolf's mannerisms and hunting techniques, 78 p.

$5 copy plus $2 postage & handling ($5 overseas)

HOSKINS REPORT Newsletter

Current events. $48/yr. - monthly (add $7 overseas)

PORTFOLIOS INVESTMENT ADVISORY

Since 1973

Economic Newsletter

$150/yr - monthly. (add $7 overseas)

Va. residents add 4 ½% sales tax

Introduction

The Merchant

PRIME DIRECTIVE: *The merchant must find a market for his goods."*

The historical geographical center of world trade is India. Its products - spices, gems and gold.

The King

The merchant must establish a king to protect him and promote his interests.

To ensure a constant supply of trade goods the merchant hires a king to protect and keep order in his trade markets. The king is a key part of the trade system called *feudalism*. Feudalism maximizes production. It assigns every man to a job which he becomes very good at performing. In time, feudalism caused maximized production which in time saturated Indian markets.

The Priest

Before The Merchant can trade in a market he must first secure the blessing of its god, or the people may kill him.

Feudalism's *over-production* forced Indian merchants to open markets in other lands. Often, the gods of these foreign nations were hostile, and they ordered their people to kill the Indian merchants. Being killed removes the profit from trade for the merchant. This is a very real problem to the trader. The problem with foreign gods was solved by the merchants of India developing a *trade-religion* and sending missionaries to take this religion and with it to change the minds of foreign gods - to make them more friendly and receptive to Indian merchants and their trade.

Buddhism's Dharma

The religion developed by the Indian missionaries to help their trade effort is called *Hinduism.* The missionary part of Hinduism is called Buddhism. Buddhist missionaries are charged with the basic work of changing the attitudes of the people who live in new markets from hostility to acceptance. This is done by teaching potential customers *Dharma* - "acceptance." Dharma changes hostile separatist religions into warm, friendly integrationist religions. The customer loses nothing. He keeps his own god, his own customs and rituals, and makes money. Dharma only asks that its customer- converts adopt two simple beliefs:

- (1) All gods are basically the same, and
- (2) Since all gods are basically the same, there is no reason not to tolerate all religions without regard to race, creed or national origin.

If a land targeted by the merchant learns these two simple concepts - "all gods are one" and "toleration;" it then follows that the land and its people will also accept the international merchant and his wares. The merchant and his wares must be "tolerated" before the trader can trade. This is why the Buddhist missionaries see to it that native Dharmatized churchmen living in targeted markets are provided with big houses and big cars. The missionary agents of Indian merchants spend tens of billions spreading Dharma - which in time returns hundreds of billions in trade profits. The Buddhist *missionary* and his converts among the native clergy must obtain customer good-will before the merchant can trade.

Media

The Merchant's media control customer attitudes to prevent rebellion against king, priests, and merchant.

Formerly, a steady flow of gifts to local dignitaries provided the goodwill needed to protect the merchant's interests. Later, the purchase of local media through native agents provided the same service. The media glorified the merchant's agent who was elected "king." Thus the merchant had his own king to rule his market. The merchant's media vilified the merchant's enemies and the people were taught to scorn them also. Priests who blessed the king and merchant were praised and their wealth increased. Priests who cursed the king and merchant were ignored and remained poor.

The Trader

India sold her products both to the Far East and the West. The ones who carried the products and operated the spice routes were the *traders.* These trade and transportation specialists gradually became a closed union. They developed their own rules, passwords, and customs. To protect themselves in lands not yet tolerant, they adopted the customs of the land, including the local religion. If the customers were tolerant, they openly practiced their own ancient trade-religion.

The Wholesaler

In the Far East, the Chinese emperor operated a closed franchise. He required that all spices, gold, and gems arriving from India be sold to the Empire, which in turn resold them through imperial outlets. The spice trade from India was an imperial monopoly. Because of the great profits to be gained, many smugglers attempted to secretly bring in goods in spite of the risk of losing their heads.

The effort to break the Imperial monopoly resulted in the rise of competing *war lords.* In time, internal dissension provided outsiders an opportunity to get part of the profits of the spice-trade. European war fleets gathered off the coasts of China. Western technology prevailed in the ensuing conflict between East and West and European nations occupied Chinese coastal cities and proceeded to distribute Indian goods, as well as their own. Chinese merchants selected by Western interests replaced the Chinese rulers.

In the West the early Indian trade franchise was operated by the Roman Empire. This franchise was continued by the *Roman Catholic Church* which also operated as a monopoly - a monopoly that has existed for more than a thousand years. Just as had happened in the Far East, the tremendous profits generated by the spice-trade monopoly brought competition from war lords in England, Germany, and Scandinavia who broke away from the Roman Catholic Church to compete with its trade monopoly. To regain this trade and secure markets in new lands, the Roman church sent out a cloud of Catholic *missionaries* called *Jesuits* to dispense Dharma. Protestant war lords sent a cloud of missionaries into Catholic lands and third world nations to do the same. Converts to either Protestantism or Catholicism supported the god of the missionary that had converted him - in both trade and war. Thus, the missionary was a very important instrument of state and trade policy in spite of the Christian prohibition against such things.[1] In Protestant lands *Dharma* was dispensed by newly created episcopal protestant churches whose priests had been appointed with the approval of the local war lord. The episcopal church in England was named the *Anglican Catholic Church;* the German and Scandinavian episcopal church was named the *Lutheran Church.*

Attempts by protestant Christians to reform the protestant state religions were dealt with by allowing them to establish state approved episcopal sects such as the "Methodist" in England

1 GOD'S LAW: "Go not unto the way of the Gentiles, and unto any city of the Samaritans enter ye not: But go rather to the lost sheep of the house of Israel." Matt 10:5-6; "I was sent to the lost sheep of the house of Israel, and to them alone." Matt 15:24

and "Reformed- Lutheran" in Germany. Keeping them episcopal took reform into harmless channels because it allowed the war lords to continue appointing ecclesiastics who approved their rule. The Catholic Church met the problem of reform by allowing the reformers to establish a new order. When the reformer died a new head of the reform order was appointed by the Catholic Church who was "conservative" and all was as it had been. The reform lasted for the life of the reformer.

The roving traders of the spice routes dispensed Dharma through their media monopoly. All parties, while intolerant of each other, were vitally interested in teaching potential customers to be tolerant of the trader and his wares.

Presbyterian

The protestant episcopal religion spawned a breakaway sect that was more difficult to handle. It was called presbyterian. Presbyterian was the type of organization - rather than belief. While episcopal prelates were appointed from the top down - presbyterian speakers and teachers were selected from the bottom up. They claimed to follow God whose commands were to be found in the Holy Scriptures. The teaching of the Holy Scriptures placed this group at odds with local rulers and with the International Trade Cartel composed of *merchants, traders, missionaries,* and *kings.* Strict adherence to the WORD resurrected the old Christian prohibition forbidding trade with strangers.[2] This impacted trade. Destroying trade was the reverse of what the episcopal church had been established to do. Establishment religion existed to open and expand trade markets - not close them. The establishment church was the natural enemy of those who followed the presbytery form of church government. Historically, the episcopal Protestant church treated these breakaway Protestant-presbyterians almost as brutally as did the Roman Catholics.

---

2 **"If thou has stricken thy hand with a stranger, thou art snared." Pr. 6:1; "Ye shall make no league with the inhabitants of this land." Judges 2:2; "Thou shall make no covenant with them." Deut 7:2**

The Contenders

There is much written about "The Great Conspiracy," the New World Order, and secret organizations of one kind or another. People are asking - what is the game and who runs it?

The answer is simple. The game is the same game that has always been played for the profits from international trade. The International Trade Cartel (ITC) is a confederation of international merchants, war lords and priests to monopolize international trade distribution. Their wholesalers are the great billionaire business barons of today. Their retailers are the Western corporations. The great battle is between the episcopacy of the ITC and the presbytery of people who refuse to accept their lot as "wage-slaves." The Christian speaks of the end time conflict between the WORD and Babylon as Armageddon.

Table of Contents

LIST OF CHARTS

Chapter 1

THE CARAVAN

The Caravan

In the Holy Land during the Wars of the Crusades, crusaders defended a seaport being besieged by Muslims. The siege had lasted almost a year. The fighting had been violent, many had died.

Suddenly, trumpets sounded. Instantly the fighting stopped. A camel train appeared, one camel plodding along in front of the next - a long line stretching back into the distance. The Arab armies parted; the gates to the city opened, the drawbridges dropped. One after another, camel after camel - an endless chain of camels plodded into the city. Two thousand of them.

It was a smaller camel train, all that was left of 20,000 animals that had arrived at a terminal city inland and had been divided into smaller trains and sent on to their final destinations. On the back of each animal rested a cargo so precious that it could have made a man rich for life - if he could but seize it. But few tried. Those who tried and failed were punished with a painful death.

Once in the city the camel drivers directed their charges through twisting, narrow streets down to the harbor. There their cargoes were off-loaded by sweating stevedores who re-loaded them on waiting Christian ships. Then, flying flags bearing the Christian cross, the ships set sail through the blockading Saracen fleet, which parted to let them pass. As soon as the last ship had departed, the Saracen ships re-established their blockade, the camels departed, the gates closed, the drawbridge raised, and arrows began to fly and large rocks again were catapulted against enemies as the fighting re-commenced.

How was it possible for both Christians and Saracens, enemies to the death, to suddenly stop their warfare and cooperate to protect and help the caravan owner taking his goods from the point of manufacture to the point of sale?

This is the same situation we have in the world today. It is a situation that takes careful planning and numerous private agreements. It can best be understood by telling the story of the wolf and the sheep.

First Problem - Unfriendly Gods

In order for a wolf to eat sheep he must first gain entry into the sheepfold. If he can't get into the sheepfold, he can't eat sheep.

His first major problem is to pass by the watchman to get into the sheepfold. If the watchman objects, this can be difficult, as shown in the following example of Josephus.

Josephus was the general in charge of putting Galilee in a state of defense against Roman invasion. The province desperately needed cooking oil. The Greek merchants nearby had abundant cooking oil for sale, but Josephus would not buy from strangers. Instead, he wrote the following letter to the authorities in Jerusalem:

> "Now I (Josephus) was entrusted with the public affairs there (in Galilee) by the people of Jerusalem ... since they had not oil ... (Jerusalem should) provide a sufficient quantity of such oil for them lest they should be forced to make use of oil that came from the Greeks, and thereby transgress their own laws." *Life of Flavius Josephus*, v13.

Josephus explained the reason for his stand so that it would be understood by the readers of his history:

> "Nor do we delight in merchandise, nor in such a mixture with other men as arises from it ... having a fruitful country for our habitation, we take pains in cultivating that only. Our principal care ... is ... to educate our children well; ... to observe the laws that have

> been given us ... Since ... there was no occasion offered us ... for intermixing among the Greeks, as they had had for mixing among the Egyptians, by their intercourse of exporting and importing their several goods; as they also mixed with the Phoenicians, who lived by the seaside, by means of their love of lucre in trade and merchandise." *Flavius Josephus Against Apion 1:12*

Josephus spoke of transgressing the Law. He was speaking of the Law of his God dealing with strangers. This Law nullified the statutes of Rome whose reason for existence was the trade profits to be gained with different nations and peoples. The Law of Israel caused foreign goods to lie unbought. This impacted business, cost taxes, and undermined the reason for the existence of the Roman Empire. These are some of the Laws:

> *"If thou has stricken thy hand with a stranger (Heb: zûwr - racial alien), thou art snared with the words of thy mouth." Pr. 6:1-2*

> *"They shall not dwell in thy land; and thou shall drive them out before thee." Ex 23:31.*

> *"They shall not dwell in thy land, lest they make thee sin against me." Ex 23:33.*

Laws such as these hindered trade. The God that demanded obedience to them was the prime enemy.

Second Problem - Protection

The second great problem that the wolf must overcome is the problem of rams angered by the violation of the Law. An aroused ram is a fearful animal. He can kill a wolf. If a wolf enters a sheepfold and the alarm is given by the watchman, the rams will surround the wolf and kill it in minutes. If the wolf enters the sheepfold with the permission of the watchman, he may still have to deal with upset rams who sense the wolf's presence. The wolf first needs permission and then he needs protection.

The problem of protection is solved when the wolf finds a ram whose greed transcends his loyalty to his God. The wolf uses his wealth to make that ram a powerful war lord - a king. As king he can then be an efficient bodyguard for the wolf.

A successful wolf must deal with both problems. He must first bribe the watchman, and then he must hire a king to be his bodyguard. Only then can the wolf safely enter the sheepfold and eat sheep.

When both of these problems were solved, the rich camel caravan was able to pass through the Saracen army into the besieged Christian city and load its goods onto Christian ships. This is why the Saracen fleet parted to let the Christian ships sail through unmolested. The merchant had persuaded the Saracen religious leader to let him pass. The mullahs told the Saracen Emir that Allah approved of the trade. The Saracen Emir told his army to let the caravans through - and they did.

Next, the merchant persuaded Christian priests to let the camels pass. The priests persuaded the Christian king that God found no fault in taking a bribe to let the camel train pass. The king instructed his army to allow the camels to pass - and they did.

Who is this mysterious merchant? Who is it that corrupts priests and kings - mullahs and emirs? Who is it that can put together gigantic camel trains of 20,000 camels, trains worth more than nations themselves, who in the middle of wars can command warring armies to be at peace with each other while their goods go to market to be sold for immense profits?

How were the merchants able to manipulate both kings and priests so effortlessly? Does someone know something that they are not telling?

You bet they do!

Chapter 2

TURKS

Roman Shops

When the Vandals invaded Rome, they discovered warehouses loaded with spices, silks, and expensive goods from the Far East.

Most Romans had only a vague idea of where these costly goods had come from. It was a trade secret. All they knew was that they had come from somewhere on the other side of the deserts beyond the borders of the Roman Empire. Those who knew didn't talk.

The thing that everyone understood was that a pound of pepper was worth a pound of gold. The spice trade delivered coveted goods, while bags and chests of gold and silver were returned in payment. Rome was drained of its gold and silver. Someone on the other side of the desert collected it. At the last, Rome had no gold and was forced to adopt the barter system. The spice merchants in the Far East owned the world's supply of gold. That gold allowed the spice merchants to buy anything that gold will buy - priests, kings, armies - anything!

Basic Geography - Deserts

There are four major deserts that run from the Atlantic in the west to the Pacific in the Far East. The Sahara runs the width of North Africa, with the Arabian Desert further to the east. To the east of that comes the Iraq-Iran Deserts, and still further to the east - the Gobi Desert to the north of China. An "Arab" could slip into the Sahara Desert within sight of the Atlantic

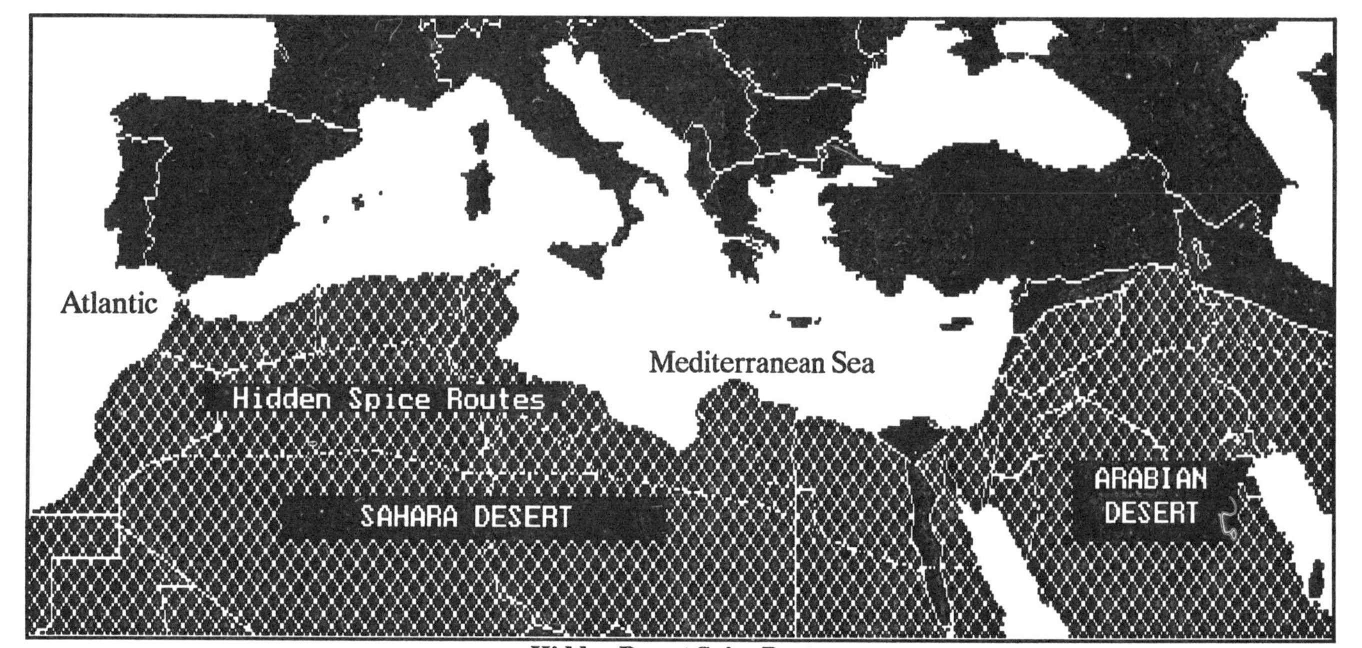

Hidden Desert Spice Routes

Long hidden from Western eyes, the spice routes carried goods worth billions of dollars. Thousands of camels reached terminal cities, paid a fee, and passed on to their destination. No one stopped them - Christian, Mohammedan, or Jew. Seizing camels was roundly condemned. Unseen, the spice merchant ruled the world through his agents. His caravans proceeded quietly - protected by the king and blessed by the priest.

Ocean in N. Africa and emerge in China without having been seen by anyone who was not like himself.

Individuals, groups, caravans, armies, and entire nations have disappeared into the deserts, and have followed this route in whole or part secure from the observation of Westerners. Westerners are always surprised at what emerges from these mysterious deserts.

The Desert Caravans

Camel caravans were massive, expensive affairs. In an age where the capture of a single camel would make an Arab rich for life - a train of 5,000 animals was ordinary, and 20,000, frequent. The goods had to be warehoused until shipping time and food had to be provided for both man and beast. Drivers and armed guards had to be arranged, and a paymaster had to pay "protection-money" to local rulers for safe conduct. Insurance agreements had to be arranged to guard against pilfering and the occasional caravan raid that captured a few camels. Messengers had to be dispatched ahead, advising outlets that trade goods were on the way. Schedules had to be met. Marshaling yards had to be ready to receive the thousands of camels and drivers, and then the goods had to be divided and new trains created to take the goods to their ultimate destinations. The details were endless - but worth it. The desert route hid its treasures from prying eyes and that alone provided relatively safe travel.

Local kings were paid to protect caravans. Part of the trade agreement between merchant and king was that the local ruler had to make good anything looted from the train while it was under his protection. This encouraged extra vigilance. All who profited from the spice trade had a vested interest in protecting it. They still do.

Marshaling Yards & Terminals

There were major marshaling yards - great trade centers such as Baghdad, Damascus, and Mecca. The city of Jerusalem was

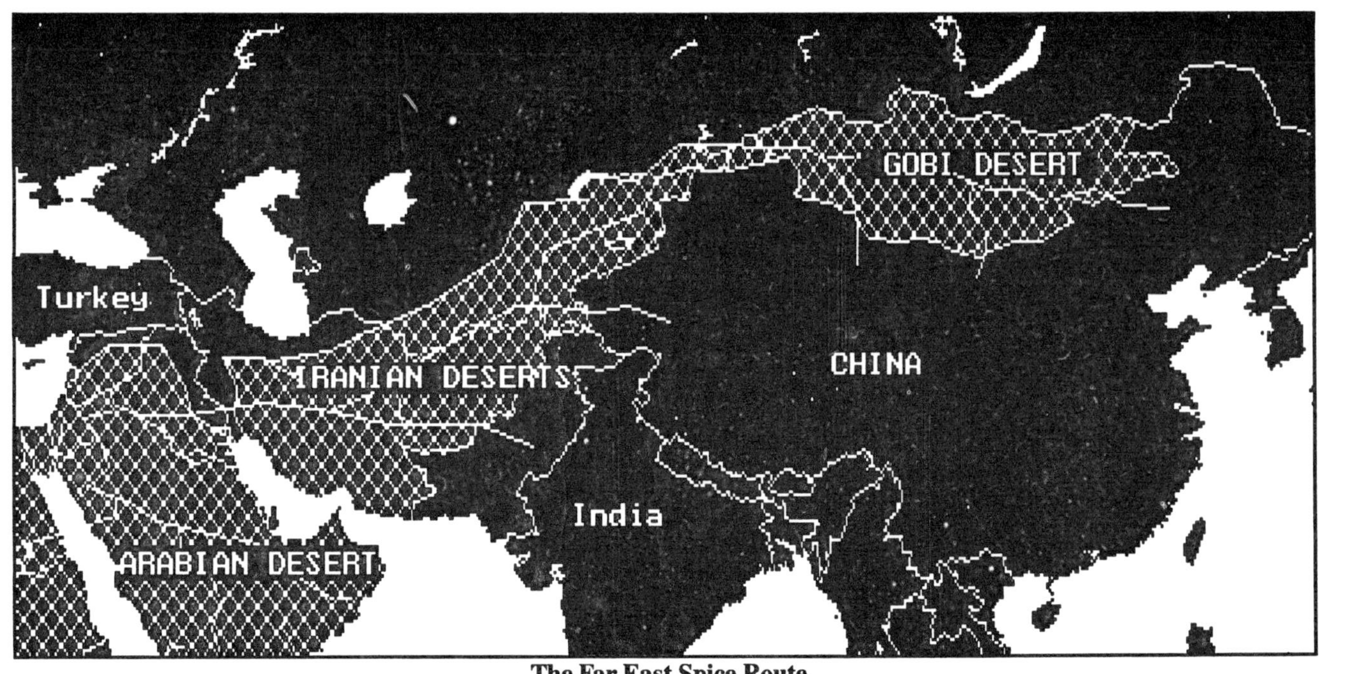

The Far East Spice Route

Marco Polo was the first to return to the West with fabulous stories of the spice routes and Cathay. No one believed him. It has ony been in relatively recent years as the overland desert route has been superseded by ocean routes that the knowledge of the trade routes has become public. This forbidden desert roadway is the historical super highway of the wandering Turk.

another - a fact of geography that helped launch the crusades. From these extensive marshaling yards smaller trains were re-routed to the seaports of Aden, Alexandria, Hifa, Beirut, and Istanbul.

History reveals that there is an international trade that operates during war or peace. It does whatever is necessary to perpetuate itself. It bribes priests and hires kings to allow its goods to enter forbidden markets. This trade emanates from a central place.

Arab-Turk Invasions

A recurring phenomenon is the periodic invasion of the world markets by the nomadic Turks who in other times have acted as international merchants. China has been invaded most often and once was completely conquered by the Mongol-Turks. China gave the Arab-Turk tribes their names based on the time of their invasions. India, the central exporting nation, has not been spared. It too has suffered many invasions and one time was completely subjected by the Moguls.

The many invasions of our own West capture our attention most closely. Note the map on the next page showing the Arab-Turk invasions. The natural state of these Arab-Turk tribes is that of continuous warfare among themselves. But, this has limits. In the past they have set aside their differences many times to form a joint effort to invade the West. Turkish tribes who are enemies today are tomorrow's allies. It's a fact that we dare not forget. It is history's wild card.

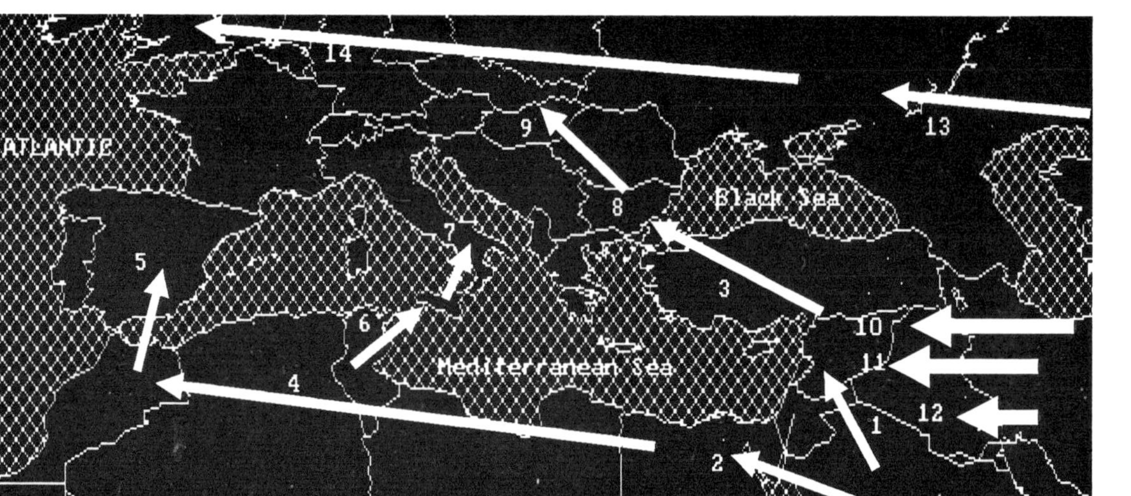

Arab-Turk Invasions:

Arabs poured out of Arabia into the Near East (1). They next invaded Egypt (2). Then they crashed through the defenses of the Byzantine Empire and annexed what is now Turkey (3). Failing to take Constantinople, they changed direction and poured across N. Africa (4) and invaded Spain (5). Failing in their effort to invade France, they invaded Sicily (6) and S. Italy (7). The Arabs, now called "Turks" - overwhelmed Constantinople and drove into Europe proper (8), where they were aided by the Huns of Hungary (early Arab invaders) (9) in their attack on Austria. Additional invaders - Seljuk-Turks (10), Ottoman Turks (11) and Mongols (12) added numbers at various times. The most recent and most successful is the Khazar-Turk invasion (13) which subdued Russia and smashed a German revolt. It is under their auspices that (14) today the Turks are flooding Italy, France, Germany, Britain, Scandinavia, America, S. Africa, and Australia in a massive, and thus far uncontested, continuation of the crusades.

Chapter 3

INDIA

Strategic Location

India lies midway between the world's two principal markets - China and the West. Historically, it occupies the most strategically important trading area in the world.

Products transported by Indian merchants journeying to and from China and to and from the West use the overland spice-route and the sea routes. India is the most important point of the East/West trade.

Indian Products

India's major export products are gold, jewels, and incense. These items are extremely profitable if sold in the proper markets.

Hindu Religion And Priests

Much of India's effort is directed toward developing markets - creating proper attitudes and conditions in foreign markets so that Indian products will be accepted there. India's religion, Hinduism, was created to change negative market attitudes into positive attitudes of acceptance. Unless foreign customers accept Indian products - no sales can be made.

To aid this change - the gods residing in lands that have been targeted as markets for Indian goods are added to the galaxy of Indian gods. Indian merchants say that they too worship the gods of the nation in which they wish to trade. India has collected thousands of gods in this manner and worships them all.

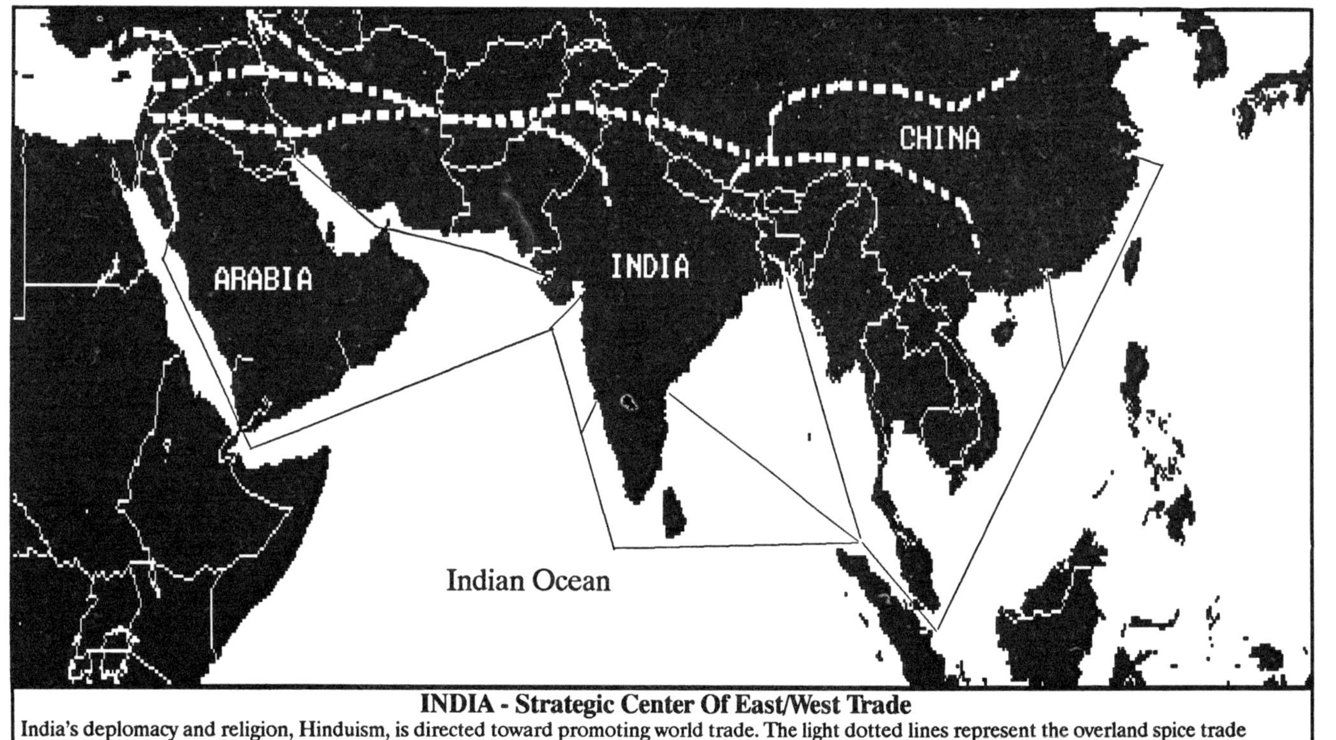

INDIA - Strategic Center Of East/West Trade

India's deplomacy and religion, Hinduism, is directed toward promoting world trade. The light dotted lines represent the overland spice trade routes. The black lines represent the sea routes. It all origionates from or passes through India.

Foreign religions are often separatist. India's trade religion is of necessity integrationist. Hindu priests study foreign religions and re-interpret them so that they can be comfortably merged with Hinduism.[1]

Indian missionaries carry the message of integration to foreign nations and teach foreign priests how to explain to their own people how their god and the Indian Brahma are one and the same. "All gods are one." This indoctrination is done in the terminology of the religion of the targeted nation. It changes Islam into Islam- Hindu. It changes Christianity into Christian-Hindu. This done, the sheep are conditioned to accept the wolf.

1 **"Cast (not) your pearls before swine, lest they trample them under their feet, and turn again and rend you." Matt 7:6**

Chapter 4

HINDUISM

Yogaville

Yogaville was written up in the Lynchburg, Virginia paper. It's about 60 miles from Lynchburg down in Buckingham County on the banks of the James. It is a Yoga settlement. The word "Yogaville" conjures up visions of "Disneyland" - or something else outlandish. That is a wrong impression.

The route led through Buckingham's back roads. Buckin gham is a poor county. There aren't many people living there. The winding road through the pine forests seemed interminable. At last I encountered a sign pointing to a left turn which said "Welcome - Satchidananda, Ashram, Yogaville. Lotus Shrine 5/8 mi, Visitors 3/4 mi."

When I was getting out of the car at the visitor's center, a bearded individual of unidentifiable ancestry confronted me in a hostile manner, demanding to know who I was and what I wanted. He instinctively knew me. There are people like that. A few pleasantries seemed to mollify him. Passing on to the visitor's center, I passed a pleasant young blond girl carrying her black, kinky-haired baby.[1]

The center is a modest one-story building that doubles as a bookstore. Attached is a conference room with movable benches. There were a number of women about, part of whose dress included the color orange. These turned out to be female

1 (1) "If the priest's daughter also be married unto a stranger (Heb: zûwr - racial alien), she may not eat of an offering of the holy thing (daily food that is blessed), But if the priest's daughter be a widow or divorced, and have no child, and is returned unto her father's house .... she shall eat of her father's meat; but there shall no stranger (Heb: zûwr - "racial alien") eat thereof." Lev 22:12-13 (2) "When they had heard the law .... they separated from Israel all the mixed (mongrel) multitude." Neh 13:3

priests, or "swamis." They were there to answer questions and help visitors. The one who approached me was a knowledgeable young woman.

From her I learned that there are 750 acres in Yogaville, and perhaps 60 Swamis (teachers), both male and female. Private interests have bought 250 acres across the road which are in the process of being subdivided into building lots. Homes are already built and others are under construction. There are more than 250 permanent residents.

The library consisted of books of teachings by gurus. It also included a selection of sweatshirts for sale decorated with likenesses of Indian gods and a selection of jewelry which included different types of rosaries.

Assembly Hall

One must remove his shoes to enter the moderate sized assembly room - about 40 feet across. Candles had been lit to celebrate the Jewish Hanukkah. Swamis celebrate the religious holidays of all religions. There are many holidays and religious celebrations. People were busy at work at tables collecting and wrapping presents for 900 needy families in Buckingham County. Yogaville makes a practice of "good works." It builds trust and good will in the community.

High on the wall were pictures of the world's men considered great by the Hindus. Martin Luther King was one - Mahatma Ghandi another. I didn't recognize the rest.

Under the pictures were symbols of the world's religions, and quotes from their prophets. The religious symbols included those of Hinduism, Judaism, Shintoism, Taoism, Buddhism, Christianity, Islam, Sikhism, African faiths, Native American faiths, "other known faiths," and last, a place for the unknown god whose place was marked with the symbol "O".[2]

My guide suggested that I might like to see the Siva Temple and the Lotus Temple.

---

2 **Paul stood in the midst of Mars' hill, and said .... I found an altar with this inscription, To The Unknown God." Acts 17:22-23**

Siva's Temple

Siva's Temple was in an isolated area about a mile away high on the bluffs overlooking the plains of the James River. Siva is enclosed in glass. Parking the car and walking a hundred yards or so one reaches what amounts to a promenade about 50 feet long pointing to the river. At one end with his back to the river is Siva, a dancing Siva. At the other end sat a statue of a guru whose teaching was responsible for establishing Yogaville.[3] In between were glass enclosures containing statues of Indian gods.

The focal point was the spectacular four-armed statue of dancing Siva, one foot lifted in the position of the dance. One of Siva's four arms holds a drum representing change through sound. The second - the "fear not" seal of preservation. The third hand points to the raised left foot - showing "grace" for those who come to the feet of Siva. The fourth hand contained a fire - the symbol of death and destruction of the body.[4]

Hindu Trinity

Brahmanism or Hinduism has three basic gods - or three gods in one. Brahma is the spirit permeating everything in the world. He is the father creator. Brahma created Vishnu and Siva. These are the three - Brahma, the creator; Vishnu the genial god of ordinary life, business, social contacts, and Siva, god of death, and since Hindus believe in reincarnation, death is instantly followed by rebirth. Siva is also god of pro- creation (sex). After creating Vishnu and Siva, Brahma retreated into the back-

3 "Since all perfect Masters are sons of God and one with God it follows that this is true of the living perfect Masters of today. If we want God, we should seek him there; and if we want to worship God, we should worship Him in them. There is no other living form of God in the world today than the person of the perfect Master and consequently God cannot be worshiped **directly** here in any other way than by worshipping the Master." **Yoga & The Bible,** by Joseph Leeming, Virginia Publishing Co, P.O. Box 997, Lynchburg, VA 24505, $10/copy

4 "The image of a god is believed to be the god .... worship in a temple centers on the daily life of the god, involving preparation of the god for worship - waking him up with bells, purifying him with incense, bathing him, dressing him, and feeding him. The worshiper comes to the temple to view the god and to receive the food that the god has touched." **Academic American Encyclopedia**, Hinduism, Temple Worship

ground as a grandfather figure and left the world to Lord Vishnu and Lord Siva.

Lord Siva

Siva, the god of birth and death, is today portrayed as the Dancing Siva. Kali, his consort, is the black female god of death and destruction, another incarnation of Siva.

Dancing Siva's symbol is the phallic symbol - the male sex organ. Sex definitely occupies a substantial place in Siva worship. Hindus have erotic sacred manuals dealing with sex. It is not an accident that the owners of the Western media make sex the focal point of TV, or that astrology has suddenly become prominently available in newspapers, or that fortune telling is prominently advertised on TV with "900 numbers" to call. It is not an accident that today almost every newsstand is a miniature porno- parlor, or that the capital crime of homosexuality[5] is acceptable. These beliefs are Hindu beliefs. One religion's sacrilege may be accepted ritual to another.

The Rest Of The Gods

Hinduism has countless other gods. Most represent special attributes of existing gods reincarnated as other gods. One is chief of monkeys and is worshiped all over India. Then there is a class of genie represented by snakes.[6] Each of the gods has a wife. From this is further division of both the male and the female attributes of the god. Added to this is a veritable army of local saints or deities. Millions of Hindus acknowledge Siva and Vishnu - but it is the local saint who looks after the village when it is in trouble.[7] The local saint is the one they pray to.

5 **"If a man also lie with mankind, as he lieth with a woman, both of them have committed an abomination: they shall surely be put to death."** Lev 20:13

6 Hindu worship is represented by the "serpent." The snake sheds his skin and is "reborn." The Hindu sees it as reincarnation - an example of immortality. Eve was deceived by a serpent. Vishnu, brother to Siva, rests on a great snake. The "serpent" is always presented as the enemy of the WORD.

7 "In India the perfect Masters are referred to as Saints." **Yoga & Christianity**, p. 42

There are thousands of major and minor gods, all resting comfortably and on a first name basis in the unity of the Hindu universal "one god" - Brahma.[8]

Caste System

In the second millennium B.C., early Aryan Brahman invaders established the caste system to prevent racial interbreeding. White Brahman Aryans were at the top and the black Dravidians were at the bottom. History teaches that two races cannot occupy the same land without interbreeding, and in time the caste system failed to maintain racial purity.[9] Pictures of modern members of the Brahma caste, such as Mahatma Ghandi, show him to be obviously of mixed race. India's four basic castes today more accurately reflect protected occupations - "caste occupational unions," if you will, rather than racial castes.

The four basic castes are (1) Brahmans - or priests; (2) the warrior and ruler caste; (3) the merchants and farmers; and (4) the peasants and laborers. The untouchables, those whose occupations require them to handle unclean objects, have no caste. In practice, Brahmans occupy the first two castes. The Brahman priests of the first caste rule through their claim to be the sole possessors of the knowledge of the way to salvation. Hindu priests generally are not permitted to marry. While sex may be tolerated, marriage involving legal inheritance is discouraged. Individuals entering the priesthood give their worldly possessions to the religious organization they join. The organization is consequently wealthy while those who work for it are poor. Certain Christian denominations copy these practices.

The lavish offerings to the temples have accumulated wealth for the priestly caste that cannot be measured. Marco Polo tells of an invading Mongol army which used all its transport to carry the loot from a single temple. This reduced the army to want

8 It is interesting that while most local Indian gods are female - Indians treat the female as inferior in the episcopal manner - and not equally basic to family unity in the Western sense.

9 See **Our Nordic Race**, Hoskins, Virginia Publishing Company, PO Box 997, Lynchburg, Virginia 24505, $7/copy.

from lack of transport to carry food, causing the army to turn back.

In 1980, when the price of silver reached $38 an oz., the outpouring of hoarded Indian silver broke the back of the American silver boom. It should be no surprise to find Indian immigrants to America paying cash for million dollar motels, hotels, and businesses. Brahmans are the world's original usury bankers.

In the field of trade, the modern Western equivalent of the eastern Hindu-Buddhist property holding organization is today's "corporation." The four castes are organized into the Indian business system known as "feudalism" in the West.

One is born into the Brahma Caste. It has now evolved into a religious/ economic/ political/ commercial caste. This caste furnishes a self-perpetuating priesthood. In its furtherance of trade, it has become the father of the world's episcopal religions, and the world's episcopal governments.

Magicians

Teachers, who by word or deed gain a substantial following, may be elevated to the priestly caste.

The teacher who openly or secretly gathers followers from whatever religious background to Lord Brahma, may be elevated to the ruling Brahman caste. Bringing successful religious leaders into the ruling Brahma caste results in more wealth accruing to the ruling caste. Hindu temples and their Western copy-cat followers are notorious for their accumulation of lucre.[10]

Feats performed by Yoga adepts often border on the miraculous - the ability to move articles without touching them,

10 Unless corrupt enough to be an embarrassment, Western televangelists are immune from really hard criticism. They bless "political correctness" and give god's blessing to practices and individuals the Christian God rejects.

springing 10 feet into the air, etc. Hindus devoutly follow the almanac. Astrology is part of their life. They refuse to do things during inauspicious times. It is noteworthy that President Reagan was greatly influenced by his wife who followed a teacher of signs in California.[11]

Reincarnation

Hindus believe in rebirth. In the words of Guru Nanak: "Our life is the farm where the seeds of karma are sown." A person is the sum total of his past lives; and when he dies he will be reborn as another human or animal to continue his odyssey until he gets life right. This is his "karma." The result is a veneration of all living things and an absolute refusal to kill the smallest animal if at all possible. There are cases where people starved while cows grew fat.[12]

It is difficult not to attach too much importance to reincarnation. The caste system (feudalism) and reincarnation permeates Indian life. A devout Indian will have his body burnt at death rather than have it placed in the ground where worms will feed upon it, and after having consumed it - starve. The starvation death of the worms will rest on the head of the departed who did not make arrangements to have his body cremated.

Yoga

Actions committed in past lifetimes result in present events (Karma). Release from the cycle of death and rebirth is accomplished by practices called Yoga. Liberation from the cycle is the core of Indian philosophy. Yoga practices are supposed

11 **(1) "Thou shall not be found among you anyone .... that useth divination (ouija boards, taro cards, fortune telling), or an observer of times (horoscopes), or an enchanter (Hex, voodoo) or a witch (witches, witchcraft). Or a charmer (potions), or a consulter (fortune teller). or a wizard, or a necromancer (contact with the dead)." Deu 18:10-11, (2) "A man also or woman that hath a familiar spirit (medium), or that is a wizard, shall surely be put to death."** Lev 20:27

12 When Hindu beliefs control those in authority, they become slaves of their "perfect Masters." They cannot execute criminals guilty of Christian capital crimes. Those who do evil are immediately punished by "karma." Their bad deeds cause them to be reborn as rodents or insects - so, in effect, they punish themselves. This is the reason for the extreme reluctance to execute rapists, kidnapers, and murderers. They have already punished themselves and if put to death will have no chance to redeem themselves.

to subdue and train mind and body to the end that the individual no longer needs to be reincarnated and can merge with the Brahma. Most of its practices are practical. Some in fact are quite beneficial. Its devotees may sit and hum "om" in unison to develop close attention and harmony. Oma is the name of the consort of Siva, the mother goddess, whose other name is Kali, the goddess of death.

To reach the Divine Spirit one must have a perfect Master to lead and teach him.[13] There is no direct communication with a god. One must reach him through a mediator.

Accepting an earthly Master to direct one to "the way" forces one to accept the teachings of the Master as revelations from god. This is in direct opposition to the Christian belief that there is no priest between the Christian and God, since God made the Christian both king and priest.[14] Astrology is also forbidden to Christians because it, too, can become a Master (Deut 18:10-11).

Hare Krishna

Hare Krishna is a Hindu movement founded in 1965 in the US. The name comes from the chant "nantra Hare Krishna" (meaning "O Lord Krishna") chanted by group members. The repetitious chant brings merit to the worshiper. They are Hindu proselyters who actively seek converts. In the mid 1980s the movement had more than 200 centers worldwide. In the US, internal disputes resulted in a number of killings and allegations of sexual misconduct. In spite of the stated ideals of honesty, courage, service, faith, self-control, purity, and nonviolence -

13 "The living Masters who now carry on the Father's work are the modern Christs, the elder brothers, and saviors of mankind." **Yoga & the Bible**, p. 54; "Inwardly, the Masters are one with the universal Holy Spirit .... They are the WORD personified, or in the Biblical phrase, the Word made flesh which dwells among us." p. 56.

14 "Jesus Christ .... hath made us kings and priests unto God and his Father." Rev 1:5-6; "For there is one God, and one mediator between God and men, the man Christ Jesus." 1 Tim. 2:5

Hinduism does have a violent face, a face carefully concealed behind the professions of love and desire for peace.[15]

The Hindu ritual, quietly promoted by followers using its unlimited wealth, permeates Christendom. Jewish rabbis claim to have received special instructions from God while in heaven during a previous existence. The Catholic Pope claims to be God's infallible representative on earth. The Brahma caste claims its divinity from God. It has been said that there are more Hindu- Christian priests in the West than followers of Yahweh.[16]

Buddha - Christian Saint

The following story shows how closely Hinduism-Buddhism has become interwoven with Western religion.

> "The strange parallel between Buddhistic ritual, discipline, and costume, and those which especially claim the name of CATHOLIC in the Christian Church, has been often noticed; and though the parallel has never been elaborated as it might be, some of the more salient facts are familiar to most readers. Still, many may be unaware that Buddha himself, Siddhárta the son of Súddodhana, has found his way into the Roman martyrology as a Saint of the Church."[17]

> ".... it was Professor Max Müller .... who first pointed out the strange fact - almost incredible, were it not for the completeness of the proof - that Gotama the Buddha, under the name of St. Josaphat, is now officially recognized and honored and worshipped throughout the whole of Catholic Christendom as a Christian saint!"[18]

15 The "love" of the Hindu is uncritical and total. Opposed to that is Christian love which is one kind only, **"If ye love me obey my commandments." John 14:15**

16 Christians, finding comparisons with Christian-Hindus distasteful, often refer to the **"WORD made flesh"** by the ancient title **"Yahweh."**

17 **Marco Polo**, Book 3, Chap XV. p. 324n, Yule-Cordier Edition, Dover Pub, NY 1993

18 Ibid. p. 326

From its inception, the papal seat has been occupied largely by strangers.[19] There have been Edomite-Jewish popes, innumerable "christianized" Tartar popes from the descendants of the Tartar invaders of Southern Italy, and the present pope who is a christianized Slav. The Catholic church does many things forbidden by the Christian religion but permitted by the Hindu religion, including the operation of usury banks,[20] and forbidding its priests to marry.[21] The result of this can be seen on the front page as pedophiles, lechers, and homosexuals are exposed. Some believe that the Catholic, Eastern Orthodox, and most protestant churches follow Hindu practices even more than their own Christian teachings.

The insistence of certain Christian sects on incorporating the Hindu practice of auricular confession makes those sects the most effective intelligence-gathering organizations in the world. Confession makes a security risk of anyone making such confession. The intelligence gathered daily from millions of unknowing "agents" makes that organization gathering the information invincible in politics and business. There is no business deal, political decision, war, revolution, drug operation, or moral peccadillo of the high and mighty that is not known to religious and political organizations which require confession from its followers, and who use this knowledge to advance its program.

Hinduism Moves West

From the time of Alexander's return from India in the 3rd century BC, the classical religions of Greece and Rome bore all the hallmarks of the Hindu religion. The world was in complete subjection to Rome and her gods and the Roman gods were likenesses of Hindu gods.

19 **"Thou mayest not set a stranger (Heb: nokriy - racial alien) over thee, which is not thy brother." Deu 17:15**

20 **"Hath given forth upon usury, and hath taken increase .... he shall surely die." Ezek 18:13**

21 **"Be fruitful and multiply." Gen 35:11**

Buddhism

The Hindu religion goes back into antiquity four or five thousand years and has spawned many sects. One of the best known is Buddhism. Buddha lived in the 6th century B.C. and discovered the middle way between harsh aestheticism on one hand and surrender to fornication and license on the other. Its followers wear saffron yellow robes and follow most Hindu rituals. Buddhists consider themselves "Hindu."

Zionists

The "Star of David" is a new name for an ancient Tibetan Hindu holy symbol, and many Talmudic teachings, such as the reluctance to put criminals to death, parrot Hindu teachings.[22]

Some believe that the Zionists have a plan for Palestine to be the headquarters of a Pan-Turkic confederacy that will include Mohammedans and Hindus, with themselves as leader. This appears to be in conflict with the plan of monied Hindu-Jews who plan to have Zionist Palestine integrated into a "one world." One may expect that a flat refusal by the Zionists who are to be integrated will be met with "the Kahane treatment." Rabbi Kahane was shot. Separatism is not permitted in the Hindu "One-World" - not even by Zionists boasting their own elitist agenda.

22 The Law demands the death penalty for the following causes: Worshipping other gods Ex 22:20, sorcery and witchcraft Ex 22:18, blasphemy Lev 24:16, perjury (capital cases Deut 19:18-19, defiance of the law Deut 17:12, adultery Deut 22:20-25, rape Deut 22:25-26, prostitution Deut 22:20-21, incest Lev 20:11-21, sodomy Lev 20:13, murder Deut 19:11, manslaughter Num 35:24-29, kidnaping Deut 24:7, carnal knowledge of beasts Lev 20:15-16. **"The Jews said unto him, It is not lawful for us to put any man to death." John 18:31**, It is in direct opposition to the Law of Israel. Rabbanic opinion continues: "As to the spirit of later rabbinic legislation, it clearly appears that there was a tendency to reduce capital punishment to a minimum, if not to abolish it altogether." Jewish Encyclopedia, p.558. The Edomite Jewish religion shows its Hindu underpinning. Hindus are reluctant to put criminals to death because reincarnation automatically punishes the crime.

Tibetan Hinduism

Tibet is considered by many to be the source of Hinduism. The leader is the Dalai Lama. Tibetan Hinduism spread to China where it became extremely influential. The "confessions" required of its adherents give information to the Tibetan Dalai Lama that allow him to exercise tremendous influence within the Chinese Empire.

> "Tibet, always to China a matter of prime importance by reason of the religious authority exercised by the Dalai Lama in Tibet, Mongolia and Manchuria."[23]

Hinduism permeates Chinese converts reducing them to servants of Tibet's priestly caste. This has forced China to keep a military presence in that tiny country to keep it from continuously meddling in its affairs.

Taoism

Hinduism, in Buddhist form, reached China and soon the indigenous Taoism was interpreted from a Hindu viewpoint. The two faces of the gods - the male and female - became the "Ying" and the "Yang" of Brahma. Much of Taoism became Hindu.

Mohammedan

The usury activity of Brahma priests spread to Babylon, and from there to Islam. As long as Islam's priests, the Imams, forbore to condemn usury, and as long as Islam remained open to the Hindu, matters rested comfortably. In time, devout Muslims attempted to enforce the Koran and coerce Hindus to accept Allah - not Allah reborn as Siva - but Allah as revealed by Mohammed. They banned usury. Hindu adherents worldwide began a "war of acceptance" against Islamic "fundamentalism." Islamic Mosques at this writing are being burned almost daily in India and the conflict has thus far cost millions of lives.

---

23 **Enclyclopedia /Britannica**, 14th Ed., Vol 22, Tibet, p. 183.

Sikhism

The Sikh religion is a Hindu sect born in the 15th Century. It was a revolt against the Brahma caste system and their suppression and exploitation of the Sikh peoples. While this sect is wholly acceptable to the Hindus, Hindu practices are unacceptable to most Sikhs. The result is an ongoing war of acceptance waged by India's Hindus against the Sikh nation with Sikh temples and holy places continually being occupied by Hindu soldiers.

Hindu Tolerance

> "Hinduism has absorbed much and rejected little. It has been a great proselytizing system .... It has accepted something from its opponents, but kept them at arm's length. Its strength lies in its eclecticism[24] and in its insistence on the divinity of its own sacred caste, the Brahmans. .... It has undergone never- ceasing changes and is still unchanged." *Encyclopedia Britannica*, 14th ed, Vol 12, India, Religion, p. 160.

Hindus accept all religions. They are tolerant toward the claims of rival deities. They are able to do this because they identify divine beings who are newly sprung into popular favor as another facet or incarnation of the personality of either Vishnu or Siva. In other words, Mohammed, Buddha, and Jesus are accepted as the rebirth of existing Hindu gods with new names. A follower of Islam sees "Allah" as God. A Hindu will agree - but sees him as a reincarnation of Vishnu or Siva. To the Hindu all is one. There is a "one world" of the gods. It is the original "ecumenism." The "one world" belief that "all gods are basically the same" is the basic Hindu belief.

This belief is diametrically opposed to the Christian belief - "*No one cometh to the Father but by me.*" *John 14:6.* To the Christian, the words "Jesus" and "Father" are translated as being the actual WORD. "*In the beginning was the WORD, and the*

24 Eclecticism: picking, choosing, and interpreting beliefs of one's opponents.

word was with God, and the WORD was God."John 1:1 and "*The WORD was made flesh, and dwelt among us." John 1:14.* The WORD is understood to be the will of God most easily understood in the Commandments - the Laws, statutes and judgments.

In spite of the clear teachings of the WORD, secret Hindus have converted many to the basic Hindu belief that in God - all is one.

> "Surveys show that most Protestants .... along with the Pope and liberal Roman Catholics .... maintain that members of other religions, such as Islam and Judaism, all worship the same God Christians worship but call Him by a different name." *Christian News*, Vol 30, No 20, May 18, 1992, p.1, RR1, Box 309A, New Haven, MO 63068. $20/yr.

Centripetal vs. Centrifugal Forces

Hindus endlessly speak of tolerance and nonviolence, but, Hindu violence is worldwide. The thing that triggers Hindu violence is - rejection. Hinduism is a CENTRIPETAL force - it attracts and gathers many separate parts into one whole.

A competing god who insists on remaining separate, on being EXCLUSIVE, the ONLY god of its people, one who refuses to become one with the world force of Brahma and be integrated into the Hindu pantheon. That god is looked upon as an opposing force - a CENTRIFICAL force - one that tears apart the holy Hindu ecumenism. If, after a reasonable period of proselyting in which every attempt is made to peacefully merge dissident groups and their gods onto one, and their efforts have been rebuffed, then the opposing god and his followers become enemies of the state (Brahma) and must be exterminated so that Brahma will not be torn apart.[25]

India's Buddhists accepted the ecumenical call to become one and be absorbed into Hinduism, or be banished. Buddhism now

25 Ghandi preached non-violent protest while his followers shot British soldiers; Martin Luther King's non- violence left cities burning; America's rulers preach non-violence but leave Ruby Ridge, Waco, and a dozen invaded and devastated separatist lands in their path.

lives only in foreign lands - Indo-China, China, and Malaysia. Christians who refused to merge were simply exterminated. The Muslems refused integration and were forced to flee for their lives. Millions fled from India into Pakistan. The millions of Mohammedans, Buddhists, and Christians who remain in India today are integrated into the oneness of Brahma. They are called "Muslem," "Buddhist," and "Christian," but most include Siva and Vishnu in their worship. Like many Western christians - they are Hindu - but with another name.

Wars Of Oneness

"Centripetal-oneness." Ecumenism. The gathering of many into one. This is the imperium of Hinduism. It explains wars that are otherwise inexplicable, i.e, the apparently irrational single-minded insistence on incorporating the independent and separate American states into a single union of states. The same irrational insistence to destroy the "separatist" Southern Confederacy. Brahman "oneness" explains the insistence to incorporate the independent American farms into corporate "oneness."

Brahmanism explains Britain's insistence on destroying the independent South African farmers and integrating them into its empire; it explains the hysterical reaction to the "separatist" National Socialist Germany which tried to escape the sticky, cloying grasps of One-World oneness. It explains the Brahman use of Western armies to invade and conquer Islamic Egypt, N. Africa, and Iraq. It explains the West's support of Mao's communists to exterminate China's Buddhist and Confucian landlords, independent warlords, and priests.

Hinduism explains Perry's insistence that Japan enter the world's mainstream, and it explains the war to incorporate Somalia into a Brahman One-World. Hinduism explains why Marcus Garvey was imprisoned when he tried to return his fellow Blacks to Africa;[26] it explains why the separatist "Malcolm X" was murdered; and it explains why there was a bloody sup-

26 **Vigilantes Of Christendom**, Hoskins, Virginia Publishing Co., PO Box 997, Lynchburg, VA 24505, $22/copy

pression of America's "Black Panther" separatist movement. Brahman ecumenism excused burning out 14 blocks to cremate Philadelphia's Black separatists. It explains Brahman rage over the separatist family at Ruby Ridge and the massacre of the Waco separatists. The "centripetal-force" of Hinduism explains Siva's never-ending war with anyone who wishes to pull away - the "centrifugal force" of separatism. It explains the absolute insistence on forcibly integrating America, and it explains the encouragement of illegal immigration in spite of the almost total opposition of the American public. Almost as an afterthought, it explains the insistence on NAFTA, a European Common Market, and guns owned only by the servants of Kali - the goddess of death.

Brahmins

The Brahmin caste long ago escaped from their confines in northern India and spread wherever their interests lay. The caste has accepted all of like mind as equals and now the caste includes Jews, Mohammedans, Taoists, Shintoists, Buddhists, and Christians.

They rule the world with their immeasurable wealth collected over 5000 years. Wealth itself is power, they need no armies of their own when the armies of the world are theirs whenever they choose to hire them. Their interconnected usury banks are headquartered in Switzerland, Germany, England, Japan, America, and India. These banks own or control the world's corporations through stock held in hundreds of bank nominee names, and, through bank trust departments which vote corporation stock placed in their trust.

Their corporations and foundations make grants to "deserving" colleges and seminaries to teach "political correctness." They support "deserving" charities and make million dollar grants to "deserving" writers, thinkers, inventors, and politicians.

Brahmins and secret-Hindus own book /newspaper/ TV/ radio chains that channel the public's thinking. The media chains promote reliable televangelists to bless their acts. "In-house politicians" are selected and elected, and hostile politicians are defamed and defeated. The same corporations contribute to political "pac's."

World leaders are hired and fired as circumstances dictate. They are "hired help." Chairmen of corporate boards, the top bankers of the world's most prestigious bank chains, and prominent religious leaders - they, too, are hired help. Powerful media billionaire owners are found to be just millionaires after they die mysteriously - and the media-chains that they were managing are revealed to be owned by Brahmin banks. Most "billionaire world leaders" are only managers - "hired help."

True Brahmins, the owners of the world, have no face that is readily recognizable. They have ruled the world for millennia - they need no worship from their feudal wage slaves.

All Gods Are One

As Siva does - so do they. Siva does not condemn homosexuality, pedophilia, or infidelity - neither do the Brahmins. Siva attacks theistic[27] religions - so do they. Siva smashes and obliterates separatism so that Siva can live - so do they. This is the reason the separatist Christian nations of the West are marked for destruction. Christian people have always rejected other gods. They are Christian or nothing. This racial trait is the reason they have been condemned to death.[28]

Fingering Secret-Hindu Priests

Christians love *God the WORD.*

> *"If ye love me obey my commandments." John 14:15; "And this is love, that we walk after his commandments." 2 John 6*

The hallmark of secret-Hindus is their insistence on integration - the integration of practices, beliefs, things and persons cursed by the WORD.

27 "One god" which excludes others.

28 Write for a free copy of **The Balak Plan**, PO Box 997, Lynchburg, VA 24505. Enclose a self-addressed envelope.

"Ye shall know them by their fruits. Matt 7:16; "All flesh consorteth according to kind, and a man will cleave to his like." Ecclesiasticus 13:16

That Special Place In Hell

Before the wolf can enter the sheepfold to eat sheep, he must first secure a safe-conduct pass from the watchman. If he does not, the rams will gather and kill the wolf.[29]

The password for all the peoples of the world who would be free of each other and free of the oneness of Brahma, Siva, and Vishnu is - SEPARATISM!

"Come out from among them, and be ye separate, saith the Lord." 2 Cor 6:17

The *WORD* prophesies what will happen to those who are late in doing so:

"They will each turn to his own people, and each one will flee to his own land. Anyone who is found will be thrust through, and anyone who is captured will fall by the sword. Their little ones will also be dashed to pieces." Isaiah 13:14-16.

In spite of the seeming chaos of thousands of gods and strange rituals - Hinduism works! It has worked for thousands of years. Within Hinduism there is "something" that holds these wildly different religions together and dissolves opposition. The name of this "something" is *Dharma*!

29 **Wolf & The Sheep**, Hoskins, Virginia Publishing Co., PO Box 997, Lynchburg, VA 24505, $7/copy

Chapter 5

DHARMA

Asoka - Father Of Dharma

King Asoka of India (d. 232 BC) is known as the St. Paul of Buddhism. He is known by more people in the world than is Jesus Christ.

In the India of Asoka's day Hinduism was in decline. It had degenerated into its thousands of component parts, each with its own gods and priests, squabbling and fighting amongst themselves. To bring peace into the chaos, Gautama Buddha started a movement called Buddhism. It professed to be Hindu, but was dedicated to reform and self improvement rather than the worship of gods. In other words, it was not a religion but a method of self- improvement. It declared that all people should worship their own gods, but temper that worship with Dharma. Dharma was defined as *non-violence, obedience* to authority and the gods, and *tolerance* of all races, creeds and nations.

Buddha's teachings required priestly poverty and celibacy to remove the conflict that exists between individual inheritance and the inheritance required for their organization's supremacy. The above should be read carefully. Celibacy means no marriage - not necessarily "no sex." Organizational supremacy meant that all effort and all wealth went into the advancement of the Hindu religious ideal at the expense of the individual. The individual priest might be penniless, without wife and child, but his organization was incredibly wealthy and powerful.

King Asoka ruled India. He used his great political power to instruct his polyglot Indian subjects in Dharma, and he used the Hindu priesthood to spread Dharma into neighboring nations with whom he wished to trade.

He did all in his power to advance the interests and power of the Brahmin priesthood. With the guidance of the priests he codified Buddhism and erected 10,000 great monuments inscribed with his edicts and placed them at crossroads all over India. They were like giant billboards instructing his subjects what was required of them. His edicts follow:

Edicts Of Asoka

- **Open Housing** - Rock Edict VII. People may live wherever they choose without fear that their religion, profession, or race will offend others.
- **Honor all faiths** - Rock Edict XII. One may not criticize another's god in word or deed.
- **Concord** - Rock Edict XII. Concord alone is commendable.
- **Message To Unconquered peoples** - Kalinga Edict II. Trust Asoka and learn Dharma to have peace and prosperity in your own land.
- **Appointment of Dharmamatras** - Kalinga Edict II. Government enforcers, "civil rights division," will be appointed by government.
- **Dharmamatra enforcement:** - Rock Edict V (cont. from IV) - (see KEII). Dharma enforcement is a function of government Dharmamatras and is state policy.
- **Teaching Army Personnel & Prisoners.** Army personnel and prisoners held by the state as well those who receive and dispense **charity** and other such organizations, will be taught Dharma.
- **Unjust Imprisonment & Unjust Torture** - Kalinga Edict I. Great care must be taken that unjust imprisonment and torture is avoided. All districts must expect periodic state inspections; at least once every 5 years.
- **Medical Treatment** - Rock Edict II - Medical treatment must be made available by the state for both men and animals.

- **Road Waysides** - Pillar Edict VII (cont. from IV.1). Rest stops for travelers must be made available and provided with water, shade, and medicines.
- **Living Animals** - Pillar Edict V. Living animals may not be fed to other animals.[1]

Using the above Edicts, Asoka fashioned the invincible Hindu weapon of conquest called - Dharma!

Dharma is the glue that holds the 5,000 active religions and 200,000,000 Hindu gods together. It is the most important single teaching of the Hindu-Buddhists. In essence the basic teachings of Dharma are:

NONVIOLENCE: *Ahemsa* - one must be non-violent to all other races and religions in both word and deed. Violence in word or deed is criminal.

OBEDIENCE: One must be obedient to the statutes, provide the needs of one's family, neighbors, workers, and be especially obedient to the ruler, which makes all else possible. It is a crime to be disobedient and take the law into your own hands.

TOLERANCE: One is required to be tolerant. Dharma directs that one may not discriminate because of race, religion, or national origin.

Tolerance also means - "not to criticize." One must not criticize other gods or their practices, regardless of how much they offend. Hindus believe there is no reason not to be tolerant since all gods are basically the same god. Each seeming difference is only a different manifestation of Lord Brahma, the universal creator, or of Brahman, the unknown world force, or, of his sons Siva and Vishnu, who are different manifestations of the same force. Thus, it is illogical to criticize someone else's

1 **Edicts Of Asoka**, Translated by N.A. Nikam & Richard McKeon, Univ Chicago Press, 1959, Univ of Chicago.

god, for to do so is to criticize a different manifestation of your own god.

Millions of Hindus easily accept Jesus as their god while also worshiping Siva - the sex god. While Jesus condemns sin - Hindus don't recognize sin - Siva allows almost anything. A Christian- Hindu may honor the WORD of Jesus one moment, and in the next moment honor the teachings of Siva. It makes an interesting combination.[2]

The Hindu "Thuggee" cult followed Brahma and Siva his creation. At the same time they also worshiped Kali, Siva's wife, goddess of death. Brahma forbids harm to others. Thuggees believed that Kali wanted them to cause the death of travelers of good character before they had the opportunity to do evil. In this way they might be reincarnated in a higher station in life, perhaps as a rich man or even a ruler, instead of possibly an insect. In this context a Thuggee murder was believed to be a righteous act. The murderer was paid for his devotion to the gods with money taken from the dead traveler's pocket.

Following the right gods allows a Hindu to do as he likes. Following more than one god is normal. The interesting thing is the extreme reluctance of Indian rulers to condemn the Thugs.

One would think that many different beliefs would cause perpetual war and chaos among Hindus. Such is not the case. King Asoka's *Dharma* was introduced to calm the land and help him rule. He boasted that with it he had already conquered many kings of the West and in time would conquer the world.

Dharma does not require conversion to conventional Hinduism, it only requires obedience to the king, tolerance of all other religions, and non- violence in word or deed to other religions and races. *Dharma* in targeted nations is brought by Hindu missionaries. The bandying about of words such as - obedience, tolerance, and non-violence provides evidence of their success.

---

2 Follow the antics of America's Judeo- Christians ministers in the newspapers, or those of Episcopal and Catholic priests. Sin to many is getting caught.

Introducing Dharma

Hindu priests re-interpret the teachings of the god of a targeted trade area. Hindu missionaries arrive to explain the necessity for tolerance, obedience, and non-violence. The missionaries don't try to change the local religion, they merely attempt to persuade them to add "tolerance" so that future customers will learn to tolerate alien merchants and will buy their goods.

Dharma

Indian Brahmins took the Dharma concept and developed it into a full blown creed. There is Dharma-morality - conquest by morality, Dharma-gift - gift of morality, Dharma-rich - moral distribution of riches, Dharma-one-blood kinship among men based in morality, Dharma-sacraments - rites and ceremonials unimportant, Dharma-pleasure - pleasure in morality, Dharma-tour - shrine visitation, Dharma-supervisor - high officials charged with the promulgation and supervision of morality, Dharma- mahamatras - enforcers, Dharma-tolerance, Dharma-noncritical, Dharma-acceptance. Each of these categories is a study requiring special priests. Below is a summation of what Asoka tried to accomplish with Dharma:

> "The Edicts of Asoka ... combine the instrumentalities of power with those of education and meditation, and they transform law by love, reason, and tolerance."[3]

The practical definition is:

> DHARMA: Buddhist teaching to pacify divergent populations; to facilitate rule and expedite trade. Dharma - acceptance, non-violence, and tolerance of different peoples and their gods and obedience to one's rulers.

---

3 **The Edicts Of Asoka**, N. A. Nikam & Richard McKeon, Univ Chicago Press, Chicago, Chicago 60637, 1959, p. viii

Hinduism is the religion of the international merchant. Hindu- India with 200,000,000 gods and 5,000 active religions maintains order by enforcing Dharma-brotherhood. Dharma is the single thread of conformity required of each of its vastly different religions.[4]

Dharmamatras

To make sure that *Dharma* was doing its job, King Asoka employed *Dharma* enforcers called *Dharmamatras.* This is the enforcement arm of the Hindu priesthood. Those who violate *Dharma* face Brahma's wrath.

The three functions of *Dharmamatras* are 1) to teach *Dharma,* (2) to punish violators, and, 3) to reward excellence in *Dharma.*

Unrepentant religious zealots that cause dissension between religions and races are punished. If incorrigible, they are visited by SWAT teams and liquidated. Under the watchful eye of the *Dharmamatras* the worship of many different gods is accepted in relative peace. Traders trade, lenders lend, and the country is quietly absorbed.

AGAIN: People may object to Hinduism and prefer their own religion. This is their privilege. All that is required is that they practice *Dharma* - tolerance - and not criticize other religions. *Dharma* is the key the "tolerant Christian" uses to unlock the gate of the sheepfold to admit the wolf. Christianity plus *Dharma-tolerance* is an animal unknown to the WORD.

Hindus Always Have Another Name

The Hindu priesthood in foreign nations seldom operates under the Hindu name or the many names of its Buddhist offshoot. It usually functions under the name of the local god who is reinterpreted as another manifestation of their own Brahma. Muslim-Hindu followers of Islam are called "muslims"

---

4 The religion of the French Revolution's terror was atheism. Its motto - **Liberty, Equality, Fraternity.** This was French Dharma-brotherhood. France's warring factions were made subservient to this Dharma - the religion of the international trade cartel. Everyone was equal except the new rulers who were selected by the cartel. The same was true of the communist government of the Soviet Union.

- not Hindus. Christian-Hindus in America call themselves "Christian." Jewish-Hindus are called "Jews." But the names merely conceal the Lotus and the Serpent - symbols of Hinduism. "*By their acts ye shall know them.*"

King Asoka's Bequest

The colossal wealth of the Brahman priesthood is in large part based on King Asoka's bequest.[5] Before he died, King Asoka gave the Hindu priesthood one thousand million pieces of gold to advance the missionary work. This wealth has increased many times since then. Some contend that the Brahma priesthood controls most of the wealth of the world through their banks and their hired agents. The Hindu priesthood uses usury banks.[6] Their surrogates and agents have created the corporation and the trust. These techniques remove the ability to trace ownership. The practice of usury and feudal corporate- monopoly in the Christian West would be impossible without the connivance of Christian-Hindu priests whose professed religion forbids both.[7]

Christian-Hindu Counter-Reformation

To neutralize priestly opponents in a targeted nation, Hindu priests thoroughly study the opposing religion. They ask for teachers to come and instruct them. With the knowledge gained, they re-interpret the religion so that the new god may easily and comfortably merge with existing Indian gods. The new god may be called Jesus. He may retain his teachings of grace, salvation, repentance, and the parables, but the meanings are changed into Hindu concepts. Jesus becomes a manifestation of Siva. Many Western Christian-Hindu priests have learned the following as if it came from the Christian God:

---

5 **Asoka The Great**, India's Royal Missionary, by Emil Lengyel, Franklin Watts, NY, 1969, p. 136.

6 The very word usury means "To bite like a serpent."

7 **"Unto a stranger thou mayest lend upon usury; but unto thy brother thou shalt not lend upon usury." Deu 23:20; "Woe unto them that join house to house, that lay field to field, till there be no place, and they may be placed alone in the midst of the earth." Isaiah 5:8**

"What, then, is the Divine Word?

"It is a power, the omnipresent and omnipotent creative and sustaining spiritual power of the supreme Lord God. Emanating from the Creator in the form of a current or wave of spiritual vibrations of immeasurably powerful intensity, it flows outward without ceasing to permeate and penetrate all worlds and all created things and beings."[8]

Hindus believe that the Christian WORD is "energy." Energy is the supreme being - not the Laws, Statutes, and Judgments.

"Guru Nanak declares 'the Steward of God becomes God Himself; do not be deceived by his human body.'" p. 40.

In this manner the preacher himself can become a god.[9]

"The living Masters who now carry on the Father's work are the modern Christs, the elder brothers, and saviors of mankind." p. 54

This teaching allows morally corrupt priests the power to sexually abuse and steal from their flocks.

"Inwardly, the Masters are one with the universal Holy Spirit .... They are the Word personified, or in the Biblical phrase, the Word made flesh which dwells among us." p. 56

RAPTURE: "Nay, only through the Masters do we .... experience true rapture." p. 66

Christianity has no rapture. This Hindu concept was introduced into Christendom in the early 1700s and is now a central part of Judeo-Christianity. Judeo-Christianity is a cult that has

8 **Yoga & The Bible,** by Joseph Leeming, Punjab, India ©1963. p.23.

9 "The pope is as it were God on earth, sole sovereign of the faithful of Christ, chief king of kings, having plenitude of power, to whom has been entrusted by the omnipotent God direction not only of the earthly but also of the heavenly kingdom." **Prompta Bibliotheca Canonica, Vol VI, p. 438, 442, Pope. (The Catholic Encyclopedia** 1913 edition, Vol VI, p. 48, speaks of this book as 'a veritable encyclopedia of religious knowledge,' and "a precious mine of information."

evolved since the 1950s to comply with Jewish religious demands made on infidels wishing to use their media.

Christian-Hindu converts often know more scripture than Christians. They have been expertly taught by Hindu-priests who re-interpret other religions.

The corrupted priest will quickly give a dozen reasons why he cannot follow this command of Jesus Christ. In fact, to follow it would slam the gates of the sheepfold on the wolf and he would lose the wolf's reward. The result is that the Hindu priest learns about Jesus, and the WORD is quickly reinterpreted to return to destroy the sheep. Establishment-christianity has become Christian-Hindu. It has been reinterpreted into Brahma. In Brahma - "All gods are one."[10]

> "Billy Graham, in an interview last January with David Frost said:
>
> "Only God working through these men (can govern the world). That is why it is so important for us to have prayer groups and prayer meetings, and join hands together, whether they're Protestants, Catholic or Jews, and pray, because we're praying to the same God." *The Protestant Challenge*, 600 Woodview Rd., Burlington, Ontario, Canada L7N 3A3, Volume XXII, No 6, Nov.-Dec. 1994

This is the mark of the Christian-Hindu. Christian priests willing to advance this changed version of the Christian WORD, or who merely agree to include Hindu *Dharma-tolerance* and tone down the strident demands of the WORD, are the ones who are rewarded by receiving prominent media coverage and financial backing. This provides a royal road for scoundrels to rapidly float to the top of theological cesspools and, all too often, from there straight to prison.

Cooperating "Christian" seminaries receive largess; gifts and endowments miraculously appear. They may keep their religion,

10 "Surveys show that most Protestants .... along with the Pope and liberal Roman Catholics .... maintain that members of other religions, such as Islam and Judaism, all worship the same God Christians worship but call Him by a different name." **Christian News**, Vol 30, No 20, May 18, 1992, p.1, RR1, Box 309A, New Haven, MO 63068. $20/yr.

but embrace *Dharma* and teach it to their young priests-in-training. Offending "*Commandments, Statutes, and Judgments*" condemning other religions and beliefs are quietly ignored. *Dharma* teaches tolerance, love,[11] non- violence,[12] and obedience to the king. Most Christian seminaries now actually have Hindus, Buddhists or Jews teaching on their faculty, teaching future establishment priests to become Christian-Hindus. A degree in theology today is sufficient cause to arouse a congregation's suspicions - if not rejection out-of-hand.

11 Dharma love is kissy- kissy, huggy- huggy, Hindu kind. It is different from GOD'S LAW: **"If you love me obey my commandments." John 14:15.**

12 God the WORD is NOT non-violent toward those who disobey. He demands capital punishment for murderers, rapists, kidnapers, and the like.

Chapter 6

ASOKA To JESUS

Asoka was the grandson of Chandragupta, the Indian king who successfully negotiated the purchase, for 5000 elephants, of the entire Indian empire that Alexander had conquered. Chandragupta's grandson, Asoka, ruled this extensive Indian kingdom. Asoka's vast empire adjoined another vast kingdom that had been handed down to successors whom Alexander had appointed - that of Greek-ruled Syria. Asoka inscribed on the Indian monuments his boast that he had conquered the mighty

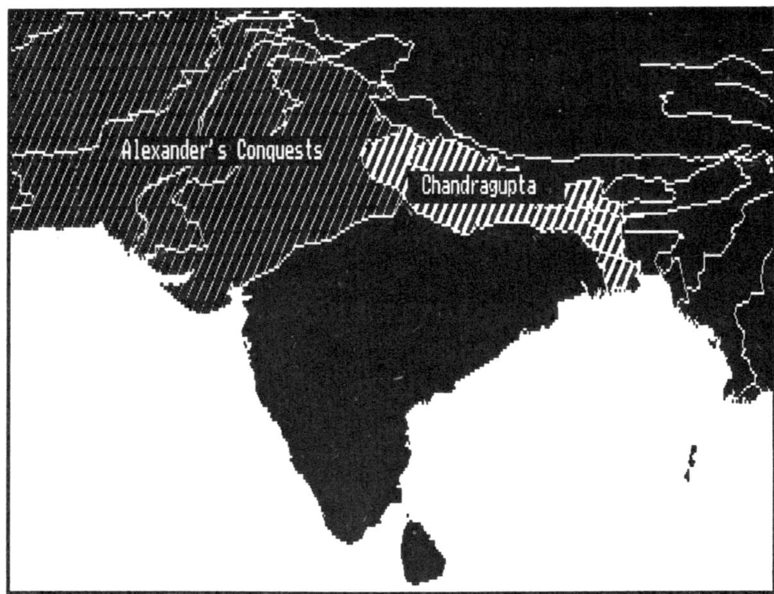

Alexander's Indian Conquests

Alexander's army stormed over the mountains into India conquering all before it until he reached the borders of Chandragupta's kingdom. At this time Alexander appointed a Greek governor and went home - taking with him "DHARMA!'

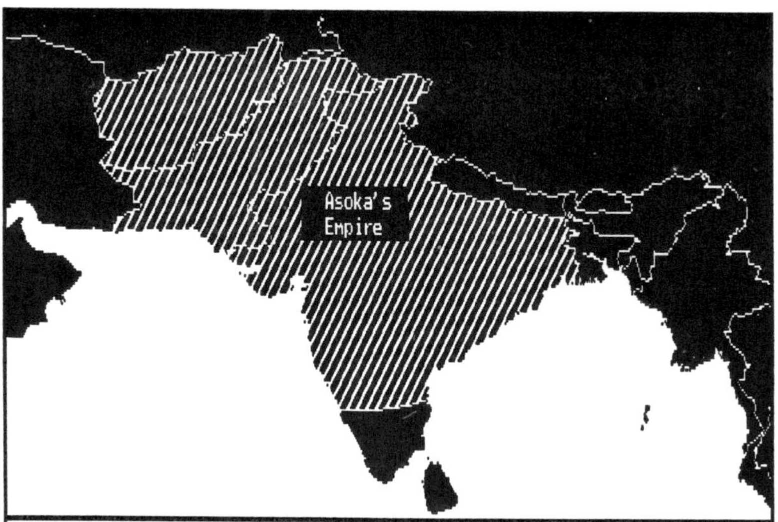

Asoka's Indian Empire c. 250 BC

Asoka inherited his grandfather's Chandragupta's kingdom. Chandragupta's family was placed on throne as a result of a plot by Hindu priests. The kingdom grew into an empire with land purchased from the Greeks combined with Asoka's own conquests. Asoka is best known for his bloodless technique of conquest called "Dharma."

Greeks also. He had conquered them without armies. He had conquered them with "Dharma."

Rulers Need Subjects Dharmatized

The great problem of conquerors is the extreme reluctance of the people they have conquered to accept other alien subjects of the conqueror. Attempts by the king to integrate them into one easily-ruled homogenous mass are often met with fierce resistance. Unruly and rebellious empires whose peoples refuse to accept each other's money, goods, services, and trade produce poor tax-collections.

The Hindu-Buddhist priesthood of India removed this problem by devising the Hindu ecumenical system.[1] "System" is the word - bringing- together. Removing strife is its purpose.

1 Ecumenism: "A movement seeking to achieve worldwide unity among religions through greater cooperation and improved understanding." **American Heritage Dictionary**

Ecumenism is a religion without a god, unless ecumenism itself is a god. All Dharma-ecumenism does is to require everyone to worship his own god and at the same time tolerate other gods. In this way there can be no friction between gods, trade moves effortlessly, and tribute collections are maximized.

Greeks Conquered By Dharma

In about 250 BC King Asoka carved on one of his monuments his boast:

> "*(King Asoka) considers .... (conquest by Dharma) the most important conquest. He has achieved this moral conquest repeatedly .... even as far away as 600 yojanas (about 3000 miles, where the yona (Greek) king Antiyoka rules, and even beyond Antiyoka in the realms of the four kings named Truamaya, Antikini, Maka, and Alikasudara ...*"[2]

The footnote to the above quote states that the five kings mentioned have been identified as Antiochus II "God of Syria" (261-246 BC), Ptolemy II Philadelphos of Egypt (285-247 BC), Antigonos Gonatas of Macedonia (278-239 BC), Magas of Cyrene (300-258 BC), and Alexander of Epirus (272-258 BC).

"Hellenization" Is Greek Dharma[3]

To tear aside the paper curtain that conceals the past, one must carefully examine historical dates and events. By following dates it is often possible to expose a condition that once seen becomes obvious to everyone. Ecumenical-Dharma is such a condition. It is so explosive that it has the potential to cause discontent if widely exposed. Therefore, such things are often

2 **The Edicts of Asoka**, N.A. Nikam & Richard McKeon, Univ Chic Press, 1959. p. 29

3 Indians taught the Greeks that they were improving the Greek empire by making its diverse conquered peoples accept each other and the Greek civilization - "Hellenism." Hellenism was Greek-Dharma.

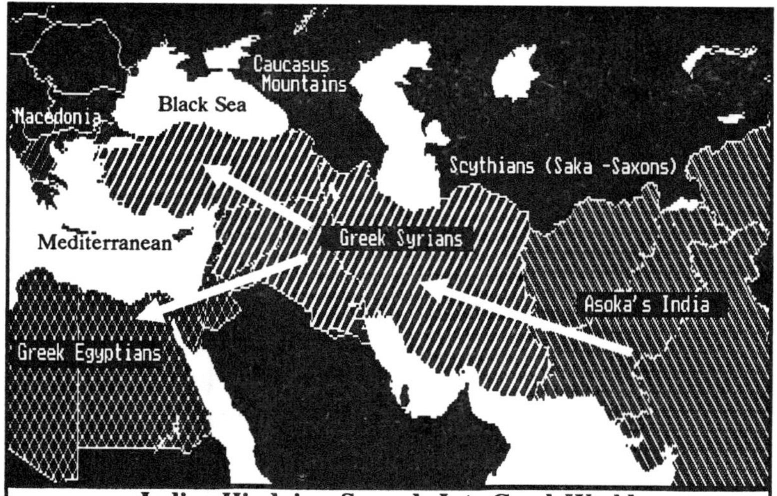

Indian Hinduism Spreads Into Greek World
Revolts by nations conquered by the Greeks resulted in Greek enforcement of "Dharma-Hellenization." "Toleration" of other gods and races was required by Greek edict. The white arrows show Hinduism's spread. The attempt to enforce Hellenization on the Israelites of Judea, who recognized only God the WORD, triggered the Maccabean Wars.

forbidden knowledge. It is the kind of thing that establishment historians overlook, and are rewarded for so doing. If they insist on exposing the situation they may be punished.[4]

The chronological progression we wish to follow starts with Alexander.

- 323 BC: Alexander The Great. Greek conqueror, died age 33. King Chandragupta, Asoka's grandfather, bought his Indian empire for 5000 elephants.

4 The most widely published historian in the English language, David Irving, is presently being punished, ostracized, and shunned by the establishment media who once doted on him. His crime? He published his discovery that there were no gas chambers at Auschwitz, no planned extermination of 6 million, no 6 million, and the entire thing is wartime propaganda that has outlived its time. Such a thing is made possible only because of the lack of challenge to today's media monopoly.

- b. 291- d. 232 BC. King Asoka the Great.
- c. 250 BC: Asoka boasted that he had conquered the Greeks.
- 261-246 BC: Antiochus II "God of Syria." This is one of the four Greek kings Asoka boasted that he had conquered.[5]
- 223-187 BC: Antiochus III - Suppressed revolts in Medea and Persia (220 BC).
- Seleucus IV - son of above. Ruled 187-175 BC: Murdered.

Hellenization Forced On Israel

The Dharmatized Greeks attempted to pacify their rebellious, conquered subjects with Greek Dharma which they called Hellenization.

- Antiochus IV - brother of above. Ruled 175-163 BC. In 168 BC declared obedience to the *WORD* illegal. Mattathias and his sons rose in revolt.

Their religion was the reason for the revolt. It was a tough nut for even the king's experienced Dharmamatras to crack. The Israelite God was not like the other gods of the empire that could be seen, touched and felt. Instead, this God was a strange collection of "sayings" that summed the nature of this God years later in the following manner: "*In the beginning was the WORD, and the word was with God, and the WORD was God.*" *John 1:1.* In essence, the *WORD*, or *Commands*, of this God - WAS God. To violate a *Command* was sacrilege. Example: Eating swine was forbidden. To force Israelites to eat swine, as was approved by

5 Once a king accepts ecumenical-Dharma as state policy to help him rule his people - Dharma becomes STATE POLICY; the accepting king and his subjects are then reluctant to violate Dharma by denying a stranger's god, the god's customs (homosexuality and usury are accepted by Indian gods), the god's people, or any other practices - even when the practices are forbidden by the **WORD.** Greece learned ecumenical-Dharma from India. Palestine and Rome learned from the Greeks. Historians state that "eastern religions" were a major factor in Rome's fall. The fact that Dharma, as state policy - was the reason Eastern religious practices appeared in the West - is suppressed for obvious reasons.

other gods, was high treason and blasphemy to the WORD. Severe punishment failed to make them do it.[6]

There was also this thing about the word "man" and "son-of-man." "Man" was a Hebrew word meaning "blush red."[7] Those who were not "man" were branded "strangers," and Israelites had no dealings with strangers. Even their holy books were addressed to "son-of-man."

Their God named them "Israel." This meant in the Hebrew language "Having God's power-of-attorney." With this authorization, each Israelite man felt empowered to enforce the WORD without consulting any higher authority. For strangers, this made a healthy and profitable stay among these people a problematical affair.

Their God, the *WORD*, proclaimed that it made them and made them different from all other people in the world.[8] This made no sense at all until it was explained that the *Commands* demanded obedience - that death was to be meted out for such crimes as murder, kidnaping and rape. Those who committed such offenses were to be put to death. Those who didn't - lived. Like produces like. The Israelites were descended for many, many generations from those who did NOT commit such offenses. Further, it was the duty of a witness to a crime to instantly enforce the *Law*.[9] This WORD that was salvation and life to the Israelites had the smell of "death" to strangers who come from afar to buy and sell. They hated this God.

The WORD pointed out that strangers were not made "*in the image of God*" - they were the exact opposite. In the merchant's lands the greatest murderer rose to the top and became king or chief; the greatest thief became banker and merchant; and rape was ignored, or if considered a crime, the punishment depended on the whim of the king. Like produces like. Strangers were

6 **Apocrypha,** Book of the Maccabees

7 MAN: Heb: Adam 119 - "to show blood(in the face), ie: to flush or turn rosy: - be (dyed, made) red(ruddy). **Strong's Concordance**

8 **"God (the WORD) created man in his own image (the likeness of his Commands), in the image of God (the Commands) created he them." Gen 1:27-28**

9 **"The hands of the witnesses shall be first upon him to put him to death, and afterward the hands of all the people." Deut 17:7**

murderers, kidnapers, and rapists. Their fathers for a hundred generations were made in the image of their own lawless gods.[10] The Israelite Laws had specific instructions for dealing with strangers; "*If thou has stricken thy hand with a stranger, thou art snared with the words of thy mouth. Pr. 6:1;* They slighted Greek merchants, "*They shall not dwell in thy land, lest they make thee sin against me.*" *Ex 23:33,* and they made disparaging remarks against the Greek king: "*Thou mayest not set a stranger over thee, which is not thy brother.*" *Deu 17:15.* They hindered Greek rule all they could.

In spite of the official ecumenical-Dharma proclaimed as law of the land by the Greek king, the Judeans rejected it. This was the problem. If the Israelites of Judea were not broken, others would follow their example and also revolt. Chaos would spread in the rest of the Greek empire. Antiochus III came down hard on these rebels. His ruthless behavior brought on the Wars of the Maccabees (167- 160 BC).

- 166 BC - Mattathias died. He had defied Antiochus IV of Syria which started the Maccabean Revolt in 166 BC.
- 166-160 BC: Judas the Maccabee, 3rd son of Mattathias, became leader, was killed.
- 163-162 BC: The Maccabees won. Antiochus V made peace with the Judeans.
- 160-143 BC: Jonathan, youngest son of Mattathias, succeeded Judas.
- 143- 134 BC: Simon, 2nd son of Mattathias, succeeded Jonathan as leader, was chosen civil governor and high priest in 141 BC, was murdered.

"Sadducees" - Hebrew Converts to Hellenism

Israelites in Judea who were converted to Greek Dharma-Hellenism were known as Sadducees. They gave lip service to the *WORD* that was God, but they also accepted the Greek gods

---

10 **"There are many nations ... all are his, and over all has he appointed spirits to rule ... but over Israel ... he alone is their ruler." Jubilees 15:23**

and Greek customs. The Dharma-Hellenist had a new name, he was now called a "Sadducee."

Those Israelites who refused and demanded strict obedience to the *WORD* were known as "Pharisees."

- 134-104 BC: John Hyracanus, son of Simon, extended his kingdom to include Samaria, Idumaea, and lands east of Jordan.

Religious Problem - Idumaea & Samaria

John Hyracanus was a military genius. He inherited the conquering tradition of the Maccabees. He conquered Idumea and Samaria, both formerly lands of the Israelites, and now both inhabited by alien peoples cursed by God. In spite of God's warning to Israel to have nothing to do with strangers, Hyracanus wanted to annex these two conquered states and their alien peoples into his own budding empire.

To be obedient to God the *WORD* required that his only Lawful choice was to withdraw and abandon his conquests, or, remove the alien populations so the lands could be re-settled by Israelites.[11] This last choice had drawbacks. It would provide the powerful Greek-Egyptian Empire in the south, and the powerful Greek-Syrian Empire in the north, an excuse to go to war against him. Or, he could enforce Dharma- toleration on Israel to make his Israelite subjects accept the new tribute- paying strangers recently conquered by their king.[12]

Hyracanus the Great found a solution. If his God would not allow him to do as he wished, he would find a god who would. He became a Sadducee to force tolerance of that which was evil in the sight of God - the integration of Israel with strangers.[13] By edict, Hyracanus required that the Idumean wolves be declared sheep by having them swear to obey the *WORD* and by being circumcised. By edict, he created a new kind of animal - a "wolf- sheep" Israelite. In numbers, Hyracanus Kingdom

11 GODS LAW: **"The inhabitants of the land .... thou shall drive them out." Ex 23:31**

12 GODS LAW: **"The stranger that is within thee shall get up above thee very high .... he shall be the head and thou shalt be the tail." Deu 28:43**

13 GODS LAW: **"There is no hope: no; for I have loved strangers (Heb:"zûwr - racial alien), and after them I will go." Jer 2:25.**

doubled and trebled almost overnight. It became filled with "instant Judeans." They all took the name "Jew" after the land. But, one people they were not. The rulers who succeeded Hyracanus continued his policies.

- 140-103 BC: Aristobulus I. Son of John. High priest and king of Judea. Was a Sadducee.
- 103-76 BC: Alexander Jannaeus - Brother of above. Assumed title of "priest-king." Continual intrigues, conflicts between Sadducees and Pharisees. He was a Sadducee.
- 76-67 BC: Alexandra - Wife and successor of above. Ruled. Switched her support from Sadducees to Pharisees.
- 67-63 BC: Hyracanus II - Son of above. Appointed by his mother as high priest. Was nominal ruler.
- 63-40 BC Aristobulus II, brother to above, actual ruler.
- 40-37 BC: Antigonus was son of Aristobulus II. His niece Mariamne was second wife of Herod the Great.
- 40-4 BC: Herod the Great, King of Judea 37-4 BC. Son of Antipater of an Idumean family. Killed his 2nd wife Mariamne. Fled to Rome (40 BC) and there appointed king of Judea. Rebuilt Great Temple at Jerusalem. Supported any form of religious ecumenism that did not reject him because he was a stranger,[14] or the Roman gods since the Romans had appointed him king and he did not want to offend them. It was Herod who killed the Hebrew children. It was he who officiated over the corruption run rampant in Palestine. His soldiers hunted down "followers of the Way" deep into caves in the deserts. There they were given the choice of "Dharma or death." Most chose death and stepped off cliffs or received arrows from Herod's SWAT Teams rather than live under Herod. Indian Hinduism - called at first Dharma, then called Hellenism, then Saduceeism, and at the last - Phariseeism - had a strangle hold on the people of Palestine. Israel faced extinction but God remembered:

14 GODS LAW: **"Thou mayest not set a stranger over thee, which is not thy brother." Deu 17:15, "Their nobles shall be of themselves, and their governor shall precede from the midst of them." Jer 30:21**

"Thus sayeth the Lord, who giveth the sun...and the ordinances of the moon and of the stars .... who divideth the sea .... If those ordinances depart .... then the seed of Israel shall also cease from being a nation before me forever .... If heaven above can be measured, and the foundations of the earth searched out beneath, I will also cast off all the seed of Israel for all they have done, sayeth the Lord." Jer. 31:35-37

- 1 AD: JESUS - "THE WORD MADE FLESH" was born. He came to save that which was lost - His people Israel.[15]

15 Israelites bear the 3-proofs of Israel: (1) God's name - CHRISTIANS - **"They shall put my name upon the children of Israel." Num 6:27** (2) Isaac's name, SONS OF ISAAC - ISAACSONS - SAXONS, **"In Isaac shall thy seed be called." Romans 9:7**, and (3) Adamic descent. **"God said, let us make man in our image." Gen 1:26**. "Man" in **Strong's Concordance** is the Hebrew "Adam". "Adam" means to "blush red." "Show blood in the face." GENUINE ISRAELITES CANNOT BE CALLED "ISRAEL." - **"Ye shall leave your name (Israel) for a curse .... the Lord God shall call his servants by another name ('Saxon'-'Christian'-'Man')." Isaih 65:15.** True Israel today produces the 3 proofs. "CHRISTIAN"- "SAXON"-"MAN." No one else can.

Chapter 7

SADDUCEES

Israel Into Captivity

"Sadducees" are mentioned for the first time when King Hyracanus conquered the Idumeans to gain control of the Idumean spice- route. While theory supports an Indian origin for the Edomites, the Scriptures state that the Idumeans (Edomites) were descendants of Esau and a daughter of a Canaanite. The Idumeans were thus doubly cursed by God. Once by descent from Esau[1], and also by descent from a daughter of a Canaanite.[2]

The conquest of Esau-Edom (Idumea) took place after Israel was taken captive into Babylon, and before the time of Christ.

Israel had violated God's Laws. God sent the Babylonians and Assyrians to punish them. Assyria conquered Israel, and took millions captive and moved them to the region northeast of Palestine, just south of the Caucasus Mountains in what is now Eastern Turkey. This was about 700 B.C.

> *"The 10 tribes .... whom Salmanasar the King of Assyria led away captive .... took this counsel among themselves, that they would leave the multitude of the heathen, and go forth into a further country, where never mankind dwelt, that they might there keep their statutes, which they never kept in their own land. And they entered into Euphrates by the*

1 "**Son of man**"(Heb: "adam," "he who blushes red." Strong's Concordance), **set thy face against mount Seir** (mount Seir - pertaining to Edom - sons of Esau, those who occupied the land of Judah after the nation of Judah was taken into captivity) .... **and say .... I am against thee .... because thou hast .... shed the blood of the children of Israel." Ezek 35:2-5. (Ezek 35:9- 10), (Ezek 36:4-6)**

2 **(1)"And Esau there saw in the land of Seir the daughter of a man of Canaan .... And Esau took her for a wife." Jasher 29:20-23; "Cursed be Canaan." Gen 9:25; (2) "Esau the father of the Edomites in mount Seir." Gen 36:9.**

Captivity

1: Millions of Israelites taken into captivity. 2: The nation of Judah taken into captivity. 3: Israel flees through Turkey. Some leave by the Black Sea and go onto the Danube and the Russian rivers where they are known as Goths. Some cross the Caucasus Mountains and are known by its name, and some move overland and are known as Sythians and Saxons. 4: Less than 50,000 return to rebuild the temple.

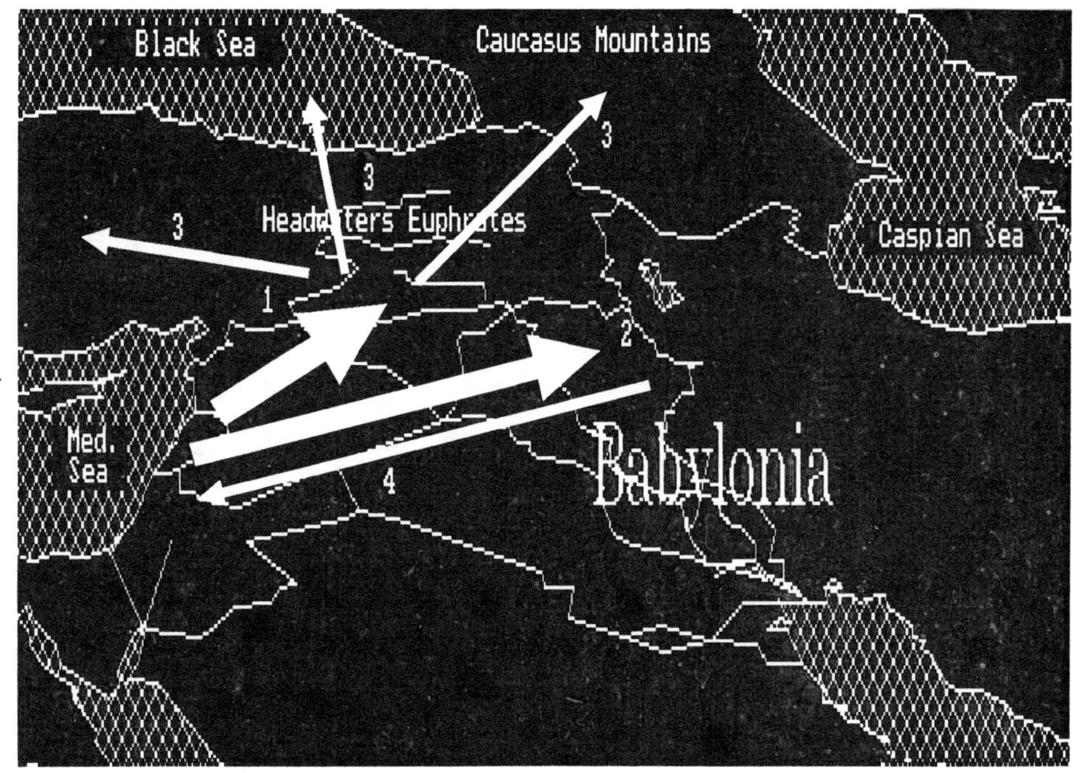

> *narrow passages of the river.... For through that country there was a great way to go, namely of a year and a half, and the same region is called Arsareth." II Esdras 13:39-45*

The narrow passages spoken of are the shallow headwaters of the Euphrates near the northern border of Assyria-Babylonia. Traveling only 8 miles a day, a minimum of 4000 miles might be covered in a year and a half - a distance covering Europe and Asia. American settlers crossed the North American continent in two centuries. The Israelites could be expected to go many times that distance in the 700 years before Christ.

The rest of Judah was conquered later and taken to Babylon. Fifty thousand returned to rebuild their destroyed temple. When they got back to Jerusalem, they found much of Judea was occupied by Idumean squatters from the south. They asked the king of Babylon to write them a letter to vacate.[3]

The Edomites had long been cursed by God, and they were a mixed people.[4]

Sadducees - Counter-Reformation

John Hyrcanus, king and high-priest of the reconstituted Judea, invaded Idumea and conquered them to take control of the spice routes. The WORD prohibited transacting business with Edomites or allowing them in the land.[5] But, Hyrcanus insisted. He needed them to keep the caravans moving, and he needed their taxes. In any event, he was high priest as well as king. The people had allowed the king to become too strong and were unable to prevent him from violating the WORD. He forgot that the King of Kings watched.

To protect his people against the snares of the priest, organized religion, and the local ministerial association, God had

3 "Darius the king .... wrote .... that the Edomites should give over the villages of the Jews which they held." 1 Esdras 4:47- 50

4 "A bastard (Heb: mamzêr - mixed breed, mongrel) shall not enter into the congregation of Israel." De 23:2

5 "Thou shall make no covenant with them .... For they will turn away thy son from following me, that they may serve other gods." Deu 7:2,4, (2) "They shall not dwell in thy land, lest they make thee sin against me." Ex 23:33.

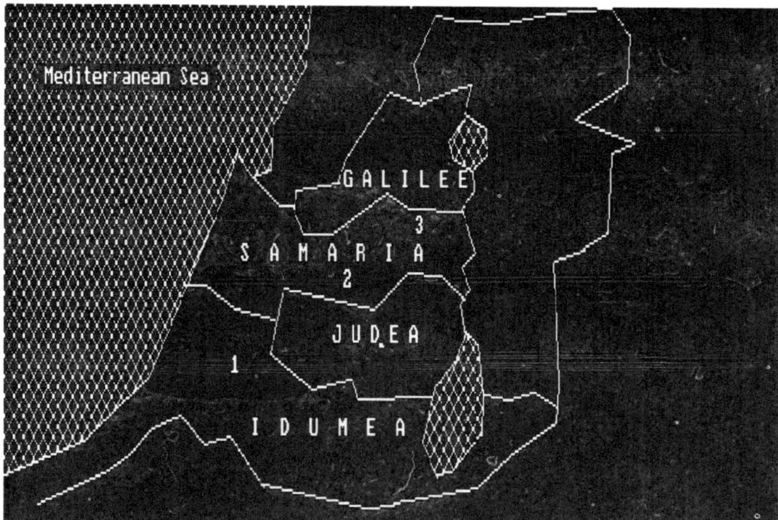

Hyrcanus Conquests 134-104 BC

The Israelites returned from Babylonian captivity to rebuild the temple. They complained about Edomites in Judea (Esau's descendants mixed with Canaanites). Centuries later King Hyrcanus invaded Idumea (1) and forced the acursed Idumeans to accept The WORD - a violation of the Law. From this time there are two kinds of Jews - "Judean-Israelites" from Judea, and "Idumean-Jews" from Idumea who were proclaimed "Jews" by Hyrcanus. 2: Hyrcanus invaded Samaria, peopled with Arabs brought in 600 years before to replace Israelites taken into captivity. Palestine was a sandwich affair: Galilee-Israelite, Samaria-Arab, Judean-Israelite, and Essau-Idumea whose influence over the whole land through the Herod kings subverted everything The WORD stood for. This required Christ himself to set matters right.

Moses instruct the Levites to put God's Law in the Ark of the Covenant so that everyone would know when the Levites were lawless:

> *"Take the booke of this Law, and put ye it in the side of the Arke of the covenant of the Lord your God, that it may be there for a witness against thee. For I know thy rebellion .... ye are rebellious against the Lord: how much more then after my death? .... For I am sure that after my death, ye will utterly be corrupt and turne from the way which I have commanded you: therefore evill will come upon you at the length, because ye will commit evill in the sight of the Lord,*

by provoking him to anger through the worke of your hands." Deut 31:26-29 Geneva Bible.[6]

Hyrcanus professed to be a Pharisee, which at that time meant that the WORD must be obeyed exactly. The WORD forbade Hyrcanus from doing what he wanted to do, so he abandoned the Pharisees and joined the Sadducees sect.[7] Sadduceeism permits one to do that which is forbidden by God.[8] The king declared that it was his divine right to rule any way he chooses to rule.

Four Philosophies

Josephus said that there were four philosophies among the Jews - Sadducee, Pharisee, Essenes, and Zealots. Each had its own beliefs. According to Josephus:

> *"The Pharisees regard observance of their doctrine and commandments as of most importance, and they believe that souls have power to survive death and receive rewards or punishments."*

The Pharisees of the early period may be compared to Scottish Presbyterians or hard-shell Baptists of yesteryear. They were strict and looked to the WORD as final authority down until the time of Hyrcanus (about 100 B.C.). Some, like Josephus, kept the WORD on through the destruction of Jerusalem and Judea in the Roman War.

Next, the Sadducees and Essenes:

> *"The Sadducees teach that the soul dies along with the body, and they observe no tradition apart from the [king's]*

6 Geneva Bible margin note: "Of thine infidelity, when thou shalt turne away from the doctrine contained therein."

7 The Sadducees believed that one should prudently give lip service to the WORD, but, that if the WORD conflicted with the edicts of the king - obey the king.

8 "Hyrcanus went over to the party of the Sadducees, that is, by embracing their doctrines .... added to the written law, and made of equal authority with it .... ." Antiquities fn 13:11:5

laws. Whenever they assume office, however, they submit to the formulas of the Pharisees (lip service), because the masses would not tolerate them otherwise.[9]

"The Essenes believe in the immortality of the soul and strive for righteousness, but they use a different ritual .... and so are barred from the temple sanctuary. .... this sect holds their property in common, and do not bring wives or slaves into the community, but live off by themselves.[10] *.... they are also extraordinarily interested in ancient writings. So strictly do they observe the Sabbath that they will not even defecate on that day."*

The Essenes believed everything the Pharisees believed, plus "something else." The something else depended on the sect of Essene being discussed. America has a hundred such groups today.

"[The Zealots'] .... have an overwhelming desire for liberty with the conviction that God alone is their leader. They will easily endure any sort of pain or death so long as they do not have to call man their master.[11] *These, then, are the philosophies among the Jews."*[12]

The West has many groups of Christian Zealots. There were scores of such groups just before the American Revolution. The original KKK formed after the War Between The States was one of many such groups. There are presently several score of the same kind. The Order is perhaps the best known.

9 "When it became necessary to make new legislation, the Sadducean priests issued decrees without looking for support in the Torah .... " **New Jewish Encyclopedia**, Pharisees

10 Keeping wives and children elsewhere prevented family disputes; "no servants" prevented the attitude of the rich.

11 **"Thou mayest not set a stranger (Heb: foreign, adulterous.) over thee, which is not thy brother." De 17:15** The king of Judea was Herod - descended from the accursed Edomites. He was their enemy.

12 **Jewish Antiquities,** Roman Judea A 18:1:WII,117. Josephus, the **Essential Writings,** p. 260, Paul L. Maier, Dregel Pub. Grand Rapids, MI 49501, 1988

Sadducees - Their Beginnings

The Sadducean sect is believed to have come into being when Palestine was occupied by Greek and Syrian invaders. These foreign rulers passed statutes enforcing Dharma, statutes that violated the WORD, and they punished those who disobeyed with confiscations, dismemberment, and even by frying some in great frying pans.[13] To avoid the displeasure of the king, some Israelites of Judea became Sadducees and supported whatever the king demanded, even when it meant disobeying the WORD and incurring the wrath of the Pharisees and Zealots. This anti-God choice denied them heaven, so they went all the way and denied the existence of heaven. Most Sadducees were rich people, or people trying to become rich, who traded with the stranger. They still are.[14] The Maccabean Wars against the alien invaders forced the people to choose either to obey the WORD, or to obey the unLawful decrees of the king - hence the constant struggle between the Pharisees and the Sadducees.

When Hyrcanus became a Sadducee the political and religious leadership of Judea passed into the hands of that sect until just before the War with Rome that resulted in the destruction of the Temple. The Sadducees presided over a state-religion, which gave lip service to Pharisee beliefs, but which introduced heresy after heresy into Israel. Even the Pharisees became corrupt by accepting Sadducean decrees which became known as "oral traditions."

---

13 See **Vigilantes of Christendom**, Hoskins, PO Box 997, Lynchburg, VA 24505. 472 p. hb. $22/copy

14 (1) "The Sadducees are able to persuade none but the rich." Antiquities 13:6:6. **(2)"It is easier for a camel to go through the eye of a needle than for a rich man to enter into the kingdom of God." Matt 19:24**

Transforming Edomites Into Jews

"Hyrcanus .... subdued all the Idumeans; and permitted them to stay in that country, if they would circumcise their genitals, and make use of the laws of the Jews .... at which time .... they were hereafter no other than Jews." Antiquities 13:9:1.[15]

"Thou has forsaken thy people the house of Jacob, because they be replenished from the east .... and they please themselves in the children of strangers." Isaiah 2:6 (Heb: nokrîy: non-relative, adulterous, calamity.)

Before the time of Hyrcanus, the word Jew referred to the Israelites of Judea who had come back to rebuild the temple. The Samaritans tried to join with them, but were rebuffed. Even the strangers who accompanied them from Babylon had been discarded. When Hyrcanus turned Edomites into instant Jews he did a revolutionary thing - a thing that brought chaos and destruction to the nation of Judea.

This let the wolf into the sheepfold in violation of the Law of the Shepherd. To survive in the sheepfold (a forbidden zone to wolves) the wolves must have friendly gatekeepers to sponsor them and friendly kings to protect them from irate rams. Hyrcanus was their man. To survive, wolves MUST always deny that the WORD forbids their presence, and they must also have someone convince nearby sheep that the WORD does not forbid wolves. Wolves are Sadducees by nature.

Once in the sheepfold it was only a question of time before an Edomite ruled the entire mixed flock. Herod, the Edomite king who killed the Israelite children, was an anti-Israelite Edomite. Ruling as king, his views and opinions permeated everything. His spies were everywhere. He had his own

---

15 Sadducee priests do this today. They bless what God has cursed, they say that wolves are sheep. They combine accursed Edomites with blessed Israelite- Christians into a mixed flock and say that "Jews are God's Chosen people" as if Edomites and Israelites are one and the same. Jesus answers the question by calling himself Son-of-Man. **Strong's Concordance** translates son-of-man to something like "son of one who blushes red." Only certain people blush red and not all of them are Israel.

"Herodian Party" composed of Sadducees. Jesus spoke of them, *"I know the blasphemy of them which say they are Jews, and are not..."* *Rev. 2:9* King Herod, of the cursed Edomite/Canaanite line, built the Temple in which Israelites worshiped. Herod helped shape their beliefs. The wolves ruled Judea. Even the formerly Law- abiding Pharisees became corrupted as they were forced to accept Sadducee rulings. Matters were bad by the time of Jesus. The "*WORD made flesh*" came to save his people - Israel - who were truly lost.

"I was sent to the lost sheep of the house of Israel, and to them alone." Matt 15:24 N.E.B.. This followed the instructions gaven Ezekial by God, *"For thou art not sent .... but to the house of Israel." EZ 3:5*

Chapter 8

STRATEGIC IDOMEA

Gulf Of Agaba

The spice trade by sea from India to the West passed across the Indian Ocean, up the Red Sea to the Gulf of Agaba. There, goods were offloaded onto camels and passed overland to port cities on the Mediterranean Sea (see map next page). Whoever ruled this strategic piece of real estate and protected the caravans could get rich from protection money.

Idomea

The name of this strategic piece of real estate was Edom, or Idomea in the Greek. The barren country of Idomea was rich because of the spice trade. It was this trade the scriptures were speaking of when in 950 BC it was written that "*Solomon .... had .... of the traffic of the spice merchants.*" *1 Ki 10:14- 15*

Idumeans

Who were the Idumeans - the people who manned the ports and handled the caravans? Answers vary. Ammonius, a grammarian, in the footnote in "Josephus," *Antiquities*; 13:19:1[1] provides one opinion:

> "The Jews are such by nature, and from the beginning, whilst the Idumeans were not Jews from the beginning, but Phoenicians and Syrians; but being afterwards subdued by the Jews and compelled to be circumcised and to unite into one nation, and be subject to the same laws, they were called Jews."

1 **Antiquities**, Josephus, Krugal Pub., Grand Rapids, MI 49501, 1981

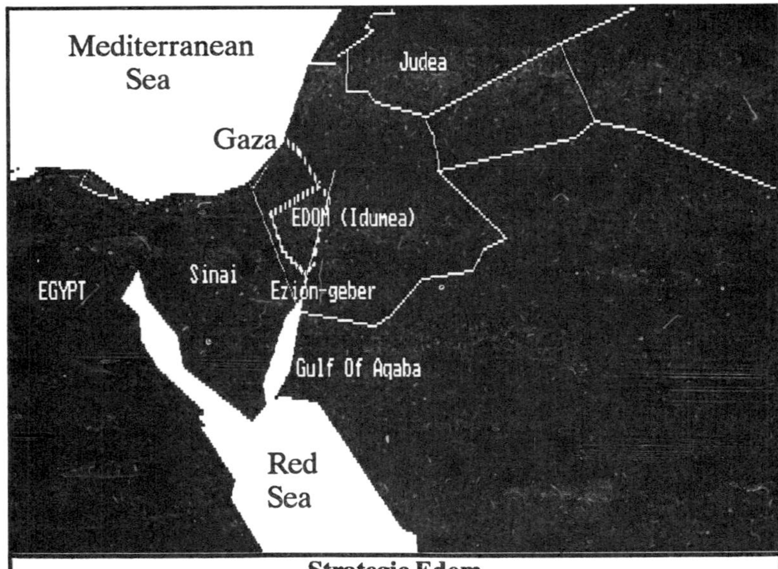

Strategic Edom

Edom was one of the principal terminals of the Spice Trade from India. Ships leaving India sailed up the Red Sea and the Gulf of Aqaba. Reaching Ezion-geber they off-loaded their goods onto camels for the overland journey to Mediterranean seaports.

Cochin Jews

The Rev. Commander L. G. A. Roberts in an article in *The National Message* of June 10, 1922, discusses the Jews of Cochin in South India.

His article points out that there are two kinds of Jews - black Jews and white Jews. There appears to be no intermarriage between the two, and the white Jews regard the black as an inferior race. The popular theory is that the dark completions of the black Jews is owing to intermarriage with natives when the Jews first settled in Cochin.[2]

2 He also points out the interesting parallel that there are also "two distinct branches of the Chozars - the white and the black." These "Chozars" are the Turkic Khazar tribe, related to the Mongols, who lived in Southern Russia and which converted first to Islam and then to Judaism in the 7th century AD. The black and white Cochin Jews operated the silk trade by sea, and the black and white Khazar Jews operated the northern overland silk and spice route - an interesting parallel.

When asked where these Indian Jews came from, the answers varied. Some of the white Jews said that they came during the reign of Emperor Titus after the destruction of Jerusaelem. The black Jews claimed descent from still earlier colonists who they say were sent there in Nebuchadnezzar day. Other white Jews said that they came from a large colony in Bombay which moved steadily down the coast. They came to the state of Kerala whose Raja needed protection from his own people. He gave these new arrivals land surrounding his own palace - rent free and tax free. In the language of nations - this made the new arrivals an independent nation within a nation. The Cochin Jews have been there ever since.

Each of these stories may be true, but they appear to be stories within a still larger story. Look at the map on the next page. Cochin is on the Malabar Coast on the southern coast of India near its tip. The silk and spice trade from China to Bombay, India, touches at Cochin for water and supplies before continuing on to Bombay. The merchants who operated the trade had an outpost at Cochin, one at Bombay, and still another at the Gulf of Agaba in Edom - where they were known as Idumeans. While living there they intermarried with Arabs and Canaanites.

Forced Conversion

The Idumeans were conquered by King Hyrcanus of the Israelite nation of Judea. The story the history books tell is that he forced the Idumeans to become circumcised, accept the Law, and become Jews.

The more likely story is that Idumean merchants approached Hyrcanus and persuaded him to open the gate to the Israelite sheepfold - a gate tightly shut by the Law.

> *"Thou shall make no covenant with them .... they shall not dwell in thy land, lest they make thee sin against me." Ex 23:33.*

Idumeans were a merchant race; their interest was in trade. It was perfectly agreeable to them to have Hyrcanus rule

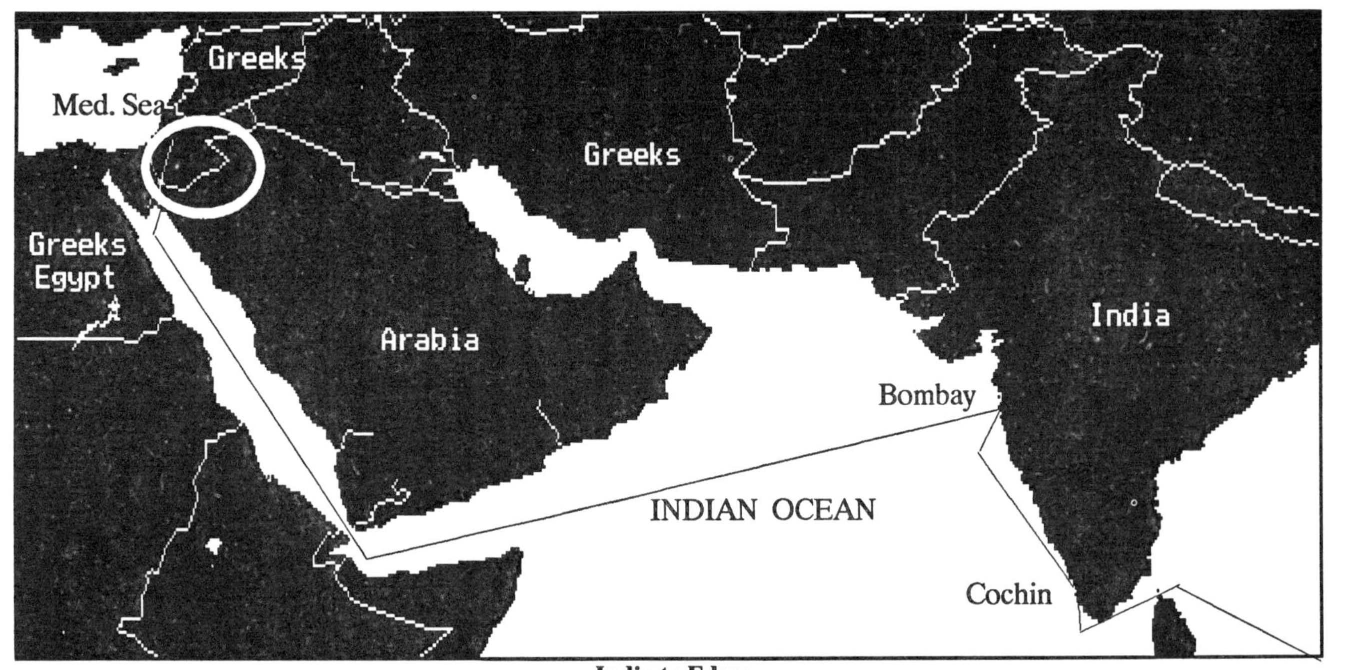

India to Edom

The circle shows the strategic location of Edom. Ships bearing Spice Trade goods left India, crossed the Indian Ocean, sailed up the Red Sea and into the Gulf of Agaba. There they off-loaded the ships, transported the goods overland to the Mediterranean Sea, or to other terminal cities inland. Whoever "protected" this strategic piece of real estate was well rewarded. The Idomeans (Edomites) grew rich on this trade.

Idumea if they received something of value in return. That something of value was the right to trade in Judea. This had been prevented in the past because the Laws of the Israelites prevented them from trading with strangers. It was to get around these Laws that Hyrcanus made them honorary Jews.[3] Since the Pharisees supported God's Law, King Hyracanus became a Sadducee. This allowed him to give lip service to God and do whatever else he wished. This opened the gate of the sheepfold to the Idumeans, now made into Jews by decree.

In exchange for this service, the Idumeans would keep the trade routes open, would operate them, would furnish Hyrcanus his share of the profit and also a share of the profits they would make from the stingy Israelites. Hyrcanus got a great deal of money, and the land of Judea was now open for exploitation by Idumean merchants.

The spice merchants took their latest adopted religion, inserted Dharma to make it harmless and universal, and spread it through the rest of Judea. They also passed this latest religion they had acquired to their co-workers in India who later gave it to their caravans as a recognizable door opener in both Islamic and Christian nations.

From Whence The Jew?

The modern Jewish race is a combination of many races. The following is a partial list: Idumean, Syrian and Phoenicican, Israelite, Babylonian, and the latest being Khazar-Turk, the largest portion.

Still, the original was Idumean. That ancient bloodline has been vastly diluted over the centuries, but many of the basic beliefs of the original people point to a strong Hindu influence, which is reasonable since they had colonies in India.

The Hindu traits incorporated in the Jewish culture are many:

- Indians are a merchant race. Jews are a merchant race.

3 "Gentiles shall ye take to wife purifying .... with an unlawful purification (baptism)." Testament of Levi 4:17

- Jews are matriarchal - they trace their descent through the female. Indian states on the spice-route are also matriarchal.
- Jewish males often change their names. Traditions of a trading society whose merchants become whatever pleases their customers could explain this.
- The Idumean Jews did not follow the Law. Neither do modern day Jews.

They follow interpretations of the law made by their priests which were compiled in their holy book, the Talmud. Neither do Indians, who are considered some of the most lawless people in the world.

- It is a Jewish custom for closely related family members to marry.

Marriage between uncles and nieces and between first cousins is common. The same is true in south India. The Cochin Jews lived in south India. The *Encyclopedia Britannica*, has this to say about the sex customs of south India:

> "Hindus and their offshoots have maintained the old exogamous principles which prevent in-breeding, though in south India cross-cousin marriage is largely practiced."[4]

The result of marriage of closely related family members today in the Jewish community is a high incidence of birth defects, nervous disorders, and perhaps the highest levels of insanity found in the world.

- Western Jews exhibit what some call an "unhealthy" preoccupation with sex. This is also a trait in southern India.

This tendency is evident in the output from Hollywood, TV and the rest of the Jewish-owned media. Cochin is in southern India and the principal god of Southern India is Siva - the sex god. What may be unhealthy to some may be someone else just exercising his religion.

4 **Encyclopedia Briticanna**, 14th Ed, #4, p979, "Caste."

- Many Jewish notables, especially in Hollywood and the world of finance, add and subtract lovers and mates with amazing rapidity.

An Indian background would explain this custom. In India "free- love" is nothing new. It's called polyandry. This is what the *Encyclopedia Briticanna* has to say:

> "In Tibet polyandry (more than one husband) has prevailed from time immemorial .... also in south India, and throughout the interior of Ceylon, and among the Nairs of Cochin ....[5]

In the Nair community of Kerala, a state in India, the mother is always the head of the house. The Arthava Veda says that a woman can even marry even after having ten husbands.[6]

The *Encyclopedia Britannica* continues:

> "According to Nayar usage every girl, before she attained puberty, was subjected to a certain marriage ceremony, after which the nominal husband went his way and she was allowed to cohabit with any Brahman or Nayar she chose, usually she had several lovers .. (who) did not live with her. Strabo asserts that polyandry prevailed in Arabia Felix. .... The peculiar polyandry of the Nayars is most probably connected with their military organization."

> "NAYAR: (Nair), the dominant lay caste in Malabar on the west coast of southern India. The Nairs were originally a militia .... but many Nairs now enter civil professions. The caste is split up into numerous groups of varying status, but all are or were curiously submissive to the Nambutri Brahmans. To the Nair, as a soldier or marine, marriage was forbidden, and a Nair woman was therefore ritually married to anyone, even a stranger, merely as a form. After that she could be united to a Nambutri or a Nair, not below her in group-status, by the *sambandham* ceremony. It would seem that once she was permitted to have several such husbands, not

5 **Enclyclopedia /Britannica**, 14th Ed. #16, Nayar, p. 177-178
6 **Am I A Hindu**, Ed Viswanathan, Halo Books 1992, San Francisco, p. 232.

> necessarily brothers, at a time. .... From the custom, however, descent into the female line naturally ensued, and it involved also inheritance in that line, a man's heir-at-law being his (uterine) sister's son. But a woman's property was managed by the senior male of her own kin.[7]

Deva Dasi

- The Deva Dasi system in India was composed of girls who serve the gods.

Most southern Indian temples are dedicated to Siva the sex god. Girls, often of good families, were donated to the gods. The priests used them as temple prostitutes.[8]

In the book, *By Way Of Deception*, the former Mossad agent Victor Ostrovsky relates how the Mossad secret service headquarters, which many say is the real government of the Israeli nation, is like Sodom and Gomorrah. The agency's female employees are selected because of their beauty; and like the Indian Deva Dasi they service the directors, male agents, and staff. Office parties are described as orgies. This same book alleges that the wives of Israeli agents in the field are serviced by their handlers who remain at headquarters. Jewish TV comedians on the comedy circuit make jokes about the loose reputations of Jewish girls, who appear not to be offended. What may be unacceptable practices to Westerners can be an accepted lifestyle to others. These practices may have had their origin in India and been handed down through the centuries.

- The star-of-David symbol adopted by the Jews is the most ancient of all Hindu sex symbols.

It consists of two triangles pointed at each other. The top triangle represents the female and the lower the male. The merging of the triangles represents the union of male and female.

7 **Encyclopedia/Britannica**, 14th Ed. #16, Nayar, p. 177- 178

8 **Am I A Hindu**, Ed Viswanathan, Halo Books 1992, San Francisco, p. 234.

Other Similarities

A Hindu origin would also explain the undisguised enmity of the Hindu guru and the Jewish rabbi to the never-changing and unyielding Christian Law that condemns Jewish interpretations, statutes, and customs. A Hindu origin would explain the following conflict.

The Christian Bible says;

> "*Whoso killeth any person, the murderer shall be put to death.*" *Num. 35:29-30;* "*The hands of the witnesses shall be first upon him to put him to death, and afterward the hands of all the people.*" *Deut 17:5.*

But the Talmud re-interprets the above to mean something entirely different:

> "Capital punishment in rabbanic law, or indeed any other punishment must not be inflicted except by verdict of a regularly constituted court. (Sesser Sanh) of three-and-twenty members (Sanh J,I; Sifre, Num. 160) "The culprit must be a person of legal age and of sound mind, and .... if any one willfully kills him before conviction, a charge of murder will be against such perpetrator." (Tosef., B.C. ix, 15; Sifre, Num 161)

This interpretation would fit in with Hindu beliefs. The Hindu believes in reincarnation - that the instant someone dies he is reborn in either a better or worse state than the one he was in when he died. In other words, a man's acts in this life determine his future; he punishes or rewards himself in his next life by his present acts. Since he punishes himself there is no need to punish him further. If he is violent he may have to be restrained, but he should be kept alive so that he will be able to do good deeds to offset his bad ones.

This in effect is the justice system in operation today. It makes no difference that God's Law says that murderers, rapists, and kidnapers shall die. The Talmudic decrees are the ones being followed and they appear to be pure Hindu. Hinduism and modern Judaism have much in common.

Chapter 9

MARCION

The reason Jesus Christ came was to save his people from the Hindu-Buddhist "Dharma" that was destroying them. Israel was lost. Obedience to Dharma had displaced the WORD. The WORD was lost. The WORD demands that Israel be separate from all others - including the cursed Edomites. Jesus made it quite clear: "*I pray not for the world, but for them which thou hast given me.*" *John 17:9*

That is - Jesus Christ made it plain to all - plain to all but those who followed the teachings of leaders like Antiochus and King Hyrcanus, and had themselves become Dharmatized. Jesus said:

> "*I am not sent but unto the lost sheep of the house of Israel.*" *Matt 15:24*

> "*These twelve Jesus sent forth, and commanded them, saying, Go not unto the way of the Gentiles, and unto any city of the Samaritans enter ye not: But go rather to the lost sheep of the house of Israel.*" *Matt 10:5,6.*

When he sent his disciples forth he instructed them:

> "*As my Father hath sent me even so I send you.*" *(the Father sent Him to the lost sheep of the house of Israel. Matt 15:24) John 20:21*

The Scriptures say that Israel was scattered into all the world after being taken into Babylonian and Assyrian captivity 721 years before Christ. To reach these scattered nations, Jesus instructed his disciples to go into all the world after them. They did. Some went eastward, some went up the Danube and the Russian Rivers, others went to England,[1] and still others went to Rome.

Synagogue Abandoned By Christians

Christian missionaries, sent by Jesus, reached their kinsmen in Rome. Their arrival was like a bombshell. They found Rome a moral cesspool. They found Israelites and Edomites worshiping together as they had in Palestine. Their mission was to restore the WORD, and the WORD commands as follows:

> *"Now it came to pass, when they had heard the law, that they separated from Israel all the mixed multitudes." Neh 13:3*

> *"For thou didst separate them from all the people of the world to be thine inheritance." 1 Ki 8:53*

> *"Come out from among them, and be ye separate, saith the Lord." 2 Cor 6:17*

> *"Separate yourselves from the people of the land, and from the strange wives." Ezra 10:11*[2]

---

1 "Three great councils of the Roman Catholic Church affirm that Christianity was established in Britain, long before it came to Rome. These councils were the Council of Pisa, AD 1419; the Council of Siena AD 1423; and the Council of Basle AD 1431." **Thy Kingdom Come**, June 1994, p. 36, 7730 Edmonds Street, Burnaby BC, V3N 1B8, CANADA, 604-524-1170. See also; **The Traditions Of Glastonbury**, E. Raymond Capt, 1987. Va. Pub. Co., PO Box 997, Lynchburg, Virginia 24505, $6 plus $2 p&h

2 (Geneva Bible) **"Now when they heard the Law, they separated from Israel all those who were mixed." Neh 13:3;** Explanatory note: "That is, all such which had joined in unlawful marriage, and also those with whom God had forbidden them to have societie."

Hearing the WORD, the faithful separated themselves. It is from this era that Christian-Israel separated from and abandoned the Synagogue - leaving it to the Edomites and their converts[3] - stopped calling themselves "Israel" and began calling themselves "Christians" in fulfillment of the prophecy.

> *"Ye shall leave your name (Israel) for a curse unto my chosen, for the Lord God shall call his servants by another name (Christian)." Isaiah 66:15*

State Within A State

Always, when a Christian revival takes place, changes occur. The WORD demands it. God's people gave their allegiance to the King of Kings. Obediently, they separated and formed Christian communities which lived according to the WORD. The WORD criticized the emperor's land monopoly and demanded that the land be divided to give each his inheritance. It demanded freedom from taxes and insisted that Israel trade with their own kind. The WORD forbade marrying strangers and demanded divorce from the strangers that had been married - insisting that they give up mixed-breed offspring for adoption. Christians were creating a state within a state. The trade of the international merchant was being impacted.[4]

Roman Reaction

Rome was a business operation. Her rulers worshiped many gods because Rome had many gods. The gods of each conquered nation were added to the existing pantheon of Roman gods, and state funds were appropriated to build temples for them. Their numbers grew larger and larger. To manage them and keep the

3 "Strictly speaking, it is incorrect to call an ancient Israelite a Jew, or to call a contemporary Jew an Israelite or Hebrew." 1980 Jewish Almanac p. 1. Identity Crisis. In the 8th century the Pharisee-Edomites abandoned in the synagogues reaped a bonanza with the conversion of almost the entire nation of Mongol Khazars living in S. Russia. These converts now account for more than 90% of world Jewry. It is their value system which is presently attracting notice in Christendom. See **War Cycles / Peace Cycles**, Va. Pub. Co., PO Box 997, Lynchburg, VA 24505, $12/copy.

4 For a partial list of Christian teachings the Dharma-ecumenical "PC" teachers object to, write for **Censored Bible Teachings**, P.O. Box 997, Lynchburg, VA 24505, $10/100. Free sample. Send SAE.

peace to ensure free trade, the Roman government enforced ecumenical Dharma copied from Greek Hellenism. The enforced religious toleration caused each god to be treated as a different manifestation of the same one true universal god. The different gods and their peoples tolerated each other - on pain of government displeasure. "Free trade" was the motto.

The separation demanded by the WORD destroyed this tranquility. The WORD - God's *Commands* -proclaimed that it was the one and only true God and ruler of its people.[5] State policy could not allow this. The Christian sector of Rome, a state within a state, became "off limits" to establishment trade and rule. Something had to be done.

Marcion Discovered

The author once did volunteer work for a businessmen's organization whose mission was to distribute Bibles to school children. We spoke to local church congregations asking for contributions to buy the Bibles. Most congregations were enthusiastic.

One day, I visited several Episcopal Churches, all of which gave me permission to speak to their parishioners. At day's end I visited one last church where three Episcopal priests were present. They were hostile. I was surprised. They were the first hostile ministers I had ever met. They refused permission but would not give a reason. They asked me questions instead.

One question was why the organization I worked for did not invite Catholics to join. I explained that the organization's rule was that members believe that only the Bible contained the WORD of God. Catholics believe that the Bible AND the Catholic Church - BOTH speak for God. When the Catholic Church speaks - it is the same as if God Himself spoke.

The visit was a failure. In an attempt to try to salvage something, I discussed early church history and in the process mentioned the name "Marcion." Instantly there was silence. The three exchanged glances. Quickly, one of them asked what I

5 Matt 15:24; Matt 10:5-6; Ezek 3:5; Ps 147:19- 20

knew about Marcion. I replied that I knew little. I asked them about Marcion - they changed the subject.

I left with a deep seated urge to learn about this Marcion the preachers would not discuss with me. The information I sought was there - if one knew where to look.

Enter Marcion

To destroy the new separatist and militant Christianity that was growing vigorously in Rome and make it docile once again, it was necessary to remove the Law just as Antiochus tried to do in Palestine. The author of the Roman effort was Marcion. He sponsored a sanitized Christianity minus *God's Commands* plus Dharma.

Marcion came from Pontus. He was in Rome in the late 130s AD. He knew well the teachings of Jesus Christ and the WORD. His father was the Christian Bishop of Sinope. "Bishop" indicates that Marcion's father belonged to the Marcion cult also, because the church established by Jesus Christ had no such exalted position as bishop. "Previous orthodox Christians had possessed no monarchial episcopate, no new testament canon, and no creed."[6]

Episcopal Succession

Hindu trade-religion is of necessity an episcopal priesthood - "episcopal" meaning rule from the top down. So are its offshoots throughout the world. An episcopal religious hierarchy is absolutely necessary if kings are to rule their people in a tyrannical manner and avoid revolt. In Judea, Hyrcanus was both King and High Priest. He ruled his kingdom and spoke for God through his episcopal church government, "from the top down." He appointed his own priests to endorse his measures that profaned the WORD.

This episcopal type of church government was forever changed: "*Jesus Christ .... hath made us kings and priests unto*

6 "Die Entstehung der Kirche im zweiten Jahrhundert und die Zeit Marcions, Barnikol, 1933.

God and his Father." *Rev 1:5-6.* The people of Israel themselves are appointed to be kings and priests. It is they who are individually responsible for what happens or does not happen in their land. The government God gave His people is "from the bottom up" and is called presbyterian. Israel admits no ruler except God and His WORD as revealed in the Holy Scripture through his *Commands*. However, tyrants consider this rebellion. They favor episcopal churches. Those they would oppress favor the presbyterian system.

Orthodox Christians in the days following Christ were presbyterian in church organization - the Marcions were episcopal.[7]

Enter Paul

After the crucifixion, there remained hundreds who had personally known Jesus, thousands who had heard him speak and seen his miracles, and tens of thousands who had known those who had known Jesus. Writings about Jesus proliferated.

There was an unknown devout believer of Jesus's teachings named Paul. He was not one of the twelve disciples, had not known Jesus personally, and had never seen him; but he had spoken to those who had, and he had a personal revelation while on a trip. He had written a series of letters. Marcion took the writings of this unknown and made them famous.

Paul's Letters

Paul's writings did not dwell on the Law. They were not meant to. They assume that the reader already knows the WORD. He proves it when he writes: "*Paul, a servant of Jesus Christ, called to be an apostle, separated unto the gospel of God.*" *Rom 1:1.* Christians were expected to know that "*the WORD was God,*" and that Jesus Christ was the "*WORD made flesh.*" Paul called himself "*a servant of Jesus Christ.*" The faithful instantly translate this into - a servant of "*the WORD made flesh.*" However, the

7 Harnach pronounced that Marcion was the founder of the Catholic Church. "**Marcion**": Harnack. Das Evangelium vom fremden Gott. p. 12, (1st edition 1921, 2nd edition 1924), also his Neue Studien zu Marcion, 1923

absence of direct quotes from the Law was exactly what Marcion was looking for to build a substitute Christianity.

Marcion's Christianity

Marcion used Paul's letters as his basic literature. He then attached three-fourths of the book of Luke minus the first two chapters - this was the Marcion Canon. There was no Old Testament with *God's Commands* that judges one's conduct. "The first closed New Testament canon of which we have knowledge was made by Marcion. It consisted of one gospel and 10 Pauline Epistles,"[8] vs. 27 books now. "The orthodox contended that Christianity was 'as old as creation.' Marcion contended that Christianity started with Christ."[9] "Marcion formed his Bible in declared opposition to the holy scriptures of the Church from which he had separated."[10] Van Soden asserts that Marcion knew nothing of remorse for sin.[11] The "absence of sin" is incidently the age-old hallmark of the Hindu.

The Marcion movement was so successful that orthodox Christians were forced to bring the four gospels together to rebut wild Marcion claims. "The 4-fold gospel was made in Rome between AD 150 and 175."[12] Irenaeus in *Adv. Haer.* iii. 11 .7 tells us that the Ebionites use Matthew, the Marcionites Luke, the Docetae Mark, and the Valentinians John.[13] This was done to prove to the world that Jesus faithfully followed the Law as did his disciples.

Marcion co-opted the name Christian. He claimed that his Christianity (minus the Law) was the true Christianity - in the

8 **Marcion & His Influence, AMS PRESS, NY, E.C. Blackman, BD, 1948, p.23**
9 **Blackman, p. 36**
10 Wescott, pp297f, p. 32, "**Canon of the New Testament.**" 1855
11 das Lateinische N. T. in Afrika zur Zeit Cyprians, 1907. Der Lateinische Paulustext bei Marcion und Tertullian. Julicher Festgabe, 1927, pp228-276
12 **Blackman,** p152
13 **Ibid. p. 156**

same way that today's Judeo-Christians (minus the Law) claim to be true Christianity.

Marcion Christians were required to believe this Canon - plus his own book - "*The Antithesis*"[14] which was treated as holy scripture by his followers. Since the Law in the Books of the Old Testament was excluded - the interpretation was left to Marcion priests - and the priests practiced the ecumenism approved by the Roman authorities.

The lack of LAW produced some interesting results. The Marcions were taught that there was no law and therefore no judgment since there was no Law. One could not break the Law and win condemnation because there was no Law. "*Judge not, and ye shall not be judged.*" *Luk 6:37* meant to Marcions that the individual could not be judged.

If the state entered the picture - that was something different - and that is what Marcion Christianity was all about; giving God's power to the state. The following quotes, with no Law, gave the Roman state the authority to do anything they wanted to do.

> "*Obey in all things your masters .... And whatsoever ye do, do it heartily as to the Lord.*" *Col 3:22,23;* "*Be subject to principalities and powers, to obey magistrates.*" *Tit 3:1*

Opposing statements like those following were unknown to Marcions - they were not in their canon:

> "*If ye love me keep my commandments.*" *John 14:15;* "*We know him, if we keep his commandments.*" *1 Jno 2:3;* "*Fear God, and keep his commandments: for this is the whole duty of man.*" *Eccles. 3:1;* "*Not everyone shall enter into the kingdom of heaven but he that doeth the will of my Father which is in heaven.*" *Matt 7:21*

Marcion taught that Paul was the only true apostle, to whom Christ committed his gospel. The other "apostles" were false and

14 Marcion's "Antithesis" has been lost. The Antithesis technique is a well known Hindu change method. If the ITC cannot get what it wants it takes a radical position and settles for a compromise. This achieved, it takes another radical position and settles for another compromise. A step at a time, it reaches its objective which is a complete episcopacy controled by the ITC.

misled the church. Marcion's enemies were Justin Martyr, Irenaous, Tertullian, Epiphanius, the early teachers of the Christian Church; but, it appeared they were going to be overwhelmed by the Marcion steamroller. There was a period between 160-170 AD when the Marcion Church threatened to win more adherents than the Orthodox Church. Converts were drawn from the heathen, but at expense of the orthodox church.[15] In about the year 200, Tertullian reported that "Marcion's heresy has filled the whole world."[16]

Marcion's teachings had taken a militant separatist religion and opened it to everyone. There were no restrictions. Nothing was excluded except those who caused dissent - the orthodox Christians. With no Law, one would think that the Marcions would run wild, and they did in places, but lewd conduct was the exception rather than the rule. Marcions were known for their passive conduct and attitude.

There was great damage done to orthodox Christianity. Young Christians not founded in the WORD began to fall away from the Law and accept the Marcion interpretation of the story in Acts 10 of Cornélius the Roman centurion - as proof that there was no Law to separate Israel from the world. If the story is judged with the Law, it becomes evident that Cornelius was descended from the Israelites who had been scattered in the dispersion. The story of Peter's vision (Acts 10:14) in which animals were let down in a sheet was proof to Marcions that all foods were acceptable.[17]

Roman life style copied many of the corrupt Indian sexual customs. The phallic symbol, the symbol of the Indian god Siva, is displayed wherever this god is worshiped. Pompeii excavations reveal the same phallic symbol. The hand of India reaches far. The Romans tolerated the gods of India and soon Rome mirrored India. They were corrupt to the extreme.

This generated a backlash among many Romans. The Marcions catered to this reaction. In spite of the lack of remorse for

15 "Ibid, p.13

16 Adv. Marc. V19, p.8

17 Roast skunk with buzzard gravy would have quickly corrected this nonsense.

sin, the Marcions were considered "good," and they were when compared with what was going on around them.

Marcion's Trinity

The "Marcion Trinity" consisted of Jesus in the center, Paul at his right hand and Marcion at his left. Marcion acknowledged a world Creator, almost precisely like the "world force" of the Hindu and Greeks; however, this god was distinguished from "the higher God as revealed in Christ. The revelation in Christ was intended not merely to supplement or 'fulfill' (the WORD) but to entirely displace it - the one had no connection with the other."[18] There was no Old Testament containing the do's and don't's of the WORD.[19]

Marcion's Dharma-ecumenical doctrine almost subdued orthodox Christianity. The spirit of the Word was replaced by Ritual. The Parables were taught without the LAW. Murder, rape, and kidnaping were no longer "capital crimes" punishable by death as prescribed by the WORD - they were only acts to be punished, forgiven, or forgotten according to the whims of the state's magistrate. The state once again relaxed and ruled supreme. Marcion's god, which he called "christian," had neutralized the WORD.

Orthodox Christian Reformation

The enemy to the orthodox church who was almost as great as Marcion was Paul. Paul, without the Law, was Marcion's prophet. But, as time passed, Christians got to know and like Paul. Controlled by the Law, Paul was thoroughly likable. Paul's teachings began to be used by Christians to illustrate the Law.

In effect, the Orthodox Christians destroyed the effectiveness of Marcion's Christianity by adding Paul's writings to their own writings. The holy scriptures, in addition to the traditional scriptures which are known as the Old Testament, now included 13

18 **Marcion & The New Testament**, John Knox, Univ of Chicago Press, Chicago, IL 1942, p.7

19 Geneva Bible: James 2:11 note 6 by Knox, Calvin et al: "A proofe: because the Lawmaker is always one and the self same, and the body of the Law cannot be divided."

of its 27 writings which are ascribed to Paul, and a 14th (Acts) which deals in large part with his career. The real strangeness of this fact does not at first strike us unless we understand the background.

> "Paul was under suspicion in wide sections of the church at the middle of the second century. ....
>
> "The choice here was so clear that it is probably false to call it a choice at all: they (the orthodox Christians) canonized the writings, but they did so by solely adding them to their traditional Scripture, not by substituting them for that Scripture... They undertook to break the force of their authorities by absorbing them into their own canon.
>
> "We have all you have and more. We have the Old Testament and the New."[20]

The Last Nail

There was one more reason that caused the demise of Marcionism - Marcion required his converts to be celibate. Marriage was banned, and like Buddhist priests, they were celibate. The Marcion movement had almost died out by the end of the 4th century.[21] They ended the same way the Shaker movement of the last century in America ended - with a handful of members, and for the same reason - lack of recruits. The almost total collapse of the formidable Marcion movement within only a century or so has been given as the reason that the Catholic Church is so adamantly opposed to birth control.

The Christian religion was left stronger than it had been. It retained the Law, and it had gained Paul who was kept safely sandwiched between proponents of the Law - and Marcionism's demise resulted in a resurgence of the Christian revival that once again threatened the very fabric of the Roman Empire.

20 **Blackman, p. 38-39**
21 Ibid, p. 54

Chapter 10

CONSTANTINE

In Rome

Rome was no longer a nation of honest independent farmers. It was a feudal Empire. The international merchant had arrived, paid the Roman priests to bless them and allow them to trade, and paid a king to protect them. The king was now an emperor, but he was still on the payroll of the International Trade Cartel. The Roman government was episcopal - rule from the top down.

The Empire taxed its subjects heavily to pay the thousands in the army, the thousands of government officials, foreign aid, and internal improvements. Imperial statutes and decrees made everything "legal."

In Palestine, the Scribes and Pharisees, surrogates of far away Caesar, tried to catch Jesus breaking a Roman statute by asking if it were lawful to pay tribute to Caesar. Jesus replied carefully; *"Give unto Caesar the things that are Caesar's and to God the things that are God's."* Knowing only Roman statutes and not the Law of God, they thought this answer meant that Caesar should be obeyed.

As Christianity spread throughout the Roman empire, Caesar's agents found themselves increasingly excluded. People refused to deal with the international merchants or their surrogates. The silk trade through the Near East on which Imperial Rule depended for much of its income was severely impacted in its collision with the Law. People began to decline to buy the stranger's goods and refused to exercise the "toleration" necessary for trade with strangers.

Constantine

Flavius Valerius Constantinus, better known as Constantine, was the first Roman emperor to adopt Christianity. Born at Naissus (modern Nis, Serbia) about 280 AD, he was the son of Constantius I, a Roman Caesar, and was educated at the Roman court. His father died at York, England, in 306 and Constantine was elected caesar in his father's place by his troops. He was a fine soldier, and by adroit footwork he managed to become Augustus Caesar of Rome, the supreme ruler.

Facts Of Life

All political rulers are surrogates of someone else and Constantine was no exception. Political rulers protect the merchant and his wares. Students do well to remember:

> "In order for a wolf to eat sheep he must first enter the sheepfold. Unless properly introduced by the watchman, the rams will surround a wolf and kill him.
>
> "First, the wolf must bribe the watchman, who then proclaims that the wolf has been magically transformed into a sheep. As a sheep he is entitled to enter into the sheepfold. Once in the sheepfold he hires rams to protect him while he kills and eats sheep."[1]

It makes no difference to the wolf how many strive to obtain the lucrative position of protector. The wolf can work with one contender as easily as the next. The successful protector is given a generous share of the prey.

Constantine's military adventures cost a great deal and his income for protecting the silk trade from the east was down drastically. Hostile Persia presented a barrier to the overland trade, and the Christian movement in Egypt and Palestine adversely modified the Indian trade by sea.

Besides the reduced flow of goods coming through the provinces of Asia, the only route remaining open was the dif-

1 **Wolf & The Sheep**, Hoskins, Va. Pub. Co., PO Box 997, Lynchburg, VA 24505 $7/copy

ficult caravan route north of the Caspian Sea whose terminal was the Black Sea. The Black Sea was also the terminal for the trade from the Russian Rivers. This rich, rich trade attracted pirates.

To protect this trade from the pirates infesting the countless Greek Islands, Constantine built a city seaport on the narrow waterway between the Black Sea and the Mediterranean Sea and named it after himself - Constantinople.

Constantine-Christianity - Counter-Reformation

After the pirates were suppressed, it was time to re-open the Roman markets. This meant the suppression of the WORD.

Force had been tried. It did not work. Marcionism had been offered as a replacement. It had failed. The Christians of Rome would follow none other than the WORD. Constantine began to make friendly gestures to the Christian community.

> "(Constantine) between 323 and 324 .... gradually adopted the Christian God as his protector and on several occasions granted special privileges to individual churches and bishops."[2]

This set the stage.

In 324, Constantine embraced Christianity still more closely and became openly involved in the affairs of the church. He saw his real opportunity in the Christian dispute over Arianism. In 325, acting as Emperor, he commanded that the leaders of Christianity meet at a great council at Nicea to debate Arianism. The leaders obeyed, thereby giving Constantine authority over them.

Constantine then proclaimed Christianity to be the official religion of the Roman Empire. This delighted many Christians who thought that the time had come when "*God's will be done on earth.*"

The many different races of the far-flung Rome Empire had been Dharmatized. Besides tolerating other gods, each temple of each Roman god also contained a statue of the Emperor who

2 **Academic Am. Ency**: Constantine I

was also worshiped as a god. It took very little persuasion for the reigning emperor-god to convince the pagan Roman population that the Christian religion was the true and only religion. While this was in progress he still gave permission to his subjects to worship him in pagan temples. The emperor had organized the Christian religion as a department of state and he, the Emperor, was its ruler.

Donation Of Asoka

The great King Asoka of India endowed Buddhism with "Asoka's Bequest." A copy of the bequest is printed below for those who may have forgotten:

> "This earth .... this land whereof the face is adorned with many jewels and gems; this soil sustaining all creatures and Mount Madura .... all of this I bequeath to the Assembly of Saints. .... "[3]

Asoka's bequest gave India, its wealth, and its teeming masses to the "saints," or the Brahman priesthood. Asoka also endowed this gift with One thousand million pieces of gold so that it would be everlasting.

Donation Of Constantine

The traditional Holy Day which had been Saturday was changed by Constantine to Sunday - the same as the Hindu holy day.[4] To make the Catholic priesthood an everlasting creation, Constantine endowed it the same way Asoka had done. The *Encyclopedia Britannica* 14th Ed, Vol #7, p. 524 states:

> "Constantine, in gratitude for his conversion by Pope Silvester, to that pope and his successors forever, (gave) not only of spiritual supremacy over the other great patriarchates and over all matters of faith and worship, but also temporal dominion over Rome, Italy and 'the provinces, places and *civitates* of the western regions.'"[5]

3 **The Edicts of Asoka**, N.A. Nikam & Richard McKeon, Univ Chic Press, 1959, p. 136

4 **Encyclopedia Britannica**, 11th Ed., Vol 13, p. 493.

5 From the 10th century on, this document was increasingly employed by popes to support their claims and became a powerful weapon to control temporal powers.

This "Donation Of Constantine" was a deathbed affair because Constantine himself had not accepted the Catholic religion that he had forced on the Roman Empire until he was on his deathbed. Pope Silvester accomplished a good day's work by helping Constantine's sinful soul along into purgatory. The Catholic Church received the entire Roman Empire as payment for praying him out again.

Roman ecumenism, learned from the Greeks who learned it from India, was now reinstated in a new format - Christian flesh hung on a Hindu-Dharma skeleton. To further the spirit of ecumenism, Buddha himself, Siddharta the son of Suddodhana, was made a saint of the Catholic Church.[6]

Constantine, the father of the Roman Catholic Church, was much like his counterpart King Asoka of India. King Asoka killed 99 of his brothers in his rise to the throne of India. Constantine killed his father-in-law, his eldest son, and his wife.

"Adding To"

> "*Every word of God is pure .... Add thou not unto his words, lest he reprove thee, and thou be found a liar.*" *Prov 30:5-6.*

Constantine's new church was called Catholic - which means "universal." It encompassed all the various sects. This church declared that the Holy Scriptures AND the Catholic Church contained the WORD. In time, the death penalty was imposed on laymen who read the scriptures to discover what God commanded. Without the WORD to contradict, the WORD was then whatever the Church said it was. The WORD so eagerly embraced by the Roman Christians was made hateful. This was accomplished in the following manner.

The law against rape states: "*The rapist shall surely be put to death.*" *Deut 22:25-26.* The Law is not the same for seduction.

6 "Professor Max Muller .... first pointed out the strange fact - almost incredible, were it not for the completeness of the proof - that Gotama the Buddha, under the name of St. Josaphat, is now officially recognized and honored and worshipped throughout the whole of Catholic Christendom as a Christian saint!" **The Travels of Marco-Polo**, Yule-Cordier Ed., Vol 2, p. 323-326

"If a man find a damsel that is a virgin .... not betrothed .... and lie with her .... then the man ... shall give ... 50 shekels of silver, and she shall be his wife." Deut 22:28-29.

Constantine's Law made the ancient Law of the WORD hateful simply by adding to it and mis-applying it. Gibbon's *Decline and Fall of the Roman Empire*, The Modern Library, N.Y., Vol 1, p. 375, relates the following story.

> "The successful ravisher was punished with death; .... The virgin's declaration that she had been carried away with her own consent, instead of saving her lover, exposed her to share his fate. The duty of a public prosecution was entrusted to the parents of the guilty or unfortunate maid; and ...if the sentiments of nature prevailed on them to dissemble the injury, and to repair by a subsequent marriage the honour of their family, they were themselves punished by exile and confiscation."

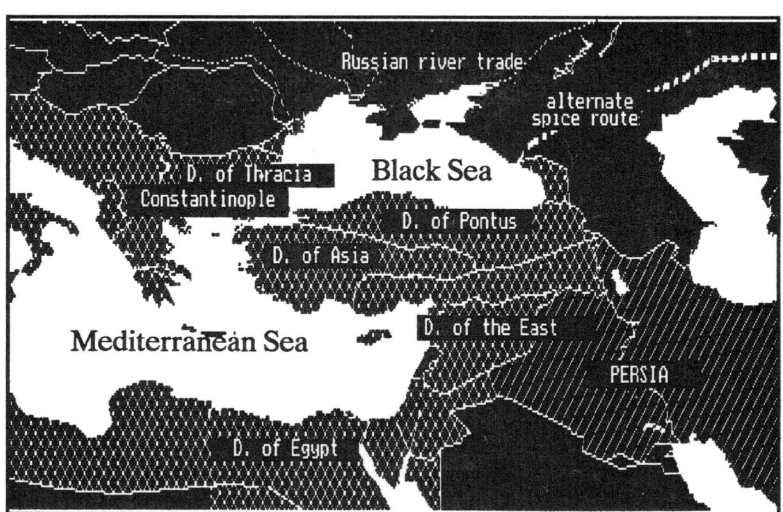

Constantinople, Dioceses, and Trade Routes

Constantine built a city at the choke point between the Black Sea and the Mediterranean Sea to protect the overland trade from the east, and to protect the trade coming down the Russian Rivers. He then converted the Roman provinces into dioceses.

By calling the above "God's Law," and forbidding the people to study scripture to confirm the Church's claims for themselves, people in time turned away from the Law. Trade with strangers again commenced, and the offending WORD - the people's salvation - was once again stripped from them and the people began their descent into the Dark Ages.

The New Rome

As the sole owner of the Roman world, Constantine's Church gave it ecclestical names. The Prefecture of Britain now became the Diocese of Britain. The Prefecture of Gaul became the Diocese of Gaul, then there was Diocese of Spain, Diocese of Italy, of Africa, of Egypt, etc. Wherever the Roman legionnaire had trod, that land was now claimed by the Catholic Church, and that Church ruled Rome through its hired emperors and their legions. The rituals of the church were installed throughout the empire, and the Bishop became the most important officer in the distant provinces.

The Roman emperors were like schoolboys playing "king of the mountain." Whoever struggled to the top was acceptable to the trade-priests, became their "protector," and received an allowance that came from the empire's trade-profits. In time the emperor was replaced by a contender - and the victor in turn was put on the payroll. Emperors came and went - but the church held the title, kept the records, collected the rents, was of God, and continued on without end.

Hindu Feudalism In The West

The Roman church introduced "feudalism" into Europe. As you recall, India's caste system is composed of four basic castes. First the Priest - the highest caste. Second, the soldier/ruler caste. Third, the farmer/merchants. Fourth, the workers. And last, those denied a caste - the untouchables and outlaws.

In India, pretenders from the ruler/soldier caste competed for the position of ruler. The victor was accepted and blessed by the priesthood caste as champion of the gods, and protector and servant of the priesthood. He also had a share of the income from the land and the international trade.

The ruler cemented his own followers to himself by grants of provinces, villages, and farms. Each of his nobles held "en fief" to his king conditioned on his loyal support and service in time of war. Each noble in turn granted a few farms to manage to each of his warriors. The system continued and remained intact until the ruling king was overthrown and a new ruler took his place and moved into his palace. Kings, nobles, and soldiers changed on a fairly regular basis, but the workers remained, and the priests who owned the land for the gods were never questioned.

Charles Martel

Charles Martel, the French conqueror of the Arabs at Tours in 732, is credited with instituting the feudal fief, although it had existed long before his time. Charles conquered a local rival. Deposing the rival and his followers, he replaced them with his own. The *Enclyclopedia Britannica,* 14th Ed, Vol 5, p. 293. states:

> "To attach his *leudes* Charles had to give them church lands as *precariuim* .... It was from the *precarium*, or ecclesiastical benefice, that the feudal fief originated."

The encyclopedia insists on using 50¢ words when 5¢ words will do as well. All the above says is that Charles paid his soldiers by letting them have a cut of the rents obtained from farmers who lived on church lands. This arrangement is in direct opposition to the WORD which requires that there be no monopolies[7] and that the land is to be divided and never ever sold.[8]

Charles supported the Catholic Church's mission of St. Boniface to Germany. St. Boniface was appointed Bishop by the Pope in 722. Charles Martel sent word to local Christian zealots not to touch him.

7 "Woe unto them that join house to house, that lay field to field, till there be no place, and they may be placed alone in the midst of the earth." Isaiah 5:8

8 (1) "The land shall be divided for an inheritance .... according to .... their fathers they shall inherit." Num 26:53-55; (2) "The land shall not be sold for ever: for the land is mine; Lev 25:23

Under Charles' protection, Boniface proceeded to talk to many of the German princes. The thrust of their talks was that 1) The Pope owned all the land, the businesses and everything else on it. 2) If the local prince wanted a cut of the tithes, offerings, and rents, and would like to continue ruling the land, the Pope would appreciate it if the prince would be the protector of Church interests; which meant "riding shotgun" and occasionally twisting the arm of a recalcitrant farmer who refused to pay "protection" or "rent" money.

Princes who did not have a working agreement with the Church received virtually nothing from their stingy, unappreciative subjects. To these, the Church offer sounded good. Overnight, entire countries accepted Catholicism. Priests and bishops were installed, the local princes got enough money to live in the style they would like to become accustomed to, the papacy got a larger share, and bishops like Boniface were appointed arch-bishops. Lands produced an income that they had not done previously. The only people to suffer were the farmers and artisans who now paid between one third and two thirds of their income to God as did their counterparts in India. Almost overnight, freehold farmers, kings living on Biblical homesteads - equal in rights and privileges to greatest kings of the earth - became near slaves.

Constantine had done his work well; his creation, the Catholic Church, spread the feudal system of India throughout the West. The Law that kept Israel free was done away - once again.

Chapter 11

PAULICANISM[1]

"We wrestle not against flesh and blood, but against principalities, against powers, against the rulers of the darkness of this world, against spiritual wickedness in high places." Eph 6:12

Hinduism And The Spice-Trade

In order to open selected geographical areas for trade, the spice-merchants spend seed-money to bring friendly priests before the public. The ones selected, whose faces you see every day, are selected with the understanding that they WILL NOT teach or honor the WORD with its offending Laws, Statutes, and Judgments. The sole reason for the existence of these priests is to open the gates to the Hindu merchant's spice-trade.

Cathars

Forbidden to teach the WORD that condemns the spice-trade and its practices, the selected religious leaders rely on: 1) Ritual, entertainment, and social activities to keep their following; (2) Reform, self-improvement, or cleansing of the individual. This "cleansing" or "purification" is called Catharism. It retains Christian parables and buzzwords while rejecting Christian Law. Catharism with ritual is all that is left once the Law is abandoned.[2] The name is often used interchangeably with "Paulicanism."

1 Christians use Paul to prove the Law. Paulican-Hindus use Paul to disprove the Law. That is the difference between followers of the WORD and Paulicans.

2 To abandon God's **Commandment** is to abandon the Christian God.

Paulicanism

Paulicanism is a later name for Marcionism. Marcion reinterpreted the WORD brought by Jesus into a substitute religion without the offending Law. He compiled a canon that left out the scriptures that Jesus used and most gospels. He retained Paul and part of Luke. Banning the Law removed the ban against the spice- merchant strangers and his employees.[3] "Paulicanism," was eminently acceptable by the authorities. To the Paulicans, the Law was whatever the preacher said it was. Each Paulican preacher had a different twist, and local beliefs ranged from the familiar to the bizarre. There were almost as many sects as there were teachers, which meant that there were many, many sects. The US has more than 300 such sects today.

Paulican Sects

> "PAULICANS, an evangelical Christian Church, spread over Asia Minor and Armenia from the 5th century onwards..."[4]

The same *Encyclopedia Britannica* article states that in 868 AD, emissaries from Constantinople visited the Paulican fortress of Tephrike to try to secure the release of Byzantine prisoners held by the Paulicans. This tells us that Paulicans were not only a strong religious power but also a strong political power.

Many of the eastern Paulican sects drew directly from Hinduism as well as from the Catholic Church. The results sound strange to our ears. The Armenian fathers held that Jesus, unlike other men, had incorruptible flesh made up of ethereal fire. Other Paulicans believed that certain of their number became the direct agents of the godhead, and they became christs here on earth. These "Perfect" or "Elect Ones" are almost

---

3 GOD'S LAW: **"And the seed of Israel separated themselves from all strangers (5236 nehkr - strange, alien). Neh 9:2; Ex 33:16; Lev 20:24; Ex 23:3l- 33; I Ki 4:21-24; Pr 6:1,2; II Cor 6:15-17; Amos 3:3**

4 **Encyclopedia Britannica,** 14th Ed, Paulicans, #17, p. 396.

identical with the Hindu Perfect Teachers or living christs. These Paulican christs were later honored as saints.

Paulican princes were in constant conflict with Constantinople. Under the protection of these princes Paulican sects sent out clouds of missionaries. Their greatest successes were in Armenia and northwestward among the Slavs in Bulgaria. The crusaders found them everywhere in Syria and Palestine. During the ages following the crusades they are found scattered all over Europe.

Paulicanism was really quite useful. One could claim to worship Jesus without having to do anything Jesus commanded if one did not want to - it recognized no Law. Their trademark today is the same as it was almost two thousand years ago - their exclusive devotion to Paul and ignoring the Law of Jesus.

Nestorians

Nestorianism takes its name from Nestorius, Bishop of Constantinople 428-431. Not having the Law to distract him, Nestorius engaged in hair-splitting theological arguments with the priests of Constantinople, in which he was rebuffed. He then went to the strangers in the East and gathered a great following.[5]

Nestorianism was even more successful in the east than its Roman Catholic competition was in the West. Its center was at Ctesiphon on the Tigris, a major trading center. Nestorian missionaries were sent to local rulers with offers to split with them the expected income to be gotten from their subjects. In exchange for endorsement and protection, the Nestorian Christians became established among the people and the income was divided with the ruler.

They founded bishoprics in Syria, Armenia, Arabia, Sarmarkand, Buluk, in Peking and Hsien fu in China, and Kaljana and Kranganore in India. Their missions extended to Japan. In China several emperors became "Christians." They allowed spe-

5 GOD'S LAW: **"I was sent to the lost sheep of the house of Israel, and to them alone." Matt 15:24 N.E.B.**

cial privileges for the Nestorian-Christian traders from India that were not given to native Chinese.[6]

Nestorian-Christianity was highly respected by Genghis Khan. He fully intended to be the Nestorian's next protector as he planned the conquest of the West. "Marco Polo is witness that there were Nestorian churches all along the trade routes from Baghdad to Peking."[7]

In time, the Hindus of India and the Buddhists-Hindus of China came to look on Nestorian-Christianity as religious competitors and so they exterminated them. Their numbers were further reduced by the rise of militant Islam which triggered massacres by the Kurds and Turks. Today, out of the scores of millions of Nestorian Christians, there remain less than 100,000.

Bogomils

Paulican missionaries spread their cult to Bulgaria and what was Yugoslavia, where they became known as Bogomils after their founder. They adopted several local religious practices that added to their popularity. From there, Bogomil missionaries spread their teachings to Italy and France, where they were known as "Cathari" - the "reformers," or "the pure ones," or, "Albigenses." Presenting a choice to the existing corrupt Catholic rule, they were acceptable to many.

Albigenses

> "The heresy, which had penetrated into these regions probably by trade routes, came originally from eastern Europe. .... they kept up intercourse with the Bogomil sectaries of Thrace. Their dualist doctrines .... present numerous resemblances to those of the Bogomils, and still more to those of the Paulicans."[8]

The Bogomil-Paulican mission to Southern France in the 12th and 13th centuries took the name of the French town of

---

6 This is why China is against Paulican-Christianity today, and especially Catholics who tried to fill the vacuum left by the departed Nestorians.

7 **Encyclopedia Britannica,** 14th Ed, #16, p. 245

8 **Ency. /Brit.**, 14th Ed, #1, p. 528, Albigenses.

Albi where they were centered and became known as Albigenses. As Paulicans, they ignored the Law and substituted ritual.

> "At all events they were free from all moral prohibitions and all religious obligations, on condition that they promised by an act called *convenenza* to become 'hereticized' by receiving the baptism of the Spirit before their death or even *in extremis*."[9]

The above means that just before an Albigension died he had to say to God, "excuse me," for a lifetime of wrong doing and then he could go to heaven. "The Law is done away" has great allure for many who wish to do as they like without fear of consequences. In the Hindu manner they rejected the eating of meat since the spirit of another human soul might be imprisoned there. They also rejected the traditional teachings on hell, purgatory, and the sacraments.[10] The "perfect masters" received a baptism of the soul which was administered by laying on of hands. These "perfect masters" were expected to observe a severe ethical code that their co-religionists did not have to observe. Their reward for clean living was that they were looked upon and obeyed as living christs on earth. Even with their faults the Albigensens were comparative angels beside the worldliness of the Catholic Church.

Using the "St. Patrick" technique in France, they approached William IX, Duke of Aquitaine, and exchanging a portion of future income for his protection and endorsement, they quickly established an episcopacy led by bishops and gathered a large following. Soon, a great part of the southern nobility followed suit. This replaced the Pope's rule and took the income that had formerly gone to the Catholic Church.

Cistercians & Dominicans - Suppressing Heretics

Pope Innocent III called for a crusade against this invasion of his domain. This resulted in the infamous Albigensian Wars (1209- 1229) between northern and southern France. The mas-

9 **Ency. /Brit.**, 14th Ed, #1, p. 528

10 Hinduism has neither heaven, hell, nor purgatory. One is rewarded or punished by being reincarnated in a better or worse state.

sacre of the the villagers of Beziers and other atrocities rapidly followed one after another.

Catholic religious orders such as the Cistercians and Dominicans were entrusted with Albigension suppression and were sent in to deal with it. The French king was given authorization to do the actual fighting. He was paid by being given the rule of the lands he conquered from the Albigensian nobles in the south. His followers were rewarded by his giving them rule over conquered villages and farms. Feudalism was at flood tide.

The Inquisition was developed by the Dominican Order to deal with suspected heretics. Torture and the smoke from burning victims was the order of the day. In 1245, the Inquisition seized the Albigension citadel of Montsegur, and 200 "Cathari" were burned in one day. Severe chastisement was decreed against all suspected of sympathy with the heretics. The search for Catharists groups spread out all over Europe for the next 100 years.

Waldenses

The Waldenses in the 12th century took the name of their founder, Peter Waldo, a wealthy Lyon, French merchant. It, too, was a Paulican reform movement. They were critical of unworthy clergy, the abuses of the church, and revealed their true origins with their refusal to take human life under any circumstances in spite of the WORD's command to take the lives of murderers, rapists, and kidnapers.[11]

The Catholic Church attacked the Waldenses in the same manner as the Albigensions. After 80 of their members were burned at Strasbourg in 1211, most of the survivors hid themselves high in the mountains of Northern Italy.[12]

---

11 **The Edicts of Asoka**, N.A. Nikam & Richard McKeon, Univ Chic Press, 1959, (non-violence) "Nature of Dharma as meditation and non-violence." Pillar edict VII, (cont. from IV.1), p. 40

12 Today's surviving Waldensian church is a member of the World Presbyterian Alliance.

Inquisition-Dhamamatras[13]

To perform specific tasks, the Catholic Church creates orders. Each order is assigned a specific task. The duty assigned the Dominicans was that of Dharmamatras. They investigated, rewarded those approved, and punished heresy. The accused were brought before inquisition tribunals where they had to prove their innocence. If they straightway confessed to minor infractions they were given punishments ranging from whippings to performing penance. More serious violations were punished with confiscation and death.

If inquisitors had to spend time obtaining confessions with torture, the victims were often confiscated and then burned. If one ran - confiscation was automatic.[14]

The confiscation of the estates of heretics was a great source of income to the Catholic Church. The various Paulican and Cathar sects - the Bogomils, Albigensions, Waldenson, and others served to fill the Vatican coffers for many years.

Crusades And Pilgrimages To Palestine

It is important to grasp the unbelievable power of the Catholic entity, its strengths and its weaknesses. This organization launched a crusade that involved the entire West - all of its kings, all of its nobles, and all of its people - everyone participated in one way or another. The people were told that they were serving God. Its true motive was to gain back land that had been lost to Islam, to garner money from Palestine's holy places, and to capture protection money from the spice-trade profits that now was going to the Arabs who stood astride the trade routes. All these at one time used to be the exclusive monopoly of the Catholic Church and they wanted it back.

13 Dharmamatras: A Buddhist Dharma-supervisor - a category of high officials charged with the promulgation and supervision of morality. "Dharma- mahamatras."

14 This policy is copied in the 4th plank of the Communist Manifesto requiring "confiscation of rebels and emigrants." Confiscation is also US government policy toward those they "criminalize."

The organization that launched the crusades was efficient. It has launched many other crusades since then using the same techniques and the same system of rewards and punishments.

Pilgrimages

Hinduism requires *pilgrimages* to holy places. Most holy places contain relics consisting of body parts of saints long dead, or is a place where a miracle occurred. India has many such holy places. Reaching *nirvana* requires many good works. Making a pilgrimage to a shrine is considered a good work. Leaving a rich gift for the priests is a good work. The greater the gift - the greater the good work. Such good deeds count for much to the one seeking *nirvana,* or attempting to shorten his stay in purgatory.

The Roman Catholic religion also has many important pilgrimage shrines. They are established in the same way in every land where Roman Catholicism is practiced. The most important are in Palestine and consist of Jerusalem, Bethlehem, Lydda, and Nazareth. If one were unable to make a planned pilgrimage, contributing an amount equal to the total expenses of the trip counted as making the pilgrimage and was counted as merit by the Church. The wealth left by pilgrims at these holy places by devout pilgrims hoping to buy the keys to the Kingdom is truly mind-boggling.

Chapter 12

GOTHICA

The Goths

Without a basic knowledge of Goths, the history of the Christian in the West makes little sense.

> "The Saxons were a German or Teutonic, that is, a Gothic or Scythian tribe."[1]

The name "Goth" means "God's people," and "Good People." *"They shall put my name upon the children of Israel."* *Num 6:27.*

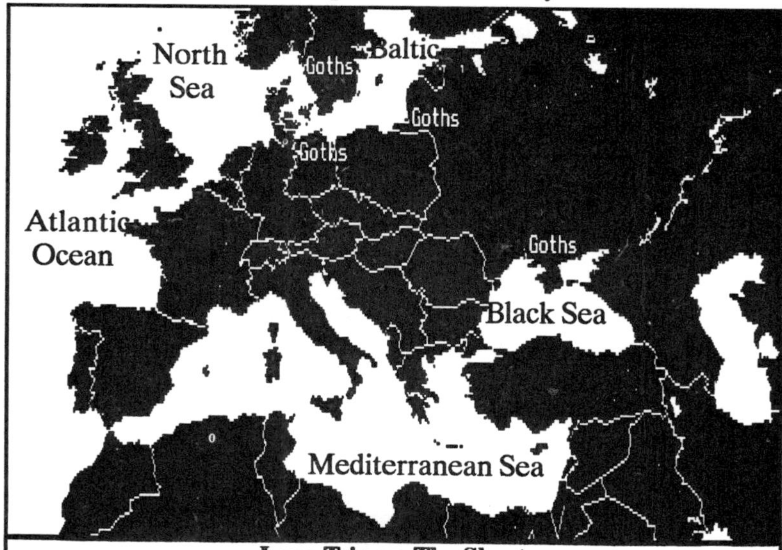

Long Trip vs. The Short

Leaving their overcrowded homelands in the north, the Goths used the Russian rivers to retrace the journey their ancestors had made 700 years earlier, and settled the vacant lands in the Crimea on the north side of the Black Sea.

1 **History of the Anglo Saxons,** Sharon Turner, Bk 11, Chapter I, p. 87, London, 1852

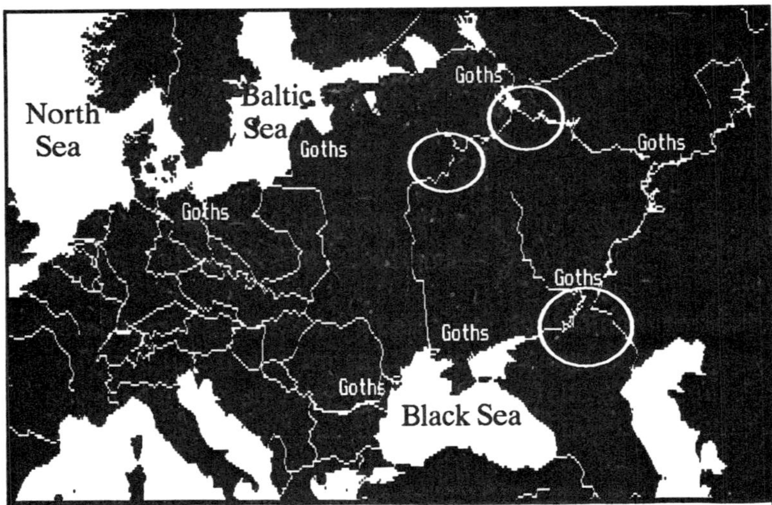

The Russian River System

Sailing up the Baltic rivers as far as they could go, the Goths pulled their ships overland to nearby Russian rivers that ran south - and sailed on down to their final destinations. The Black Sea could also be reached by sailing from the North Sea south to the Rhine River, then sailing up the Rhine as far as possible and transferring over to the Danube and on down to the Black Sea. Both the northern and the southern river routes had been well used for hundreds of years, and still are.

Their culture and architecture are called Gothic; and the lands they occupied - *Gothica!*

The words "Scythian," "Saxon," and "Goth" are interchangeable. A more recent name has been added - "German." The Romans gave the West Goths this name.

At the Battle of the Catalonian Fields, more than a million men fought, and perhaps half that number died. On one side were the invading Turkic Hun horde allied with their enemies the Ostro- Goths. On the Gothic side were the Visi-Goths allied with their ancient enemies - the Romans.

During the years 7 B.C. to 17 A.D. the Goths first came to the attention of Roman historians as living in the area from Pomerania to W. Prussia on the Baltic Sea.[2] Some historians surmise that they began to move from this northern region because of the following reason:

2 "To this day there are numerous European regions bearing the Gothic name .... Swedish Vastergotland and Ostergotland .... as well as the island of Gotland." **History Of The Goths,** p. 23, Herwig Wolfram, Univ Cal. Press, Berkeley, 1988.

> "Overpopulation led the people to draw lots and the inhabitants thus chosen emigrated. Their wanderings are said to have taken them across southern Russia into Greece."[3]

Those chosen to move boarded "dragon ships." Instead of sailing west out into the North Sea and into the Atlantic Ocean they sailed east up the Vistula River. When they could go up-river no further they drew their ships ashore, put them on wheeled cradles, and oxen dragged the ships overland to a Russian river that flowed south.

Again boarding ship, they sailed down river until they reached the Crimea - on the Black Sea. The land was vacant and rich, so they landed, put plows into the ground and began developing their new home. There were repeated arrivals of Goths from about 238 A.D., each group going farther afield searching for suitable land to settle. By 253 A.D. some groups had gone as far as Greece and, crossing the Black Sea, they ventured down into Asia Minor. By 268 the Gothic advance had reached the Aegean Sea - deep into the territory of the East Roman Empire. These new arrivals were trespassing and so the Empire reacted by sending armies to enforce their territorial integrity. This led to a series of wars between the Goth nation and Rome.

The Hunnic Attack On The Goths

The Goths had been ensconced in their new homes for little more than a century when in 375 A.D. a new and lethal enemy burst into their rear.

These were Huns. The Huns had complete knowledge about the Goths, their numbers, disposition, wealth, and their method of warfare, but the Goths had never heard of the Huns before. They had received no advance notice of their arrival - no warning. There was not even knowledge that such a people existed.[4]

3 Ibid., p.23

4 The Huns were a mixed-breed people kin to the earlier Arabs and the Turks who came later. They were given their name by the Chinese who named all these various nomad tribes.

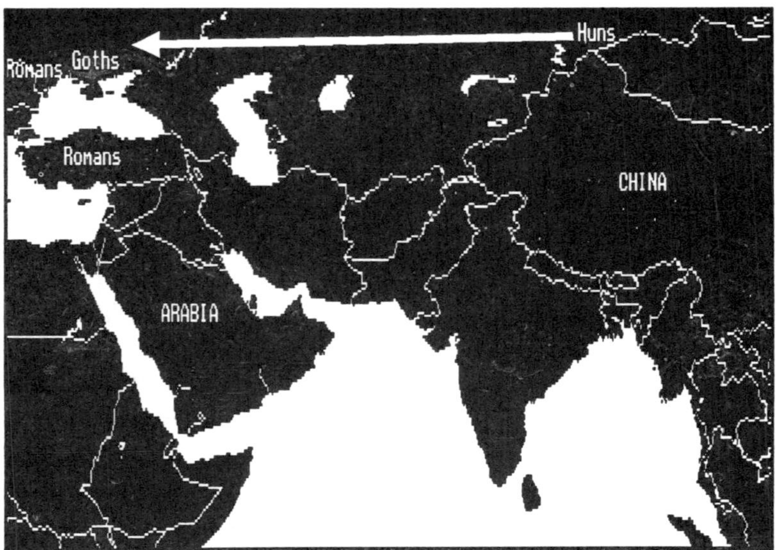

Hun Migration To Attack The Goths

Leaving the borders of China, the Huns migrated toward easier prey. Marching unseen through the Mongolian deserts, north of the Iranian and Iraqi deserts, they arrived completely unannounced in the rear of the Goths, who were occupied with the Romans. The Hunnic attack was devastating.

The Huns arrived one morning in numbers like locusts, riding little ponies, and after launching a swarm of arrows, fiercely attacked anyone in their path. They were not like any people the Goths had met before. They were extremely mobile and favored long-range fighting with the bow. Although quick to dispatch isolated groups with sword and lance,they often put captives to death in a barbaric manner.

The Goths had traditionally fought in the forest and on the sea. They were now living on the open steppes and had developed no way to effectively fight this new enemy whose method of war was adapted to the wide open spaces of Asia. This enemy was fifty miles away one day - at one's doorstep the next - and thirty miles away in the opposite direction the day after. The Goths were afoot and this fearsome enemy was mounted. While Gothic infantry was formidable, the Huns would not fight unbroken infantry. They surrounded such groups and rained a torrent of arrows on them until there was a sign of disorder, upon which signal, they charged with sword and lance.

Individual Gothic homesteads and small settlements were overwhelmed and subjected to ghastly treatment by the Huns. Thousands more poured past on their way to the heartlands of the Goths.

Overnight, the Crimean Goths found themselves inundated in a sea of Huns and fighting for their very existence. Before they could mount an effective defense, half were overrun and made captive. The rest escaped by leaving everything and fleeing for their lives.

Ostrogoths

The Goths who were overrun in the years 375-377, who were the eastern Goths or the original East-Germans, became suzerain to the Huns, and from this time on were known as Ostrogoths. In exchange for their lives, they gave hostages to the Huns, and received freedom for agreeing to acknowledge the Huns as their masters; to fight for them when called upon, and to enforce whatever rules and policy the Huns dictated to them.

The Goths gave their word, a sacred act among the Goths, and they rendered loyal service to the Huns - even to fighting their brothers the Visigoths, who had escaped from Hun captivity.[5] Privately, however, the Ostrogoths agreed among themselves that if they ever escaped the yoke of the Huns they would never allow themselves to be made captive by them again.[6]

The conquered Ostrogoths were quickly instructed in Hunnic warfare by their conquerors. They were equipped with horses in the Hun manner, and with Hunnic bows and lances. They were introduced to the mobile mounted tactics of the Huns, to their highly developed horn-braced bow, and learned to wield

5 **GOD'S LAW: "Ye shall not .... fight against your brethren the children of Israel." I Kings 12:24**

6 Informers reported this oath to the Huns, but since Goths were known to take great pride in honoring their oaths, the Huns ignored the report. Of course, honoring an oath to a lawless people, an oath that violates the Law **"Thou mayest not set a stranger (Heb: nokriy - racial alien) over thee, which is not thy brother." Deu 17:15**, put them in conflict with the **WORD** which is God and prolonged their captivity.

it from horseback. This allowed them to effectively fight for the Huns with massed firepower that often overwhelmed the more advanced armor, tactics, and might of enemies who were comparatively immobile.

Visigoths

Those Goths who escaped Hun captivity made an instant transformation in their method of warfare and civilization. From an agricultural nation rooted to the soil, they became a mobile nation at war. Farms vanished. Every man, woman, and child became a member of their mobile army. Adopting the Hun horse, wagon, lance, and most of his tactics, they became devoted practitioners of what worked for the Huns. They improved certain of their new adaptations to give them an edge - to stay a jump ahead of their fearsome enemy. Metal plates were sewn to their leather armor to help turn Hun arrows. Long lances were adapted to outreach shorter Hun lances. To counter the Hun "open order" attack, they adopted the tactic of mass-

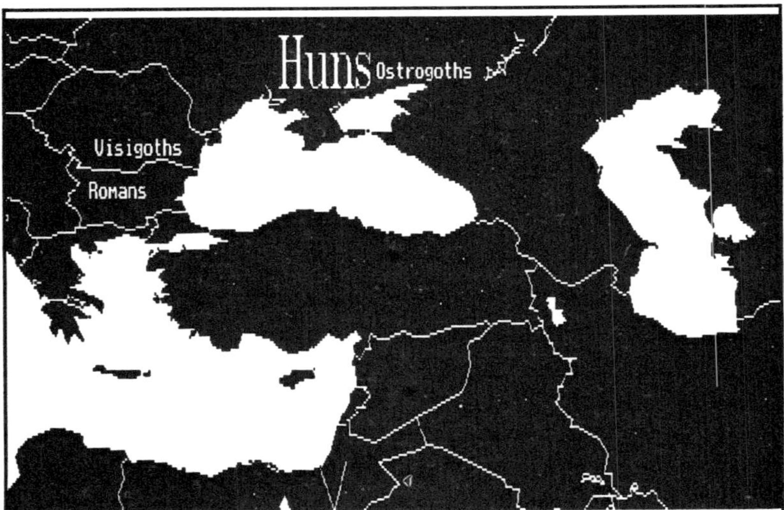

The Hunnic Conquest Of The Crimea

The Huns overwhelmed the east Goths (Ostrogoths) and forced them to fight for the Huns. This combined enemy forced the west-Goths (Visigoths) across the Danube and into conflict with the Romans who failed to fulfill their promise to provide food.

attack designed to run over the enemy not nimble enough to get out of their way.

Part of the mounted Goths dismounted to fight behind wagons or to become infantry stationed behind hedgerows of spears. While waiting for a chance to use their spears and swords, they doubled as archers. They protected themselves with shields to make the Hun mounted archery less effective. Thus, the infantry protected the wagons, the wagons protected the cavalry, and the cavalry protected the infantry. Both mounted infantry and cavalry soon matched the Huns in long marches.

The Danube - Gateway To The West

The Danube River was the boundary that protected Rome's eastern empire. Most of the land on the Roman side of the Danube lay vacant because Roman tax collectors had long before foreclosed the Roman farmers and had driven them from the land. The Visigoths offered their service as warriors to guard the Danube defenses against the advancing Huns in exchange for the right to settle and farm this vacant land. Of course, they needed food until the first crops came in.

This was agreeable to the Roman leaders who were forever short of soldiers, so they agreed to allow the Goths to cross the river and settle. They also agreed to feed them until their first crops came in the following year. Funds were allocated for this purpose and given to Roman officials to buy food. But, instead of buying food, these Imperial officers embezzled the funds for their own purposes, leaving the Goths to starve.[7]

Adrianople - 378 A.D.

The Visigoths had given their word. They were trying to live up to it, but the Romans were not living up to their part of the contract - to bring food. The Visigoths were starving. They waited as long as they could and so they requisitioned food from the Roman countryside to stay alive. They were joined in this looting by scattered groups of kinsmen Ostrogoths, and inde-

7 **The World Of The Huns.** Otto J. Maenchen-Hefew, p. 470, Univ Cal Press, LA 1973

pendent groups of Huns and Alani who had found the Visigoth passage across the Danube and had followed them. The Visigoths were now at war with the Romans.

The Goths could not re-cross the Danube - the Huns were waiting for them. They could not stay where they were - there was no food. So, they loaded their women and children in wagons and continued in the direction of Constantinople, the capitol of the Eastern Empire, eating up the countryside as they went.

To meet this invasion the Empire fielded an army and marched to meet the Visigoths. The two armies met on August 9, 378 A.D., west of Constantinople, at a town called Adrianople.

The Romans deployed their incomparable legions, and opened the battle with the *barritus*, the ancient German warrior battle song. The song began quietly and gradually swelled to a thundering roar, which revealed just how German the Roman troops really were. They then commenced their irresistible advance against the Visigoths and their allies.

The Visigoths also sang their war song in praise of their ancestors' exploits.[8] They had circled their wagons, stationed infantry to defend the gaps between the wagons, and waited. The Roman infantry reached the wall of wagons and hesitated - seeing no way of entry. While their efforts were concentrated against the wagons, Visigoth heavy cavalry rode from behind the wagons, charged the Roman cavalry armed with short javelins, and rode right over it. They then instantly reversed field and smashed into the Roman right flank, rolling it up. One Gothic regiment detached itself from the battle and circled behind the Roman lines to fall on the Roman left flank which it also rolled up. This was the first time in history that a Roman legion had been assaulted by mounted Gothic heavy cavalry armed with long lances that were pushed through infantry formations by the weight of charging horses. It was also the first charge of mounted Western chivalry that began the thousand-year reign of the mounted Christian knight.

8 The Trojans and the Greeks of Xenephen's "Ten Thousand" did the same before battle.

With lines shattered, the Visigoth infantry sallied forth from their wagon fortresses into the broken Roman lines. The battle degenerated into a massacre. Among the dead were the Roman emperor and 35 of his high ranking officers. Only the badly mauled Roman cavalry and less than 1/3 of the infantry survived. The Visigoths had shattered the defenses of the Roman Empire - and in the process opened the door wide for the following Huns.

Influx Of Goths And Germans Into Rome

The invading Goths settled Northern Italy, France, and Spain. The Germans also settled in Northern Italy, France, and parts of the Balkans. Seldom noted by historians is that the Germans and the Goths were branches of the same people. One could call the Goths the early "East Germans" and those from Germany - the early "West Germans."

River Travel And Viking Ships

From time immemorial the Goths traveled and traded on the Russian and European rivers. Their ships are described as flat bottomed with figures at the bow and stern, and large enough to transport 25 or 30 men. This is the description of a Viking ship! The Viking ship was born on the rivers of Russia where shallow draft flat-bottomed boats were an absolute necessity. The exploits of the later day Vikings were due more to the intrepid men than the flat- bottomed river boats they sailed.

Genesis

Where did these river people come from? This seldom-asked question is answered in II Esdras 13:39-45:

> *"The 10 tribes, which were carried away prisoners out of their own land.... whom Salmanasar the king of Assyria led away captive .... took this counsel among themselves, that they would leave the multitude of the heathen, and go forth into a further country, where never mankind dwelt, That they might there keep their statutes, which*

> *they never kept in their own land. And they entered into Euphrates by the narrow passages of the river. .... For through that country there was a great way to go, namely of a year and a half:*[9]

II Esdras quoted above is in the Apocrypha - one of the 10 books removed from the King James Bible in 1825. It is little wonder that people know so little about themselves.

Josephus wrote the following only 300-400 years before the Goths arrived on the stage of history:

> *"There are but two tribes in Asia and Europe subject to the Romans, while the 10 tribes are beyond Euphrates till now and are an immense multitude." Josephus, Antiquities 10:5:2.*

The two captive tribes mentioned must have been the Israelites in Palestine and the people of Britain and Gaul subject to the Romans. The 10 tribes beyond the Euphrates are obviously the Scythian-Saxon-Goths. There was only one other large group of people in that region and they were called "Sarmations" whom we believe to be ancestors of the Slavs. Slavs are believed to be a mixture of Saxon plus "something else."

River Highways

Look closely at the map of the Black Sea shown on page 116. The great river flowing in from the west is the Danube. One could sail up that river as far as he could, hike 30 miles over to the Rhine River, and sail down to the North Sea, and save hundreds of miles of dangerous ocean travel. This was done on a regular basis. The Romans were forced to keep a large fleet on the Danube to stop this river traffic.

River Fork Trading Posts

Wherever two rivers came together, one found a trading post. These trading posts in time grew into villages and towns. They

9 Traveling only 8 miles a day, 1641 miles could have been covered in a year and a half, and Israel's captivity took place 700 years before Christ. This was enough time for them to have covered the world, as recent archaeological finds are confirming.

had been there for centuries. Gothland, early Gotland, or later Russland or Russia, was a series of towns and trading posts scattered alongside rivers all over the immense land area of Russia.

Goth-Slav Relationship

The Slav-Goth, or Slav-Russ, relationship is ancient. Respect has always been rendered between the two - and a reluctance to push differences to the point of confrontation if at all possible. While the Goths settled on farms and villages located on the Russian rivers, the Slavs migrated over the endless steppes, seldom coming in contact with Goth settlements - unless there was a reason to.

Slavs have many admirable qualities, but self-discipline is not one of them. When they drink they tend to drink too much, when they fight their fights can degenerate into massacres. When they rule, they are often oppressive - good hearted - but lawless. This lack of order tended to make them easy prey for roving Turkic nomads who captured Slavs as slaves - which gave them their name - "Slav."

In time, many of the weaker bands sought protection from their more aggressive fellow Slavs and the everpresent Turkic raiders by placing themselves under the protection of the Goths. This was the basis of the ancient Goth-Slav alliance. The Turk was the common enemy.

Vikings

The Russian rivers were Gothic highways. There were few men living on the Baltic in the far north who had not made the voyage to the Black Sea and back again. Those living in the Baltic in the north traveled out to the North Sea and up the rivers deep into the heart of Germany. The Romans named these Goths - "Germans."[10]

10 In this manner another name was added to describe the same people: Goth, Saxon, Scythian, Russ, Saxons from Angleland - Anglo-Saxons, the Saxons from Jutland - or Jutes - and "Germans."

The Gothic-Germans in the north heard about vacant land in France, Spain, and Italy, and their younger sons went forth to take possession. Roman armies were paid to keep these vacant lands for their absentee landlords. To the Goths these Roman armies were a nuisance and were looked on in the same way American settlers looked on the American Indians who stood in the way of gaining land of their own. They were just obstacles to be overcome.

By this time the Roman Empire was a hollow shell. There were no Romans left and soldiers were scarce. Many of these would-be Germans settlers found it more profitable to serve in the Roman armies. It was these western-Goth soldiers, now called "Germans," who were hired to fight for Constantinople. They faced the Eastern-Goths, or "Ostrogoths," at the battle of Adrianople. Each sang their ancient war songs of their same ancestors.[11] The Roman Empire was a land-corporation ruled by ever-changing policy which they called laws. This policy was enforced by a state- religion, judges, and mercenary soldiers. The people called "Romans" had long vanished. The Empire rulers were administrators who did the hiring, firing, leasing, buying and selling, and levying of taxes. It had devoured most of its own people and managed vast vacant provinces - which is what corporations do in time.

Later, other Goths took their flat-bottomed river boats with carved animal figures at the bow and stern and went "a'roving" into the Atlantic and Mediterranean - they had gone "a'viking" in the Norse tongue. This added still another name to the long list of Gothic names - "Viking."

---

11 **GOD'S LAW: "Ye shall not .... fight against your brethren the children of Israel." I Kings 12:24 "Thou shalt not avenge, nor bear any grudge against the children of thy people." Lev 19:18. "Blessed is the man who does not direct his heart with malice against any man." Enoch 44:3.** Yankee and Southern Saxons may not fight. British and S. African Saxons may not fight. German, Danish, Australian, or Swedish Saxons many not fight. It is the law. EXCEPTION: **"When any persons would compel us to break our laws, then it is that we choose to go to war." Josephus, Against Apion** 2:38. He who would require the Saxon to break God's law, fights God, and is the Saxon's enemy.

Hanse

Still later, the Roman religious-political system spread into the north Gothic countries and took the people's land. All land now belonged to the Roman religious corporation called the Roman Catholic Church, and was managed by local princes.

Dispossessed farmers went to seaside villages where their numbers caused them to grow into cities. These cities built walls and defied the rule of local princes and kings who policed provinces and collected taxes and tithes as part of their fief obligations to the landlord Catholic Church. These cities also built ships which traded with other independent cities inhabited by the descendants of these dispossessed Gothic-Saxon farmers. These ships were armed and powerful. In time many of these cities combined into an organization called the "Hanse." They formed an early monopoly to oppose the Holy Roman Empire and the political/economic rule of the Catholic Church. They were so successful in what they did that it is said that the price of bread remained the same for three centuries in the Hanseatic League.

The League included cities in Russia, Denmark, Sweden, Norway, Germany, England, Holland, and France. An injury to the ships or trade of one was considered as an injury to all. They fought and won wars with some of the greatest of the European powers. Their leaders met periodically on the Island of Gottland in the Baltic Sea, and their Hanse was the most important economic power for centuries. It was not until the power of individual states grew greater than the confederation of Hanse cities that the organization declined in power and then vanished.

Hitler's Living Space - Russia

The Gothic-Russ, allied with Slavs, fought Islamic-Turkic invaders almost continuously from the time of the Crusades until 1917. This alliance gradually drove Turk rule from Russia and regained the land that had been lost.

In the process, several Turkic tribes were overrun - these were former invaders who had moved in and settled on Gothic-Slavic land. These conquered Turks were treated as they had treated others. This heavy-handed treatment kindled smoldering fires of hatred.[12]

Other conquered Turks, aided by kindred usury-bankers in the West, made alliances with disaffected Russian-Slavs to overthrow the Gothic-Russ. In 1917, they launched a successful revolution. The Goths, with few exceptions, were exterminated by the millions in the land they had occupied for thousands of years. The Slavs were left with a new Turk master who had always hated them.

Gothic-Russ refugees brought sad tales of disaster to the German West. It was inevitable that a Western German-Goth crusade would be made to reinstate the Gothic-Russ refugees into their ancient homeland. It would also provide a home for the surplus Goth populations living in central Europe. This German-Goth crusade to the east was crushed by a Turkic-led western confederation of Gothic states. By way of punishment additional land was taken from the German and Austrian Goths and tribute has been exacted from them for the past 50 years.

Now, after a rule of three-quarters of a century, there is nothing but ruin left in Slavic-Russia. The Turkic nomads are leaving. They are abandoning the land and moving on - leaving shambles behind them. Democratically "media-selected" Slav and Turk administrators are attempting to rule without traditional Gothic direction. The result is predictable.

Summary

"God's people" have eternally been told to flee their nemesis. Adam was instructed to flee Satan; Able - Cain, Jacob - Esau, the sheep - the wolf, the Christian - the Turk. Now there is no

---

12 The southern Turkic provinces are presently attempting to withdraw completely from Slavic Russia to join the Islamic confederacy.

place left to flee to. This is not the fault of the Turk. God told his people not to deal with strangers.[13] The fed wolf never leaves the sheepfold. The enemy is not the wolf - it is the disobedient among God's own people who feed the wolf.

For many years disobedient Goth teachers, preachers, and political leaders have misled their own people. "Goths" are not cities to rule; counties, states, and nation-franchises to sell to the highest bidder. We are not someone's property. We have been appointed Kings and Priests by our God,[14] and fully intend to take our rightful place. We know who we are - where we came from - and where we are going.

We are children of the Goth-Saxon-Scythian peoples of the Russian and European rivers. Our forebears settled Russia, Italy, Scandinavia, Germany, Britain, France, Spain, America, South Africa, Australia, and New Zealand. They are known by many names including Indo-European and Caucasian - the name of the mountain chain which contains the narrow pass called the Pass Of Alexander, through which they escaped from Assyrian captivity almost 3000 years ago. Names and peoples change, but "God's people" are still known by the three proofs of Israel.[15]

God did not bestow his name - "Goth" - without reason. He also named his people "Israel" so that they would have his "power of attorney."[16]

13 **GOD'S LAW: "And ye shall make no league with the inhabitants of this land." Judges 2:2; "Thou shall drive them out before thee. Thou shalt make no covenant with them, nor with their gods. They shall not dwell in thy land, lest they make thee sin against me." Ex 23:31- 33; "If thou hast stricken thy hand with a stranger, thou are snared." Pr 6:1-2**

14 **GOD'S LAW: "Jesus Christ .... hath made us kings and priests unto God and his Father." Rev 1:5-6**

15 (1) God's name - CHRISTIANS - **"They shall put my name upon the children of Israel." Num 6:27** (2) Isaac's name, SONS OF ISAAC - ISAACSONS - SAXONS, **"In Isaac shall thy name be called." Romans** 9:7, and (3) Adamic descent. "Man" in **Strong's Concordance** is the Hebrew Adam. "Adam" means to "blush red." "Show blood in the face." Genuine Israelites can produce all three proofs. CHRISTIAN - SAXON - MAN.

16 Israel - Heb: Yisrâ'êl - "He will rule as God .... also his posterity." **Strong's Concordance**

Chapter 13

WEST GOTHICA

E. Gothica Combines With W. Gothica

The story of the East Goths dovetails with that of the West Goths in the person of Charlemagne. His empire consisted of both East and West Goths. His feats are legendary. However, there are two facts that most historians overlook. The first is that Charlemagne was hired by the Roman Catholic Church to manage the lands of Europe which they claimed as their own. Second: the road of his military conquest was prepared for him by missionaries of the Roman Catholic Church.

Taking Farms - Making Serfs

After the wolf is in the sheepfold, his first act is to begin a tax program designed to destroy self-sufficient farms. The reason? The sheep who owns his own tax-free land is self-sufficient. He doesn't need the spice merchant or his goods, and is certainly hostile to being taxed.

The empire-building technique of removing land from freemen and reducing them to serfs is ancient. Douglas Reed in his *The Controversy of Zion*, Noontide Press, Newport Beach, CA, 1985. p. 219, has this to say about it:

> "Next, Karl Marx. The Protocols say, 'The aristocracy of the peoples, as a political force, is dead .... but as *landed proprietors* they can still be harmful to us from the fact that they are self-sufficient in the resources upon which they live. It is essential therefore for us at whatever cost *to deprive them of their land* .... "

"Karl Marx in his *Communist Manifesto* exactly followed this formula. True, he declared that Communism might be summed up in one sentence, 'abolition of private property', but subsequently he qualified this dictum by restricting actual confiscation to *land* and implying that other types of private property were to remain intact. (In the later Marxist event, of course, all private property was confiscated, but I speak here of the strict parallel between the strategy laid down *before* the event by the Protocols and Marx.)"

The transfer of free people into slavery moves in lock-step with the transfer of the ownership of their land to their rulers who are agents of the international spice merchant. But, before the transfer can take place, the ancient gods who oppose the transfer of land must be replaced with gods that approve the transfer. Only then can the transfer take place.

The Druids

As the invincible Roman armies advanced into Europe, they encountered fanatical opponents among the Celts and Saxons. If conquered, they rose again in revolt after revolt. The Romans questioned their captives and learned that this fanaticism was the result of the teachings of their Druid priesthood. In other words, for the Romans to secure peace over their conquests the Druids must be exterminated.

It was the policy of the Catholic Church to destroy the records of religions that were defiant to Roman rule. Because of this, practically all records of Druid beliefs and teachings vanished, and the vanished Druids became what their conquerors said they were. This allowed the establishment to create a picture of crazed hooded barbarians, who, in league with trolls and witches, engaged in human sacrifices at night on desolate moors. It has only been in the last hundred years that a more balanced picture has emerged. The following articles give a different view.

"The Druids may be described as an association of professional wise men, philosophers in the early Greek sense, claiming to be experts in all the higher branches of knowledge. They professed special knowledge of the gods, the other world, the future life, the form and measurement of the earth, the movements of the heavenly bodies, the history of men; and they were accepted as authorities in matters of religion and law."[1]

The following sheds even more light:[2]

"An ancient Greek manuscript translated by C. S. Sonnini, and printed in English in 1801 tells of St. Paul's visit to Britain. Verse 13 reads: 'And it came to pass that certain of the Druids came to Paul privately, and showed by their rites and ceremonies that they were descended from the Hebrews which escaped from bondage in the land of Egypt, and the Apostle believed these things and he gave them the kiss of peace.'

"Mr. Charles Hulbert, writing in 1825 says: 'So near is the resemblance between the Druidical religion of Britain and the Patriarchal religion of the Hebrews, that we hesitate not to pronounce their origin the same."

"Cassell's 'History of England' says: 'The Druidical Rites and Ceremonies in Britain were almost identical with the Mosaic Ritual."

"Crania Britannica' records: '...the unearthing of a cist or barrow at Stonehenge, in which were the remains of a Druid perfectly clad in his sacred garments, with a breastplate on his breast, the facsimile of that worn by the Hebrew High Priest."

"The Ten Commandments of the Druids, were almost identical with those given by God to Moses. The Druids worshipped a Trinity, one of Whose Names was 'Yesu,' so when the early Christians preached Jesus as God they preached the most familiar Name of its own Deity to

1 **E/B**, 14th ed, Ireland, p. 599

2 Excerpted from **Association Of Covenant Peoples**, Nov 1993, Vol 16, No 11, issn 0840-5778, PO Box 1478, Ferndale, WA 98248

Druidism. In the ancient British tongue 'Jesus' has never assumed its Greek, Latin or Hebrew form, but remains the pure Druidic 'Yesu.'

"So it seems apparent that the Druids were Levites, and that they too must have arrived in the British Isles before the Israel Nation was established in Palestine. Possibly the 'seven thousand' whom God said had not bowed their knee to Baal were these Druids in the 'Appointed Place,' the Isles of the Sea, North and West of Palestine."[3]

Saint Patrick 387-461

The conquest of Ireland took place without the need for an armed invasion. It is a textbook case.

Saint Patrick was commissioned by the Catholic Church to secure Ireland for the Catholic Church. He was an ideal selection. He knew the land and its people. He was a Briton who had been carried off as a slave to north-eastern Ulster. After laboring six years as a shepherd,[4] he was released and made his way back to the Continent and spent fifteen years studying in the Church of Auxerre. Receiving his instructions he was given the rank of first bishop of the Irish in 431 by Pope Celestine I, and set out for Ireland where he arrived in 438.

He could have gone to any one of a dozen nominal Irish kings, but he chose King Loiguire. The records say that he was vigorously opposed by local priests (Druids), but that King Loiguire, son of Niall, received him eagerly and proved to be an eager listener.[5]

Patrick explained to him the workings of the Catholic Church, how that it was God's representative on earth and its priestly administered "last rites" sent the faithful to heaven. It could also excommunicate and send people to hell. He told the Irish King

3 Jer 31:10; Jer 3:12, 23:8

4 **"And if thy brother, a Hebrew man, or a Hebrew woman, be sold unto thee, and serve thee six years; then in the seventh year thou shalt let him go free from thee. .. thou shalt not let him go away empty: Thou shalt furnish him liberally out of thy flock, and out of thy floor." Deut 15:12- 14**

5 Before the arrival of the Catholic Church, those called "kings" were often judges, or war-leaders, not a king in the modern sense - one who holds himself above his fellows.

that the Church was willing to publicly confirm him in a true kingship over such lands he would like to claim, and punish any of his subjects who objected with excommunication. He explained that the parishioners would be required to pay tithes and taxes, and pay the church to pray their loved ones out of purgatory. All this should amount to a tidy sum which would be shared with the king in return for his protection, endorsement, and help in collection. All that was needed was his blessing and protection to set up operations.

King Loiguire was an ambitious man, and in the manner of ambitious men was perpetually short of cash. This offer was the best one that had come his way. He agreed.

Saint Patrick was jubilant. He had arrived in Ireland in 438, and in 439, the short space of a single year, with the king's help he was so successful in establishing the Roman Church that his patron Germius had to send three bishops to his assistance. Their names were Secundinus, Auxilius, and Iserninus. Patrick chose Armagh for his own "see" near the ancient Ulster capital. These four bishops divided the country, and Ireland was added to the empire without the usual expense of an invading army.

Observation

It is interesting to note that Patrick bypassed the obstacle of the Druid priesthood by first securing the protection and endorsement of a sympathetic king. Once the Catholic Church was installed, the Druids were suppressed. Then the ancient laws of Ireland were replaced with Catholic Church policy, which made rule much easier. Slave ownership was abolished and the freed slaves turned into tithers and taxpayers. Feudalism was gradually introduced which reduced freemen to slaves. Monasteries were established to train priests to manage the new owner's wealth of land and money that flowed into church coffers. [6]

6 One must not forget that one of the major causes of the present problems in Ireland is that in 1155 Pope Hadrian IV gave Ireland to the English king to rule.

Charlemagne 800 AD

Charlemagne was crowned Holy Roman Emperor by the Pope. He conquered much of Germany and held it en fief from the Catholic Church. The formerly free Saxons were given the choice of Catholicism or death. Feudalism was introduced and the Saxons were reduced to serfs.

Most histories turn their spotlight on Charlemagne. He is the one who turned Europe upside down. He pulled down kings and turned mighty Saxon warriors into meek peasants who touched their caps when the empire's mighty priests and warriors rode by. Charlemagne was colorful, powerful, and an emperor in stature (almost 7 feet tall) and royal authority. He was also only the spearpoint of the Catholic-Hindu juggernaut driving into the heart of Europe. The feudal system he installed is worth reviewing.

Europe's Feudal System

India's feudal system consists of four castes:

(1) the priest;

(2) the king and his warriors;

(3) the farmer or store keeper; and

(4) the workers.

The same hierarchy exists today:

(1) *the "priest"* - the "banker" acts as surrogate for his priest. It is his god's laws which are the ones enforced today;

(2) *the king and his warriors* - the "media-elected," or "media-appointed" and their enforcers;

(3) *the farmer/store keeper* - "entrepreneurs/ investors;

(4) *the workers* - corporation president down to floor sweeper.

An empire may have ONE religion or MANY religions - one race or many races. If there are many - the unifying thread that keeps the peace is - "Dharma." Dharma becomes THE religion.

Today, we have corporations for manufacturing, service, and defense needs. Yesterday, when the Church owned practically all manufacturing and farming, and was responsible for education, religious activities, and warfare, "orders" (corporations) were created to supervise these activities. The foremen and supervisors who belonged to these Orders lived in monasteries and convents (now schools & universities) to ensure indoctrination and special education. They were as much a part of the Church as the minister who stands in the pulpit on Sunday, and the local plant manager whose corporation stock is owned through a bank whose stock is owned by the Church.

Catholic Military Orders

The "orders" of the Roman Catholic Church managed specific projects, such as manufacturing, trade, education, religious projects, and war. The Church military orders, the Templars, Hospitallars and Teutonic Knights, were spectacular. They performed feats of heroism during the Crusades that seem remarkable even to today's jaded historians.[7] However there was a drawback; as new recruits gave their wealth to the organization they were joining, most of these Orders over time became so wealthy and powerful that the military organizations they belonged to competed with the power structure of the church itself and had to be downsized or even disbanded.

One of these military Orders, the Templars, grew so powerful and became so rich that the Catholic Church, to protect itself from a possible rival, excommunicated the entire Order and confiscated its land and wealth for itself and its administrative kings.

Another, the Teutonic Knights, was threatened with being disbanded, so they took the vast stretches of land they held en fief from the Catholic Church and defected to the protestant cause. This act was never forgotten - or forgiven, as we shall see.

The third group, the Hospitallars, were downsized drastically to prevent that organization from also becoming a problem.

---

7 **War Cycles / Peace Cycles**, Va. Pub. Co., PO Box 997, Lynchburg, VA 24505, $12/copy

From this period on, whenever the Vatican had need for an army to accomplish a specific mission, it contracted with its feudal kings to use their armies. This prevented a home grown "praetorian guard" from evolving like that which caused so much trouble for the Roman Emperor. The loyalty of the church-crowned kings was ensured by the use of religious sanctions (excommunication), and "crusades" by the loyal against those branded as disloyal. Neighboring kings would have liked nothing better than to receive permission from the Pope to invade and sack the lands of their disloyal neighbors. The prime lesson the Church learned from creating their own military orders was that it was cheaper and safer in the long run to use surrogates. Surrogates involve fewer obligations, and if need be, can be controlled by the use of other surrogates.

The Western feudal system divided the Saxon nation into taxable entities called countries, states, counties, and cities. Each of these political subdivisions was "episcopal" in structure. Each country was ruled by a king crowned by the Church to maintain order and collect taxes, and the Church preached Dharma-love to the people so that they would learn to accept the feudal system, their new life as serfs, and their often obnoxious diverse neighbors, thereby facilitating commerce and trade.

Dominican Order - Inquisition 1231

Dharma enforcers (Dharmamatras) were created and named the "Inquisition" by Pope Gregory IX in 1231. It was entrusted to the Dominican Order. Working closely with local political and military forces, they proved forceful enough to eliminate powerful groups such as the Albigenses (Cathari), the Waldenses, the militant portion of the Hussites, and a multitude of lesser brushfire revolts.[8]

The Inquisition required that the person accused be brought before them to swear under oath that they would reveal everything. Failure to reveal EVERYTHING was declared to be

8 The job of Dharmamatras, or enforcing "political correctness," is now performed by other organizations.

perjury, which proved guilt. This was punished by confiscation. Confession to lesser faults resulted in minor penances like flogging, pilgrimages, or fines. Confession to major faults resulted in being made to wear a yellow cross with its resulting ostracism. Denying accusations without being able to prove one's innocence could result in imprisonment for life or execution and total confiscation. Conviction for heresy also resulted in confiscation. Flight to avoid the inquisition resulted in confiscation. Confiscations were a major producer of church wealth.

When executions were handed down, they were not done by the church since "the church" insisted that it was not permitted to shed blood.[9] The convicted were turned over to secular authorities who almost always executed sentence by burning.[10]

9 "Pilate saith unto them, If that speech of his was blasphemy, do ye try him according to your law. The Jews said to Pilate, Our law commands us not to put any one to death; we desire that he may be crucified, because he deserves the death of the cross." Nicodemus 4:15-16; Contrast this with The WORD - **"The hands of the witnesses shall be first upon him to put him to death, and afterward the hands of all the people." Deut 17:7**

10 The King of Spain used the Inquisition to ferret out Maranos and Morescoes - Jewish and Arab converts to Catholicism who, as wolves, remained secretly true to their own gods. The crusade against the Maranos and Morescoes in Spain was a case of state-Catholicism used to further state policy - not necessarily the policy of the Roman Catholic Church. The Roman Catholic Church often verbally abused the Jews, but protected them from actual harm and from the Inquisition.

Chapter 14

CRUSADE TO PALESTINE

The Background

A prophet named Mohammed arose from among the Arabs who studied the scriptures taken to them by Catholic and Jewish missionaries. He soon learned that Jesus had said "*I am not sent but unto the lost sheep of the house of Israel*" *Matt 15:24* and that "*The house of Israel, are my people ... And ye my flock, the flock of my pasture, are men (Heb: adam - those that blush rosy), and I am your God*" *Ezek 34:30-31*. Jesus was undoubtedly a great prophet, his sayings were wise, but, the WORD that was the God of the Christians left no doubt to the Arab who took time to study it, that it was exclusively the God of Israel.

The WORD demanded a standard of conduct that was impossible for the Arab to live up to. It was the opposite of the conduct that had made the Arab and his forefathers for a thousand generations. The WORD of the Christians executed those committing murder, kidnaping, and rape. The true god of the Arabs rewarded his people for committing murder, kidnaping, and rape by making them powerful, wealthy, and satisfied. It was obvious, the God of Israel could not be the god of the Arab. "Allah" was their god, and since Mohammed was the one who had discovered this fact - Mohammed was his prophet.

Gathering followers, he captured a desert city. This act shut down a major portion of the spice routes and kept them shut down for almost a year. Armies were sent to drive him away. They failed. At last, the merchants took the spice route protection franchise from the local king who could not fulfill his obligations, and gave it to Mohammed. This gave Mohammed a steady flow of income, and great prestige. Using both, his revelation from Allah rapidly gained a large following.

Mohammed's teachings were war-like. His followers quickly swept over the near east cutting the spice routes to Christendom. The mighty Christian empire of Constantinople was powerless to stop them, much less to take them back. This presented the Roman Catholic Church a magnificent opportunity. If it could drive the infidel away - the income from the trade routes would be theirs, as well as the income gained from the pilgrims' offerings left at the shrines in the Holy Land.

Proclaiming The Crusade

The Pope marshaled his armies. He proclaimed a *Crusade* to free the Holy City and rescue the grave of Jesus from the infidel.[1]

The kings of Europe were bound by feudal oath to fight for the Church, the nobles were bound by feudal oath to fight for the kings, and the peasants and yeoman were bound by feudal oath to fight for their nobles. As an added incentive, the Pope promised them "eternal merit," "land taken from the Saracens," and "indulgences."[2] He also promised to take back the fiefs and excommunicate and send to hell all those who would not honor their feudal obligations. Because of these incentives millions volunteered.

There was another result. In the process of whipping up the crusading spirit, Christians turned against the infidels living in their midst, including the Jews. The departing warriors killed Jews by the thousands and the Church was powerless to stop them without injury to the crusading spirit. The short term benefit was that each time a Jew died his land holdings obtained by usury escheated to the king who divided the revenue with the Pope. In other words, the massacre of Europe's Jews helped pay for the crusades.

1 "Bishop Adhemar of Puy, whom Urban names his legate, was made leader of the first crusade." **Ency. Brit.**, 14th ed, Crusades, Vol 6, p. 773

2 An "indulgence" was an official signed document granting God's "Pardon" for sins - a veritable passport to heaven. In time these indulgences were bought and sold in everyday business.

Fruits Of War - 1099

The Pope proclaimed the first crusade to be a success. The Roman Church got the Palestine shrines and their income, and occupied spice route cities such as Petra far out in the desert to collect income from them. The Eastern Orthodox Church got back their lost lands in Turkey. The Western kings and knights who fought the wars with their peasant and yeoman followers were decimated. Most died. By the millions they died.

Back home the nobles had mortgaged their estates to finance their part in the crusade. Since usury was a capital crime to Christians,[3] the Church used the infidel Jews to do what they could not do - lend the needed money at usury. The Church decreed that while crusaders were alive and fighting, interest on their loans only accumulated, but payment was not demanded. If they died, or returned home, payment was due. If not forthcoming, their estates were foreclosed and passed into the lender's hands.

The kings numbered and taxed the Jews to gain their portion. They also received the Jews' entire holdings at their deaths. The Church received its portion from its vassal kings according to prior agreements.[4]

3 **"Hath given forth upon usury, and hath taken increase .... he shall surely die." Ezek 18:13**

4 "The Jews could freely reside in such towns only as had an Archa for the preservation of the Jews' deeds and starrs, from which the king could ascertain their capacity for further taxation." **Jewish/Ency.**, England, p. 165; "The clergy complained that .... the Jews (did not) .... pay the tithe to the Church." **J/E,** Portugal, p. 136; "They lived on excellent terms with .. the clergy; they entered churches freely, and took refuge in the abbeys in times of commotion .... and helped to build a large number of the abbeys and monasteries of the country." **J/E**, England, p 162; "All property obtained by usury .... fell into the king's hands on the death of the usurer." **J/E,** England, p. 162; "The deeds proving the indebtedness .... to the Jews were not in the tower, the mob rushed to the cathedral, and there took possession of them and burned them." **J/E,** England, p. 162. This last proves the usury conspiracy between the Catholic Church and the Jews - conspiracy to commit a capital crime.

Business First - Constantinople's Conquest

Being an ally of the Vatican was like being an ally of the United States today - a risky business. Constantinople was wealthy and its defenses weak, so in 1204, the Pope's armies stormed Constantinople and made off with its gold. Of even more value was its treasure house of relics that had been collected for a thousand years. There were bones of saints and pieces of the cross on which Jesus was crucified.[5] These found new homes in Europe's churches and became drawing cards to the credulous. Pilgrimages to these sites deducted years from one's allotted time in purgatory - as did a sinner's donation of land to the shrine.[6]

The Vatican's occupation of Constantinople lasted for 57 years before the Greeks reclaimed their city. In the meantime all the rents and taxes from the lands, businesses, and peoples that had formerly been claimed by the Eastern Church went to the Roman Church.

Constantinople next fell to the Turks in 1453, a fall from which she did not recover. Russia then became the head of Constantine's Eastern Orthodox Church. The Czar of Russia and his church owned virtually everything in Russia and his nobles held their lands in fief from him.

When the Khazar-Turks and Slavs revolted in 1917 and killed the Russian Czar and took control of his government - the ownership of the land, businesses and peoples of Russia, as well as the Orthodox Church itself - all passed to the new government which still owns it. It was this new Soviet-Turk government that appointed and confirmed the Christian Orthodox Church officials. These new Soviet rulers were the same Khazar-Turks who converted to Judaism in the 9th century, and who were cousins to the Turks who fought against the Crusaders. The church confessionals that had worked so well as intelligence

5 It is said that there were enough "pieces of the cross" in existence to have built the Spanish Armada.

6 **GOD'S LAW: "Ye shall not offer unto the Lord .... an offering thereof in your land." Lev 22:24.** To give away one's land would nullify God's command to divide the land and never sell it. Num 26:53-55.

gatherers for the Czar's government now supplied intelligence to the new Turk-communist government of the anti-Christ.

Many Khazar-Turks switched to Orthodox-Christianity and Islam. Some became Christian priests. Today's Polish Catholic Pope was confirmed as a priest by the Soviet communist occupation government. This, plus the pope's approval of widespread Turkish immigration into Europe has fueled speculation among Catholics that this present Pope is himself a Turk.

The Latin Kingdoms

Christian rule in Palestine was doomed from the start. Instead of dividing conquered lands among the people by lot as required by scripture,[7] the Catholic Church paid its crusading kings by giving them the lands they had captured - en fief. The kings divided their allotted holdings to their loyal counts on the same basis. The counts divided their share among their surviving knights, who in turn divided their shares among their surviving men-at-arms. It was a closed monopoly-agreement. Since so few survived, the land allocations were far larger than had been planned earlier. The few controlled much and the land was sparsely settled by them. As a result, the Crusader "Latin Kingdoms" were a closed corporation - when kings, hundreds of barons, thousands of counts, and tens of thousands of men-at-arms were arriving monthly as reinforcements to fulfill their feudal obligations to the Pope, and the land was short of settlers and fighters. The Christian kings of Palestine could retain almost none of the reinforcements since there was no un- alloted land on which to settle them. Most "defenders of the cross" were forced to return home as paupers.

---

7 **GOD'S LAW: "The land shall be divided for an inheritance .... To many thou shalt give the more .... to few thou shalt give the less .... the land shall be divided by lot." Num 26:53- 55; "Joshua divided the whole land by lots to Israel for an inheritance, as the Lord had commanded him." Jasher 90:19;**

Approved Lifestyle

The Christian conquerors of Muslims, after satisfying their initial blood lust, allowed most of them to remain to work the land, and even tried to convert them.[8] The Arabs, unable to defeat the Crusaders on the battlefield, and having no religious inhibitions against racial interbreeding, fell back on the ancient "Balak Plan" used with such success by their ancestors in prior days.[9] As a consequence, and with the Church's blessing, many Christian rulers found solace in the dusky arms of comely Turk women - thereby delivering the land and inheritance to their mixed-breed Turk offspring in the next generation.[10]

8 **GOD'S LAW: "These twelve Jesus sent forth, and commanded them saying, Go ye not into the way of the gentiles .... go rather to the lost sheep of the house of Israel." Math 10:5**

9 Josephus, **Antiquities** 4:6:1-13; For a free copy of **The Balak Plan**, Send a self addressed stamped envelope to the **Virginia Publishing Company**, PO Box 997, Lynchburg, Virginia 24505.

10 **GOD'S LAW: "The lips of a strange woman drop as a honeycomb .... Remove thy way far from her .... lest strangers (Heb: zûwr - racial alien) be filled with thy wealth." Pr. 5- 10; "A bastard (Heb: mamzêr - mixed breed, mongrel) shall not enter into the congregation of Israel." Deut 23:2; "With harlots and adulteresses shall ye be joined, and the daughter of the Gentiles shall ye take to wife purifying them with an unlawful purification." Testament of Levi 4:17**

Chapter 15

WILLIAM THE CONQUEROR

William The Conqueror - Invading England - 1066

At about the same time the crusades started, William the Conqueror invaded England.

The English have long claimed that both Jesus and St. Paul journied to Britain. St. Paul's Cathedral in London is said to be located on the spot where Paul once taught. The Roman armies brought the Catholic form of "Christianity" in the 4th century. In fact, Britain is recognized as the oldest diocese of the Catholic Church. However, the Britains were fiercely independent, especially the Saxons. While rendering nominal respect to both the King and the Catholic Church, they retained their freedoms including the freedom from the feudal system and its tax system. The payment of rents and tithes to Rome by the English king were token at best. The matter was notorious. Britain was ripe to be exploited.

The Papacy contracted with William of Normandy to conquer England; "The expedition had the solemn approval of Pope Alexander II."[1]

William was the bastard son of Robert the Devil, duke of Normandy. His father, Robert, was the son of Viking invaders. He died on a pilgrimage to Jerusalem and left William his successor. With the help of his overlord, Henry I of France, William put down rebellion against his rule when news of his father's death was received.

1 **Ency. Brit.**, Vol #23, p. 609

William had difficulty securing the backing of his barons for the upcoming invasion of England. He had to go to each with promises and threats. At last, he loaded his men and horses and sailed for England. He landed at Hastings where he won a hard fought battle against the English. He then proceeded to London where papal approval was publicly bestowed on him when he was crowned King at Westminister Abby by the Pope's representative.

William proceeded to install the Roman Catholic feudal system over the rest of the land, building castles as he went to protect his confiscations from the revolts of irate Saxons. Each stage of the conquest presented a new reward for another of his warriors. Almost every English landholder, large and small, was dispossessed, although under church statutes only those who bore arms against William should have been treated in this manner. However, William decreed that those who had not borne arms against him had not borne arms against Harold, his enemy, either. This was the fault that William found. Under Constantine's Bequest, all the land belonged to the Catholic Church. Those who did not fight against Harold were presumed to have acquiesced in his "robbery" of the moneys due the Pope and were therefore enemies of the Papacy. The punishment they received was considered the punishment that was due them. All Saxon English, of whatever rank, were almost overnight dispossessed and reduced to serfs - workers of the land. "In place of the individual absolute ownerships of Saxon days, the Conqueror became practically the sole owner of the soil."[2] Without explanation this statement is misleading. The kings owned their kingdoms en fief to the Pope. This was the extent of their ownership.

The feudal Church owned the land - they were the first caste, King William and his warriors protected the land and collected taxes, tithes, and offerings. They held the land en fief to the church and were the second caste; the merchants and farmers held en fief from the King, they - were the third; and the formerly free Saxons, now virtually slaves, held only small plots

2 **Ency. Brit., 14th Ed, p. 437, Peerage**

of ground from the farmer-overseers placed over them. England had become a feudal state with its caste system. They were now well organized and were great producers of revenue for the Church.

There was no question about who ruled - "Until the reign of Edward III, the peerage consisted only of high ecclesiastics, earls, and barons."[3] The "earls" and "barons" were added to the peerage later as a gesture of goodwill by the church, but, everyone was acutely aware of the power of the papacy which cast its shadow over all the land.

The Jews

> *"Whosoever denieth the Son, the same hath not the Father." I Jno 2:23*

> *"They shall not dwell in thy land, lest they make thee sin against me." Ex 23:33*

> *"Receive a stranger into thine house, and he will disturb thee, and turn thee out of thine own." Ecclesiasticus II, 11:34*

The Jews have historically been used as a hidden order of the Catholic Church. They do things the Catholic Church does not like to be seen doing.

Jews are perfect for the job. A superficial study of their religion with its shrill and repetitious anti-Christian diatribes against Jesus; its preoccupation with excrement and sex; and their sharp practices make them an easy target for their detractors. Some people become so distraught over their practices that "Jews" become almost all that they can talk about. Good hearted patriots, wishing to uphold the Laws of God, can not understand why those in power will not do something about Jewish anti-Christian, anti-Western, anti-American acts! They spend their daylight hours uncovering more of their mis-deeds to complain about.

3 **Ency. Brit.**, 14th Ed., Peerage, p. 438

This is precisely why the Jews have been put in the position they are in - and are so carefully protected. As long as people rail at the Jews, and as long as the Jews rail back at their attackers, no one will look beyond the Jew - and that is where the body is buried.

The Church cannot lend at usury[4] because it is against the WORD and the Catholic Church claims that it is God's representative on earth and custodian of the Scriptures. Therefore, to profit from usury, they used the Jews. Jews have no inhibitions about lending to non-Jews.

To avoid the charge of using Jews as their agents - the Jews were attached to the kings to be managed. With the king's hand thus prominently displayed, no one could say that the Jews collected usury for the Pope. Sometimes the pretense was torn away and the Church was found actually dealing directly with the Jews, as revealed in the following comment in *The Jewish Ency.*, England, p. 162:

> "The deeds proving the indebtedness ... to the Jews were not in the tower, the mob rushed to the cathedral, and there took possession of them and burned them."

The Papacy saw to it that good care was taken of their charges, and this was true from the earliest days:

> "Toward the Jews he (Pope Gregory) acted with lenity, protecting them from persecution and securing them the enjoyment of their legal privileges."[5]

This was a flagrant violation of the law "*Thou shalt make no covenant with them, nor with their gods. They shall not dwell in thy land, lest they make thee sin against me.*" *Ex 23.32-33.* When the antics of the Jews became abusive enough to provoke retaliation - the Church opened its doors to protect them from victims turned hostile - as one would expect them to do if they were of value to the Church.

4 **"Hath given forth upon usury, and hath taken increase ... he shall surely die." Ezek 18:13; "Unto a stranger thou mayest lend upon usury; but unto thy brother thou shalt not lend upon usury." Deu 23:20.** To charge usury, or to condemn a lender to death by paying him interest makes one a "false witness." The punishment for a false witness is to receive the same punishment his victim receives. Both are capital crimes.

5 **Ency-Brit**, Vol #10, p. 869

William needed the Pope's permission to marry, to make war, and to invade England. William was hired help. He kept nothing hidden from his ecclestical supervisors. The Church's confessional system kept the doings of his government an open book. The Jews had been allowed to live and practice usury in Catholic- Christendom for centuries before William. William's relationship with the Jews was standard procedure, and his introducing them into Britain was to comply with general Church policy to exploit the land.

Tax & Foreclose

The usury system operated in the following manner. William imposed feudalism on England. Next he taxed the people in spite of their bitter complaints. The self- sufficient farm system of England formerly had little need of money, so to obtain money to pay King William's taxes, they were forced to pledge their land as collateral to the Jews in exchange for usury-loans. When one borrows $10 and has agreed to repay $11, and the lender refuses to accept anything in place of the 11th dollar that is needed to pay the interest, the borrower is often forced to default and surrender his collateral.[6]

The Jews naturally wanted to keep the property they had taken from those they had foreclosed. To prevent this the king instructed as follows;

> "The Jews could freely reside in such towns only as had an Archa for the preservation of the Jews' deeds and starrs, from which the king could ascertain their capacity for further taxation."[7]

In other words, as secret employees of the state, the Jews could live only where they were directed to live, and all loans had to be recorded with the government. Usury was a sure-fire money making business - and the king loyally sent the pope his share of the profits generated by the Jews.

---

6 See **War Cycles / Peace Cycles,** Virginia Publishing Company, P.O. Box 997, Lynchburg, Virginia 24505, $12/copy

7 **Jewish Ency.,** England, p. 165

Practicing their trade, the Jews in England quickly gathered 1/4 of the land of England into their hands. To secure this land from the Jews and put them to work elsewhere, in 1290, they were forced to leave England and set up business in France and Germany. The rule in effect at that time: "All property obtained by usury ... fell into the king's hands on the death of the usurer."[8]

When the Jews left "they took their portable possessions with them," meaning their working capital. Since the king held his land in fief, all additions to the kings land were automatically additions to the holdings of the Church. If the Church had wished to punish the Jews, they would have taken their money in addition to the estates they had foreclosed, but this would have left them with no way to continue the practice of their usury trade which was so profitable to the Church. The Church had no intent to punish them - it merely wished to move them to more profitable surroundings where they were instructed to practice their trade in their newly assigned territories as they had in England.

When tormented, Saxons rose in wrath against their visible persecutors, which was often. However, the King protected them, and the churches and cathedrals were thrown open as havens of refuge. As soon as the storm clouds blew over and the peasants were herded back to their cottages, the Jews were set back to their work again.

Jewish Popes

The Jews appear as abject servants of the Catholic Church. History is replete with stories of how they have been used, abused, bullied, robbed, and kept on pins and needles - but that applies only to the Jewish masses. To the "alpha-Jews," the door of the Church corporation stands wide open. There are countless Jewish priests, scores of Jewish cardinals and bishops, and some like Anaclet II, Gregory VI, and Gregory VII became popes.[9] Most Jews are Turks who have converted to Talmudism.

8 **Jewish Ency.**, England, p. 162.
9 **Popes From The Ghetto**, Joachim Prinz, Dorset & Co.

Turks as a people are a product of their own lawlessness - the most brutal and bloody rising to rule. As traders and salesmen they historically adopt whatever religion is pleasing to their customers. They do this with not much more thought than a Westerner would take when putting on or taking off a glove.

The religious dogma of the Church is subject to its primary business - which is "business." Its foremost tenant is to spread "Dharma-ecumenism" among peoples and territories it wishes to exploit. All are accepted who will work with the system - and this includes the Jews. The Catholic Church and the Jews are bound together with golden chains hundreds if not thousands of years in the making.

Why One & Not The Other?

In the next chapter we will see how that in the past the Catholic Church has blessed its followers for killing French Protestants, German Protestants, Irish Protestants, English Protestants, and Italian Protestants. This gives rise to the question; why haven't Catholics been ordered to kill Jews that they have vilified so often? Could it be that the Jews are only "cold war enemies" that are in fact "secret friends?" Could it be true that the Jews are actually a secret order of the Catholic Church whose mission is to do that which the Catholic Church dare not do directly? If this is true - it would explain what is otherwise inexplicable.

Chapter 16

SAXON REVOLTS

Wycliffe - 1328-1384

The Catholic Church and its' surrogate ruler, the English king, disagreed over the division of rents, taxes, and tithes taken from the people.

The English king had his own champion - a Catholic priest named John Wycliffe. His weapon was the Bible. A serious ecclesiastical argument by a king with the Church over money was something that had not happened in a thousand years, and it caused consternation in the ranks of the Catholic Church.

Wycliffe knew the Bible. He pointed to the place where it said that monopolies were forbidden, especially land-monopolies, that the land was to be divided and never ever sold.[1] Wycliffe had known this for a long time, but he couldn't speak out and challenge the Catholic Church unless he had someone to protect him from being burned alive as a heretic.

The princes of England were glad to give him their protection - there was a lot of money at stake. He was talking their language when he told the world that God said that land-monopolies were illegal - illegal for the Church, that is.

The princes paid Wycliffe to attend all the conferences they held with the Pope's representatives. He was their "expert witness," and they paid him 20 shillings a day for doing it - a royal income in that time. As their in-house ecclesiastic-lawyer he

1 **GOD'S LAW: "Woe unto them that join house to house, that lay field to field, till there be no place, and they may be placed alone in the midst of the earth." Isaiah 5:8; "The land shall not be sold for ever." Lev 25:23**

argued their case and they protected him from a Roman church that was irate because one of their employees had switched sides and had let the cat out of the bag on this land-monopoly thing.[2] In 1366, he published his *Determiatio quaedam de dominio* supporting parliament in refusing the tribute demanded by Pope Urban V.[3] The controversy continued:

> "As soon as parliament met in the autumn of 1377, Wycliffe was consulted by it as to whether or not it was lawful to allow that treasure to pass out of the country in obedience to the pope's demand."[4]

Wycliffe quoted scripture proving that it was unlawful to do so. Wycliffe was indispensable. From being the Pope's churchman, he was acting as the Princes'-churchman - a state priest. He said things that the Roman church burned people for saying - those people who had no protection.

Wycliffe's Bible

Wycliffe suggested to the king that the quickest way for the king to gain the support of the people was to allow them to read the scriptures and determine for themselves who was right - the prince or the pope. The King's council agreed. But to do this, a Bible in English would be needed since most of the people who could read couldn't read the Latin Vulgate. Wycliffe agreed to translate the Bible from Rome's Latin Vulgate into English - thereby depriving the Church of the monopoly on the Holy Scripture that they had had for a thousand years.

The Bible is an operation manual for all who study it. With the Bible to guide - the warts on the nose of the Roman Church became visible to all. Wycliffe not only translated the Bible, but wrote books expounding the doctrines he had discovered, things that were eagerly read by reform-minded Catholic priests all

2 "He now publicly proclaimed the doctrine that righteousness is the sole title to dominion and to property, that an unrighteous clergy has no such title, and that the decision as to whether or not the property of the ecclesiastics should be taken away rests with the civil power." **Ency. Brit.**, 14th ed, Vol 23, p. 822

3 **Ibid.**, 14th ed, Vol 23, p. 822

4 **Ency. Brit.**, 14th ed, Vol 23, p. 823

over Europe. In rapid succession he wrote the following arguments and pronouncements:

- *De civli dominio.* His argument was that for the clergy to hold property is sinful, and that it is lawful for statesmen - God's stewards - to take away the goods of a clergy no longer obedient to God.
- Wycliffe recommended that the king take possession of the property claimed by Rome, including all the Church-owned monopolies in England as a "divine right."

The king liked that. Other kings in other countries liked that. Land-monopoly, the church's biggest prize, was getting within reach. Why should kings split the peasants' tithe and the merchants' rents and taxes with the church? After all, wasn't England protected by an English Channel if the Church called down a crusade on her head?

- He declared that the doctrine of arbitrary divine decrees of papal infallibility was anathema.

The Bible determines right and wrong. Many priests liked that one.

- Based on the cornerstone truth that "*In the beginning was the WORD and the WORD was with God and the WORD was God*" - the laws, statutes and judgments - and that the Pope was violating the WORD - he found the Pope to be an antichrist (See vol. ii. of the *Sermones. Book iii.* of his *Opus evangelicum* entitled *De Anticristo.*)

Later reformers picked up on this one. The Pope didn't like being called an "antichrist" anymore than today's Pope and antichrist protestant preachers enjoy being labeled with the antichrist tag.

- Knowing that acorns don't fall far from the oak - he pronounced that all "Church Orders" were liable to the same corruption.

This put the Roman Church on one side and the king and his supporters on the other. The people were the balance.

- The argument in his last book *Opus evangelicum*, proclaimed his insistence on the "sufficiency of Holy Scripture."

Today, this argument is accepted by all protestants, and many catholics - in theory. Back then, it was heresy. It put limits on what the Church could do. The Church, (and the princes), could either submit to the WORD and obey its commandments, or fight the WORD, and destroy those who demanded obedience to it. Both chose to give lip service to the first and to follow the latter course.

- It was his discussions from the scripture that brought forth the doctrines of "free-will," "merit," and "predestination."

Calvin later added "grace," and Wycliffe's "merit" proved that the "grace" resulted in salvation. It is hard to have one without the other in spite of the thief crucified with Jesus who had no time to do good works.

- With his new Bible in hand, Wycliffe trained "poor preachers" who spread out over England taking the WORD to all who would listen.

The day of the itinerant preacher had arrived and the WORD went directly to the people, and the common people loved it. They rejoiced in the plain and homely doctrine which dwelt chiefly on the simple "Law" illustrated by the parables contained in the gospels. Unknown to both King and Church, England's people were being taught that their God, the WORD, had promised them wonderful things. These things were there - all around them - if only they would take them for themselves. After all, it was their land the King and Church were squabbling over, it was they who actually produced the wealth upon which both King and Church fed.

Each time the Church came after Wycliffe, he appealed for protection from the king - and got it.[5]

---

5 John Huss later raised Wycliffe's doctrine to the dignity of a national religion. Many of the works attributed to Huss were actually the works of Wycliffe. Huss, Luther and other continental reformers owed Wycliffe much, and the spirit of the English reformer permeated the reformed churches of Europe.

The Peasant's Revolt - 1381

While kings and prelates argued over who was to get the land-monopoly with its tithes and rents, the people had been listening and learning that God said that land was not to be a church-monopoly, nor a prince-monopoly, but that it was to be divided among the people and never ever sold. The Bible said that the land was not to be taxed, that the Bible said that God had made the children of Israel "kings and priests" - not the Kings, or the Roman Church. Of course, the poor preachers who preached to the people had no mighty protector to protect them when they condemned land-monopolies, usury-monopolies, and taught the Biblical stories about the Phineas Priesthood.[6] Both the Church and the King could hang them out to dry, so they "whispered." They were so quiet that neither the prince nor the confessionals of the priest revealed that they were whispering, or what they were whispering about.

Matters came to a head in 1381. Archbishop Sudbury ordered the king to collect from every adult additional tribute in the form of a poll tax. Rich or poor the tax was the same. The poorest family had to provide his three goats. All hell broke loose. The people weren't going to do it. Scripture said that Christians were not to be taxed.[7] All England burst into flame from coast to coast, from city to city, and town to town. Castles and manors were burned. Tax collectors, priests, and lawyers were hunted down and butchered along with proctors (overseers), unjust judges and rulers. County, manor, castle, and town militias armed themselves and gathered. In an age when 8,000 men made a respectable army, the English peasant army numbering 100,000 gathered and elected Wat Tyler their leader. John Ball, a poor preacher, was his religious advisor. They marched on

6 See **Vigilantes Of Christendom**, Hoskins, Va. Pub. Co, P.O. Box 997, Lynchburg, VA 24505, $22/copy.

7 **GOD'S LAW: "Of whom do the kings of the earth take custom or tribute? of their own children, or of strangers? Peter saith unto him, Of strangers." (Gr: allotrios - foreign, not akin.) .... Then are the children free." Matt 17:25-26.**

London. The Londoners were equally oppressed by the church monopolizing manufactures and trade. London's city aldermen opened the city's gates and the rural army joined the city's disaffected militias and together they began hunting down unjust churchmen, judges, lawyers, foreigners, and Lombards (bankers).[8] Whole areas were burnt.

They demanded to be freed from being slaves of the manor. They demanded freedom from taxes and the tithe, and they demanded the right to rent land at four-pence an acre as freemen rather than being the property of the manor. These peasants were armed with long-bows and most arrived in their manorial militia companies. Many of them had fought in the king's wars with France. The week before they were humble serfs. Now, united, they were the most powerful force in the world - and they were armed.

Wat Tyler and his followers met with the royal party of Richard II, a boy aged 14. Most peasant demands seem modest by today's standards - that they not be treated as villains (manor-slaves), be allowed to rent their land at four-pence an acre, be able to move away when they liked, be given relief from and cessation of countless rents, dues, taxes, and tithes.

These demands were granted. Royal letters were written to local governors, and everything was put in a charter. The English love charters. While this was going on, more ecclesiastics were hunted down and dispatched by peasant vigilantes. The next day when they arrived to meet with the king, Tyler had consulted with his poor-preacher advisors and had expanded the peasant demands to include the division of the land among the people as required by scripture. This was the real heart of the matter.

Taking the church land-monopoly from the Catholic Church and dividing it among the king's supporters "en fief" to the king rather than Rome was the prize the king and his party had planned to take for themselves. Now, the peasants demanded this land for their own. The peasants in essence rejected both

8 God's Law is simple and just. Most of man's statutes are unjust. Each one is passed to shave a bit from God's Law and give advantage to special interests. Judges and lawyers, instrumental in destroying justice, were hated by the people.

King and Church and meant to take what was their own land back again. A king without a kingdom was no longer a king.

The king's party made ready to deal with these trusting peasants. After all, they had a kingdom to lose or a kingdom to gain - their future rode on the success of their plans. They negotiated with the peasants to disarm their suspicions. It was planned that when next they met, a SWAT team composed of the mayor of London and twelve of his supporters would suddenly rush Wat Tyler, and cut him down. Everything went as planned. When Tyler got close enough, the assassination party drew concealed weapons and rushed Tyler, killing him.[9] The people were left without a spokesman. Thousands of peasants drew their bows and the lives of the king's party hung by a thread, one bowman loosing his arrow would have caused a thousand more to fly, but before the arrows could be loosed, the young king boldly rode forward and said that he would be their leader. In essence, the wolf told the sheep that he would protect them and the sheep foolishly believed him.

The king rode back to the safety of the Tower of London and issued orders to his armies to attack the peasants. The chivalry of England - knights in full armor - went after the peasants slaying indiscriminantly. The king quickly annulled the freedoms he had just granted and hanged the peasants by the hundreds.

Tyler's advisor, the people's-preacher John Ball, when condemned, confessed that he learned his subversive doctrines from Wycliffe. William Courtenay, who succeeded the executed Archbishop Sudbury, the author of the poll tax that had touched off the revolt - as Archbishop of Canterbury - resolved to stamp out the Wycliffe heresy, including Wycliffe himself. He called a council of bishops, theologians and canonists at the Blackfriars' Convent. But the king still needed Wycliffe, so he remained at large and was unmolested. After all, the king had to have a theological- lawyer to support his claim to the church's land-monopoly. Neither the king nor the Church needed a third

9 The eternal lesson is that violators of the WORD can never be trusted. A thief, a liar, or a usurer will also murder.

claimant to step in - peasants aroused by learning Christian teachings. The prince and church disagreed on almost everything except that. They still do.

The slaughter of peasants continued until there was no evidence of rebellion left. Those protestants who were left alive kept very quiet, but they did not go away.

Today we are regaled in story after story of how Catholics slaughtered Protestants. This is true. However, the story glossed over by the establishment church is that it was the "state-protestants" appointed by the king who slew peasant-protestants by the thousands. "State-protestantism" defends the King's gold as aggressively as the Catholic Church defends its gold.

Lollards

The Wycliffe rebellion was the emergence of something new. It was not another warmed over "Paulican" struggle for Church wealth, between Church and King, or a new "wannabe" rival. Wycliffe's Bible had released the WORD into the minds and hearts of the people. The WORD itself was the leader. It was something that could not be reasoned with, or, as it turned out, stamped out. The people were following a leader who was not "the King and his appointed preachers," nor "the Church and its appointed kings" - it was God the WORD who Himself stood against both King and Priest. It was no longer the 1st and 2nd castes of priest and king suppressing the 3rd and 4th castes of farmer-merchants and workers. The vision that was now followed was "*Thy kingdom come on earth as it is in heaven.*"

Wycliffe's secret followers were called "Lollards." After Wycliffe's death in 1384, the "poor-preachers" that he had trained quietly used Wycliffe's Bible to declare the authority of the WORD into the late 14th and early 15th centuries. They were highly critical of the wealth and power of the church. In time they won the support of Oxford scholars, country gentlemen, wealthy merchants, powerful nobles, and the masses of common people.

The Lollards were subject to more and more persecution. Executions were continuous. To set an example, King Henry V even brought his friend, the popular Sir John Oldcastle, to trial and then burned him at the stake. The Lollards remained underground where they survived to await another day. They were now custodians of the WORD. Their time would come once more - it was inevitable. Wycliffe had loosed the WORD in the land.

Huss 1372-1415

John Huss was a Czech religious reformer. He was an ordained priest who came under the influence of the writings of John Wycliffe and became the leader of the Catholic-Slav reformation. He too criticized the church's wealth and corruption and he supported Wycliffe's doctrines.

Gradually losing the support of the Catholic clergy, he was forbidden to preach and was excommunicated in 1411. One after another he was abandoned by the archbishop, king, and university. Given safe conduct by Sigismund, the Holy Roman Emperor, he traveled to Constance in 1414. He should have known better. The policy of an episcopacy may vary considerably from those of the God of the presbytery:

> "A man who has been excommunicated by the Pope may be killed anywhere."[10]

> "Any person who has promised security to the heretics shall not be obliged to keep his promise." Council of Constantine.[11]

At Constance he was arrested, condemned for heresy, and burned at the stake.

Huss rejected the absolute authority of popes and the Church. He asserted the authority of Scripture over the Church. His execution ignited the Hussite revolt by his followers who

10 **Theologia Moralis**, Busenbaum-Lacroix, 1757

11 **Fifty Years In the Church Of Rome,** Charles Chiniquy, Chick Pub, Chino, CA 1985, p. 288.

spread Slavic-Protestant teachings among the Slavs of central Europe.[12]

The Hussite Revolt

After Huss's death his followers, the Hussites, spread throughout Bohemia and Moravia teaching the supremacy of Wycliffe's teachings over the doctrines of the Catholic Church. In time they split into two factions. One faction wished to retain episcopal government and traditional ritual. The other wished to return to a primitive simplicity, conform to scriptural mandates, and proposed warfare to subdue God's enemies and transgressors of the Law. This group provided the main military force of the Hussite revolution which seized church lands and destroyed church property.

The pope called for a counter-reformation crusade against the Hussites. The Hussites, fighting from heavily built wagons containing cannon, repeatedly defeated their opponents. In time they were worn down to a handful who sought safety in the hills. Some joined the Catholic church, others joined Luther's revolt. The non-violent group of Hussites survived and has come down to us in the form of the Moravian Church.

Zwingli 1481-1531

Ulrich Zwingli was a leader of the Swiss reformation. A Catholic priest, he became a chaplain to Swiss mercenary troops hired to fight in the Italian campaigns. He became convinced that hiring men as mercenaries to kill other men was a great evil.[13]

On his return home he continued his Bible studies. This led him to drop his papal subsidy, and attack ecclesiastical abuses. He allowed his followers to eat meat on fast days, and married

12 The WORD, passing through the Slav filter, becomes Slavic. Because of the Law, it is a twisting of the WORD - a form of paulicanism. However, Slavs are our close kinsmen. We owe them and they owe us. And, they too have suffered at the hands of a common enemy.

13 This is a lesson that the U.S. must again learn. If the price is right, U.S. mercenaries will destroy any people or nation on earth.

in violation of Church prohibition. Zwingli's Sixty-seven Articles became the basis for the Swiss Reformed Church.

Zwingli was responsible for extending the reformation to other Swiss cities: Bern, Ballen, and Basel. Zwingli was killed on the battlefield of Kappel in 1531 defending Zurich from the counter-reformation crusade by the Catholic cantons of southern Switzerland who had been sent by the papacy.

Luther 1483-1546

The Reformation proper is said to have started in Germany on Oct. 31, 1517, when Martin Luther, an Augustinian Catholic priest, posted his "95 Theses." The "Theses" invited debate over the sale of indulgences by the Catholic Church. The papacy viewed this as heresy and proceeded to take steps against Luther.

Luther was protected from the Catholic Church by Frederick III, elector of Saxony. Frederick extended his protection over Luther in exchange for Luther's endorsement of his seizing church property - in the same manner as Wycliffe had been used earlier by the King of England. Luther's writings invited the Christian Nobility of the German Nation to reform the church themselves. He attacked the papacy and its view of the mass - the Catholic teaching that the bread and wine of communion was miraculously changed into the actual blood and flesh of Jesus.[14] He said that the people were being taught to be cannibal-like - eating God's flesh.

He translated the New Testament into German, and wrote the Small and Large Catechisms, countless sermons, hymns, and over 100 volumes of tracts, biblical commentaries, thousands of letters, and then translated the whole Bible into German.

In the German states where protestant princes supported him, he organized Evangelical churches. He abolished confession and private mass. Priests were allowed to marry and

14 **GOD'S LAW: "Whatsoever man there be of the house of Israel, or of the strangers that sojourn among you, that eateth any manner of blood; I will set my face against that soul that eateth blood, and will cut him off (destroy him) from among his people." Gen 9:4**

monasteries were abandoned. Preaching the WORD, he sowed the wind.

The German Peasants War 1524-1526

The Peasants' War was precipitated by Luther's Bible. Luther had gotten the backing and protection of the princes by preaching the same things Wycliffe had taught more than a century before. In exchange for being allowed to preach the WORD and to secure protection from being executed by the Catholic Church for doing it, Luther taught that the princes were more entitled to Church lands and the income from those lands than was the Church. He also taught that the Church was corrupt, which it was. Luther's message was democratic. Its force and directness added fuel to the discontent smoldering for generations alongside natural anti-clericalism.

Seven years after Luther's attack on the indulgence system,[15] the peasants had learned their God given rights and revolt broke out. It was sudden. The standard - a peasant's wooden shoe, a "clog" - on a pole.

In June 1524, encouraged by the successful bid for freedom made by the Swiss, many cities, knights, and even princes came to terms with the insurgents and joined their ranks. The rebels put forward a religious and social program. A basic demand was that each village be allowed to elect its own pastor who wasn't appointed by the Catholic Church. They made another demand - that Church land be divided among the peasants. This demand was to separate the peasants from the ruling kings.

Many of the prince-ecclesiastics felt that it would be better strategy to have the Church land that was under their management divided into many peasant's farm holdings than it was to have it given to individual protestant princes, thereby making the princes powerful opponents. Amongst these ecclesiastical "friends of the farmers" were the elector-palatine, the Bishops of Bamberg and Speyer and the Abotts of Fulda and Hersfeld.

Then too, by being agreeable and negotiating, they might save their heads and maybe retain some land and income. Being

15 Indulgences: a certificate guaranteeing forgiveness for uncommitted sins.

disagreeable put them in double jeopardy. The covetous Lutheran princes on one side were poised to seize their land and on the other side the peasants already had it.

Much of Europe went up in flames as the peasants wreaked havoc on their ancient oppressors. According to the *Encyclopedia Briticannica,* 14th Ed, Vol 23, p. 265: "There was much secularization of church property, suppression of monasteries and introduction of the Lutheran service in many churches."

However, this revolt was playing hob with the agreement that Luther had made with Philip of Hess. Philip was a major figure in Germany at that time. Luther had agreed to support Philip's claim to church land in exchange for his protection. Philip could get the land only if he secured Luther's help to suppress the peasants' revolt.

Luther was now caught between a rock and a hard place. Both the WORD contained in the Bible that he had translated and his teachings triggered the insurgents. At first he sympathized with them and wrote a pamphlet protesting the harsh measures used against them. But Philip was threatened with losing the coveted Church property to the upstart peasants. Luther was the reason for this. If he lost this land he would have no economic reason to protect Luther from the tender mercies of the Catholic Church. Being faced with the loss of Philip's protection and the possible loss of the whole reformation movement, including his head, caused Luther to reconsider.

Luther chose to cast his lot with the Princes against the peasants. He wrote another tract *Against The Murdering, Thieving Hordes Of Peasants.* This latest tract breathed fire and slaughter down on the peasants.

The main revolt was subdued before the end of 1525. It ended in disaster. Peasant outrages and propaganda against them had united the princes, and when they had the upper hand they wreaked outrages of their own in a ferocious vengeance on the people. *The protestant-princes retrieved the land-monopoly from the protestant-peasants that the peasants had retrieved from the Catholic Church.*

The Teutonic Order Switches Sides

A notable event of 1525 was the action of Albert of Hohenzollern, grand master of the Teutonic Order, who, supported by most of his knights, declared for Luther, secularized the property of the Teutonic Order and made himself the personal ruler of its territory between Poland and the Baltic.[16]

This defection was stunning. The Teutonic Order of the Catholic Church was the principal warrior priesthood of the Roman Catholic Church.

Lutheranism - A State Religion

Since the peasant rebels had in nearly all cases claimed religious sanctions for their acts, the peasants were allowed to keep Luther's Bible so as not to unduly antagonize them. However, to safeguard the possession of the new property acquired from the Catholic Church plus the property taken away from the rebellious peasants, the princes demanded that new Lutheran pastors be appointed by episcopal means, "from the top down," rather than presbyterian, "from the bottom up." The princes were to have veto power over the selection of Lutheran bishops. This gave the German princes power over what was to be taught the people by Lutheran pastors. In this manner Lutheranism became a "state-religion" in the service of the princes.

Princely selection of Lutheran Bishops forced Lutheran priests to teach only the one third of the Bible not dealing with government. State-protestantism was a revival of the ancient "Paulicanism" by which nothing but Pauline scriptures are used to disprove the WORD rather than the correct method of using Paul to prove the WORD. The protestant princes were adamant. They had no intention of losing their lands again to peasants who had become religious zealots, the way the Catholic Church lost their lands to them - just because the Bible said "*the land is to be divided and never sold.*" The blood bath that resulted from the peasants' revolt was not a Catholic atrocity, but state-

16 **Ency. Brit.**, 14th ed, Vol 23, p 265

protestantism drowning peasant-protestants in a sea of blood to prevent them from taking back their land.

Besides Germany, "state-Lutheranism" of the Princes became the state-religion of Denmark, Sweden, Norway, and Finland. As a state-religion, Lutheranism could not be turned against the rulers of the state. The preachers attempting to do would be fired. In revised form and as a popular movement, state-Lutheranism penetrated Hungary, Transylvania, Moravia, Bohemia and Poland.

Roman Catholicism, the religion of the Latin nations and Poland, except for brief periods, had always tolerated corruption as a way of life. It still does. The Protestant state-churches of Europe and America are better in degree only - if at all. The great thing accomplished by Luther's revolt is that the Bible was released from a thousand year captivity and the WORD was loose in the land.[17]

The Paulican Revival

Taking part in the Protestant Revolt were Anabaptists, so named because of their opposition to infant baptism. Most were sincere lawful reformists, but some were Paulicans - they rejected the restraints of the Law contained in the WORD. They formed communes of seized property and held it under a leader rather than dividing it. They also indulged in sexual license. These aberrations were harshly suppressed along with the general suppression of the peasants.

Thirty Years War 1618-1648

Once the peasants and their allies among the knights and nobles had been suppressed, the princes held their land unchallenged - excepted by its previous owner, the Catholic Church. The Catholic Church ordered the Holy Roman Emperor to organize a crusade to get it back.

17 At Fishburne Military School in the 1940s, the Bible instructor was a Lutheran pastor. He was one of the best. Much of American Lutheranism has been influenced by religious dissenters escaping Europe's state-religions who owe allegiance to the entire WORD - not just the politically acceptable one-third of the Bible.

The resulting war was between an alliance of Catholic princes and an alliance of princes claiming to be Protestant. Both Catholic and Protestant peasants were driven into the armies of the two factions to fight the wars, and bloody wars they were. Brandenburg, Mecklenburg, the Palatinate, Wurttemberg, Pomerania, and parts of Bavaria lost 50% or more of their population. Some estimates say that the population of Germany dropped from 20 million to 6 million. Whatever it was, the war between the Catholic Kings and the Protestant Princes over the ownership of the peoples' land was the bloodiest thing seen before the 20th-century.

The war ended when there weren't enough peasant soldiers left to fight it any longer. Catholic princes and Protestant princes then got together and made a notable agreement - one having effects down to today. The agreement was this: if a prince was Catholic, his people had to be Catholic. Those who weren't could move elsewhere. If a prince was Protestant, his people had to be Protestant: those who weren't were free to move. This resulted in most German states being either Catholic or Protestant. Today, most sons of the peasants who fought the wars have no idea why this is so, but those who profited from the war - they remember.

The peasant's enemy in Protestant lands was now the Protestant Princes and the Lutheran state-religion taught by prince-selected politically-correct priests. In Catholic lands it was the Catholic Church and their appointed religiously-correct kings. The enemy of both kings and priests was the WORD. The WORD rests ultimately with the people the WORD claims as its own.

Chapter 17

THE COUNTER REFORMATION

Tyndale 1494-1536

Wycliffe (1328-1384) set things in motion with his translation of the Bible.

About a century and a half later, William Tyndale (1494-1536) translated the New Testament into the English vernacular. Fearing that Henry VIII would kill him for making a Bible translation that would teach people their rights, he moved to Germany to get his work printed. Even there his work was protested, and legal injunctions for a time halted his printing. Beginning again, he translated much of the Old Testament and wrote many tracts, all causing consternation when they arrived back in England. King Henry demanded that he be returned to England for spreading sedition. In 1535 he was betrayed by a friend, Henry Phillips, in Belgium, condemned as a heretic, strangled at the stake and his body was burned. This was one more case of an episcopal protestant state-religion defending its master, the king.

Calvin 1509-1564

Lutheran tracts and missionaries spread the protestant movement to France. One convert was a Catholic priest named John Calvin. His beliefs came under attack, and he was forced to flee to Geneva, Switzerland, where he helped organize a great evangelical organization. His book *Institutes of the Christian Religion* (1536) had great influence in Scotland and France. In France, the Protestants, called Huguenots, became very strong.

In 1559, two thousand congregations met to organize a nationwide church.

John Calvin, John Knox, and other reformers translated the Bible into English - a different translation from Wycliffe's translation which had come from the Catholic Vulgate. It was called the Geneva Bible. The unique thing about this Bible was that it contained margin notes by the reformers in small print expounding sections that many found difficult to understand. In this way, the finest brains of the Reformation put their collective opinions into a record that was read by practically every household in Britain. The result was so incendiary that King James was forced to authorize a new Bible to replace it - the one we know today as the King James version.

The first settlers to America brought the Geneva Bible and dispenced Law from it. It referred to the patriarchs as "our fathers," thereby taking the title "Israel" from Britain's Episcopal Church and Rome's Catholic Church for themselves as being the nation of Israel scattered throughout the West. This is an important claim.[1]

Calvin is considered the father of British protestantism. Close attention was paid to the things he wrote - things such as:

> "How absurd would it be that in satisfying men you should incur the displeasure of him for whose sake you obey men themselves! The Lord, therefore, is the King of Kings, who, when he has opened his sacred mouth, must alone be heard, before all and above all men; next to him we are subject to those men who are in authority over us, but only in him. If they command anything against him, let it go un-esteemed."[2]
>
> "I know with what great and present peril this constancy is menaced, because kings bear defiance with the greatest displeasure, whose "wrath is a messenger of death" (Prov 16:14), says Solomon. But since this edict has been proclaimed by the heavenly herald, Peter - "*We*

1 Israel - Heb: Yisrâ'êl - "He will rule as God .... also his posterity." **Strong's Concordance**.

2 Calvin: **Institutes of the Christian Religion**, The Westminster Press, Philadelphia. 1960, Book 4: Chapter 20: Paragraph 32:

> *must obey God rather than men*" (Acts 5:29) - let us comfort ourselves with the thought that we are rendering that obedience which the Lord requires when we suffer anything rather than turn aside from piety. And that our courage may not grow faint. Paul pricks at us with another goad: That we have been redeemed by Christ at so great a price as our redemption cost him, so that we should not enslave ourselves to the wicked desires of men - much less be subject to their impiety. (I Cor. 7:23)."[3]

The establishment's protestant religion in the West gives lip service to Calvin, but the average protestant preacher would die before quoting the above. He would be accused of disloyalty to his country and inciting riot and rebellion against the establishment. It would be the same as insisting "*We must obey God rather than men.*" *Acts 5:29*, which puts men at enmity with Lawless governments who punish its critics by removing tax-exemption à la Bob Jones University and numerous individual churches.

Britain's Revolt - John Knox 1514-1572

The Protestant Revolt reached its most advanced stage in Great Britain. By the time John Knox arrived on the scene, Henry VIII had already seized the properties belonging to the Catholic Church. He took over the Catholic Church in England, made himself its head, and installed his own bishops whose job it was to announce to the world that what the king did was God's will. This was Henry's own new Protestant state-church. It was the old Roman Catholic Church turned into an English Catholic Church with a new name and some new rituals and beliefs. It was entirely episcopal. At the time of Knox, Henry's daughter, a devout Catholic, sat on the Scottish throne.

John Knox, too, had been a Catholic Priest. He became a protestant through the efforts of George Wishart - who was soon thereafter burned at the stake. In retaliation, Scottish protestants executed Cardinal David Beaton who had been

3 Ibid; Book 4: ch 20, PP 1.

Wishart's judge. The Catholic Church sent out a force to punish the rebels. Knox joined in the defense of St. Andrews castle and was captured. Sentenced to serve on a French galley, friends secured his release after 19 months.

In 1553, Knox sought refuge in Geneva where he met and worked with John Calvin. In 1554, Knox began to justify resistance to faithless rulers who attack their dutiful subjects. He also collaborated in the writing of the Geneva Bible.

Returning to Scotland in 1559 he was foremost in the fight against the Catholic queen who was forced to abdicate in 1567, whereupon protestantism was secured in Scotland. Unfortunately, the Church lands were promised to the nobles in return for their protection.

The English Civil War

Scottish Presbyterianism spread to England where Wycliffe's Lollards had prepared a fertile field. As people grew disenchanted with the episcopacy of the king and his Church they were added to the revolt. The king's income produced by the church and its businesses began to diminish, forcing the king to demand increased taxes. The people resisted, demanding the total abolition of the office of bishop by the Church of England, and that the Bible replace the king's Book of Common Prayer which contained neutered verses.

In time, the dispute centered in the Catholic king vs. a Protestant parliament. The king turned to his supporters who held their land "en fief" to him and commanded that they take the field with their supporters. Parliament called up the nation's militia - under command of nobles sympathetic to parliament.

Cromwell

The leader of Parliament's presbyterian forces was Oliver Cromwell. In a series of brilliant battles he defeated the forces of the Catholic king. This left a protestant parliament ruling the nation with no opposition. It was the opportunity the people had waited for. They lobbied parliament to redress ancient wrongs, and parliament began to talk about dividing the land as commanded by scripture. When it ordered Cromwell to disband his army, he refused, packed parliament with his own supporters, and set himself up as a king with the title "Lord Protector." Then, he killed the defeated king and settled his followers, en fief to himself, on lands confiscated from the king's supporters.

Protesting his reverence for God, he set about undoing the reforms of the Protestant Presbyterians. He put religious reform on hold and forbade dissenters to discuss their religious dissents in his army (Dharma). To prevent rebellion to his own rule he respected the prevailing prejudice against Catholics, still, he allowed the surrogates of the Catholic Church, the Jews, into England[4] where they took the place of the expelled Catholics who had formerly managed Church financial and business interests. Some believe that Cromwell was a secret agent of the Roman Catholic Church.

When Cromwell died the old rulers quietly stepped back into the shoes that he had kept safe from the Presbyterian Protestants. King Charles II restored the Anglican Episcopal Church, which he called "protestant," as the state religion. He banned the Presbyterian Covenanters as traitors, banned presbyterian meetings and fined, confiscated, inprisoned, transported, and executed those who were arrested attending meetings held far out in the open fields. It was called "the killing times."

Cromwell's followers were allowed to keep their lands if they transfered their enfiefment obligations to the new king. The remnant who insisted "No King but Jesus" and that "*We must obey God rather than men.*" *Acts 5:29,* were outlawed.[5]

Counter-Reformation

The single purpose of the Catholic Church's' counter-reformation was not to "reform," but to re-establish its supremacy

4 **GOD'S LAW: "They shall not dwell in thy land, lest they make thee sin against me. I Ki 4:21,24; (2) "Receive a stranger into thine house, and he will disturb thee, and turn thee out of thine own." Ecclesiasticus II, 11:34**

5 Their story can be found in **Vigilantes Of Christendom.**

over its old trade areas and to regain lost land, wealth, tax privileges, and to destroy the reformers and their reformation.

Excommunication

The first weapon of the Catholic Church is religious sanctions. In the past the mere threat of excommunication was enough to bring to heel one of their own who displeased the Roman ecclesiastical hierarchy. It was the first weapon used then and now. It is unbelievably effective among Catholic believers. Leon Degrell organized the Rexist Party in Belgium. This is what happened:

> "Contesting the 1936 elections .... the Rexists scored a smashing success against the established parties. .... Degrelle's movement gained 11.5% of the vote and 33 seats in Parliament. But the victory upset the church hierarchy in this heavily Catholic country. When Degrelle challenged the Belgian prime minister in a by-election the following year, the church ruled that voting for the Rexists was 'a mortal sin.' .... For his role .... Degrelle was excommunicated by the Catholic Church. ..."[6]

Excommunication is a tremendous power - a power that has been exercised or has been threatened to be exercised time and again down through the centuries. It is a threat that may be employed against any Catholic - king or peasant - who is not "politically correct." Members of episcopal sects can only know what they are told, and they are told only that which their episcopal hierarchy wants them to know - and they speak for God. When the hierarchy holds the keys to heaven, "true believers" must obey or risk losing their souls - a frightful option.

Inquisition At Work

The Inquisition stood ready to back up excommunication. There was little it could do in protestant lands that had been lost, but there was a great deal that could be done in lands newly

---

6 Supplement to **Gothic Ripples**, #28, December 1994, Greenhow Hill, Harrogate, ENGLAND, HG3 5JQ

re- conquered or lands still under Catholic control. The reform minded must be routed out.[7] This was the job for the inquisition's "thought police." They backed up the priests' "ex-communication" so thoroughly that where Catholicism ruled there was never again a protestant problem. Suspects disappeared. Some returned years later but refused to speak of their experiences.

The Inquisition had no hesitancy in going after anyone who stood in the way of Church policy - great or small.

Among the victims of the Catholic Inquisition were Joan of Arc, Galileo, and the entire Catholic military Order of Templars. Joan of Arc had disobediently fought the English after Papal policy had awarded a portion of France to England; the Templars committed the grievous sin of accumulating wealth desired by the Church. In time, the outrages committed by the inquisition caused it to be suppressed in Portugal in 1821 and Spain in 1834. Their job was taken over by secular government departments where state- Catholicism's influence outweighed Roman Catholicism.

It should be mentioned here that within Catholicism itself there is always a struggle going on as patriotic national ecclesiastics ally themselves with national political leaders to attempt to limit the power of the ubiquitous Roman Church. This struggle is the dirty laundry that the Catholic church hides from the public, but it can be deadly. When a Mexican bishop is assassinated, or a German Catholic banker is ambushed and killed, the immediate thought is that it is the ongoing dispute over church jurisdiction. "State Catholicism" supports the state as it strives with its neighbors. Roman Catholicism supports the international trade cartel. The objectives of the two may vary widely.

7 A free examination of "the Jewish question" would reveal ownership and surragate enfiefments, the knowledge of which would throw the West's power structure into chaos and the world into revolution. Therefore, the investigation has to stop at the "Six Million," regardless how untenable the claim.

Coup - French Huguenots 1572

When excommunication and the Inquisition failed to bring dissidents into line with church policy, a more forceful measure has been the coup.

By 1550, perhaps one quarter of all Frenchmen were Huguenots. A substantial number of noblemen offered them protection. Catholic attempts at suppression were unsuccessful. In the feigned attempt to draw the nation together, the king's sister was promised to the leader of the Huguenots to be his wife. It was a ruse to disarm them.[8] Just before the wedding the Catholics received word from the king to kill all Protestants - men, women and children. On Saint Bartholomew's Day, Aug. 24, 1572, some 100,000 Protestants were slaughtered - and over half a million before it was over. The Catholic Church struck a medal to commemorate the event. Later revolts by Protestant peasants such as the one by the Camisards in the Cevennes region (1702-1711) were brutally suppressed. The Huguenots who survived fled to Germany, America and South Africa.[9] The Catholic Church kept its lands in France and took those of the departed Huguenots. With title held in bank nominee names - they still own it.

Ireland 1641

The Irish Massacre has been censored out of the history books. The background is this:

St. Patrick annexed Ireland to the Roman Catholic Church. The Church farmed out the land and its peoples to local kings to manage. In 1155, Pope Hadrien IV gave Ireland to the English King to manage. The English invaded to exercise their contract. Later, Henry VIII made himself the English Pope and claimed the right to keep all collected tithes and offerings rather

8 The lesson to be learned over and over is that the word of the unLawful is never ever to be trusted. "We (Catholics) are also under an obligation to keep secrets faithfully. And sometimes the easiest way to fulfill that duty is to say what is false, or to tell a lie." (Catholic Encyclicals X, 195. "A false statement knowingly made to one who has no right to the truth will not be a lie." (Catholic Encyclical, IX, 471.)

9 My wife's ancestor, a little girl, was smuggled out of France in a barrel.

than sending them on to Rome. Irish Catholics led by their priests and leaders refused to recognize this claim of the Anglican Catholic Church and revolted. The revolt was suppressed and the hotbed of revolt, northern Ireland, was cleared of Catholics.

Scottish Presbyterians, also refusing to recognize the authority of the Anglican Church, had been dispossessed of their lands. They were shipped to Northern Ireland to be tenants on the vacant farms - and act as a buffer between the Anglican English land owners and the irate Catholics. The Anglican Church itself was the actual owner of the land in both the Irish Presbyterian north and the Catholic south, with English nobles appointed to manage the land for the English crown.[10]

The massacre broke forth on Oct 23, 1641, on the date of the Feast of the Roman Catholic St. Ignatius Loyola, founder of the Jesuit Order. It was led by Sir Phelim O'Neill.[11]

The Protestant inhabitants of the town and castle of Langford were massacred. Forty English Protestants at Terawley were forced to choose sword or drowning. At the castle of Lisgool - 150 men, women, and children were burned together. At the castle of Moneah - 100 were put to the sword. One thousand men, women and children were thrown from Portadown Bridge. Four thousand were drowned in different places. In Killmore 200 families were killed. At Antrim, 954 Protestants were killed in one day and 1200 more later in the county, many of whom had their heads taken. At Powerscout Church they burnt Dr. Dibles. At Clones, 17 were buried alive. Dr. Sir William Petty reckoned the Protestant loss at 110,000. One hundred and fifty-four thousand victims were claimed between 1641- 42.[12]

10 Most Irish Presbyterians in the north, and Irish Catholics in the south, to this day do not realize that the Anglican Church owns title to the very land they live on in Ireland. The fight the IRA is making against the Protestants, with the secret encouragement of the Catholic Church, is to force the Anglican landlords to share the land rents with the Roman Catholic Church. This is the reason for the Vatican visits by the British royals. Both the Irish Presbyterians and Catholics are expendable.

11 The politically astute will recognize the name in America still backing ultra- liberal political policies.

12 **Remember 1641**, Allen Campbell, PO Box 92, Belfast, N. Ireland

"At Cork, a Roman Catholic priest, named Mahoney, published in 1645 an 'exhortation' to his fellow countrymen in which he said:

"You have killed 150,000 enemies in these 4 or 5 years, as your very adversaries howling, openly confess in their writings and you do not deny .... It remains for you to slay all the other heretics or expel them from the bounds of Ireland."[13]

"A Romanish Bishop was the brain of the whole enterprise. The priests commonly anointing the rebels before sending them to their murderous work, assuring them that if they chanced to be killed they would escape Purgatory and go immediately to heaven."[14]

Remember 1641, a short booklet by Alan Campbell, states:

"The Roman Catholic rebels of 1651 feigned friendship to our forefathers right up to the day that the war of genocide began. It was the same in Paris, France in 1572. The Romanists pledged peace and brotherhood to the Protestant Huguenots; then rose up on St. Bartholomew's Eve to don white armbands and slay 100,000 of them. In August 1969 they posted 'peace slogans' while making bombs for their murderous assault upon the Apprentice Boy's parade. Many innocent Protestants have gone to their deaths by bombs and bullets as a direct result of information supplied to the terrorists by the very Roman Catholics who lived and worked with them.

"Present attempts to stage some sort of round table conference can only result in some sort of power-sharing with the Roman Catholics. It contains within it the seeds of our own destruction. In 1991 we say that 'another 1641 is just a compromise away.'"[15]

Episcopal-Feudalism, whether economic, political, or religious, cannot live with separatists of any sort - especially

13 **Fox's Book Of Martyrs**
14 **History Of The Irish Presbyterian Church**, Thomas Hamilton, DD
15 **Remember 1641**, Allen Campbell, PO Box 92, Belfast, N. Ireland

presbyteries. In time the effort will be made to force them to comply with the dictates of the episcopacy's leader. Refusal will result in a 1572, 1641, the Hindu-Islamic wars of the 1940s, the present establishment-Islamic war against the Islamic-presbytery, Waco, Ruby Ridge, Gordon Kahl, Philadelphia, and the assassination of Huey Long and Rabbi Meir Kahani. When dealing with episcopacies, and those who obey them, to survive one must be vigilant.

Naked Force

Once the protestant princes had secured their lands and suppressed the peasant's dissent, there was little chance that a threat of Roman Catholic excommunication would command obedience. Protestant theology protected the rebels against that. Nor could the Inquisition be used - the inquisitors had been banished from protestant lands. The *coup* was equally impossible - the rebels had been alerted and were on guard. All that remained was naked force - crusade.

Crusades are infrequent outside of Christendom. Genghis Khan was a rare one who was able to conquer and combine the myriad Turk nations of the world and lead them against a common foe which he selected. However, this juggernaut dissolved upon the death of its creator. Mohammed's "Islam" united the Turks once again into a crusade until the riches of its conquests distracted the conquerors from further efforts.

Only in the West exists the organization and power to launch one crusade after another. This power has been considered a Catholic monopoly. The Church's influence over its followers has been so great that diverse races and countries among its followers will unite into a common effort and will time and again step over the bodies of their own dead to get at the foe selected for them by the Catholic Church. The great crusade to capture Palestine included most of the nations of Europe. The crusade called to defend Vienna against the Saracen juggernaut was led by the Pope's Holy Roman Emperor and again included most of the nations of Europe. Other successful crusades include the ones against the Albegencions, Waldenceans, and Hussites.

Napoleon targeted himself when he took the crown from the hands of the Pope and placed it on his own head. The nations of the world were sent to crush him - and they did.[16]

The world was sent to crush Germany in World War I. In World War II fifty-two nations were sent to take Germany to pieces - and they did. The Thirty Year's War ushered in a frightful method of war - wars of annihilation. But, then as now, naked force alone is non-productive. It has to be combined with something else to be successful.

The Jesuit Order - 1534

The new strategy decided upon was to reactivate the "Dharma" system dispensed by *Dharmatras*. They were named "Jesuits."

Jesuits are ordained priests. They don't wear special clothing and are not subject to local Catholic authority. They are bound by a vow of obedience directly to the Roman Catholic Pope which causes constant friction with the governments of national states. Their training period lasts up to 15 years and they are governed by a general who lives in Rome - the "Black Pope." This is how it has always been since the Order was created. Nothing has changed.

Jesuits were insidious. Wherever they operated their grasping interference in the sovereignty of independent nations, their accumulation of money, land, and power on behalf of the Roman Catholic Church, in time, caused them to be distrusted and hated. They could be masters of disguise. Many were adept at posing as protestants. Highly intelligent, talented, and trusted, a number appointed to the highest posts of government were later discovered to be Jesuits. State secrets were passed regularly to the Roman Church.

One country after another expelled them. Powerful forces of both Protestants and Catholics opposed them. Even some cardinals in the Vatican joined the general condemnation.

---

16 The nations united against him included Catholic, Anglican Catholic, State-Lutheranism, and Orthodox - all of whom Napoleon had injured. The unifying thread was the money dispensed by surrogates of the Catholic Church.

Together, they caused the organization to be suppressed in 1773. In 1814, the Jesuit Order was re-established.

A religious feudal system is a state within a state. Its followers are in fact citizens of a foreign country. In most Catholic lands the Catholic Church cracked the whip; in Protestant lands the Protestant Princes replaced the Catholic Church, took over their organization and renamed it, and they cracked the whip. The feudal system remained the same. The differences between the priests of the Protestant Kings and the priests of the Catholic Church became a matter of "doctrinal differences" in which the Catholics were bested time and again by their better-read protestant opponents.

Catholic vs. Protestant Doctrinal Differences

"The doctrinal principle of evangelical Protestantism, as distinct from Romanism, is twofold - objective and subjective. ...

- Absolute sovereignty of the Bible vs. the Roman doctrine of the Bible and tradition.
- Justification by the free grace of God vs. faith and good works
- Universal priesthood of believers vs. exclusive priesthood of the clergy.
- Protestantism is the religion of freedom vs. Romanism the religion of authority.
- The religion of evangelism and simplicity vs. Romanism's legalism, asceticism, and ceremonialism.
- Appeals to the intellect and conscience vs. appeal to the senses and imagination.
- One is internal vs. external & with outward observation.
- Christianity of the Bible vs. Christianity of tradition.
- Directs to divine revelation vs. directs to the teaching priesthood.
- Freely circulates the Bible vs. the latter keeps it for the use of the clergy and overrules it by its traditions.

- Protestantism is the religion of immediate communition of the soul with Christ through personal faith vs. Romanism the religion of reaching the Savior through an army of subordinate mediators and advocates.
- The Protestant prays directly to Christ vs. the Romanist usually approaches him only through the intercession of the blessed Virgin and the saints.
- Protestantism puts Christ before the church vs. Romanism virtually puts the Church before Christ and makes churchliness the condition and measure of piety.[17]

The Jesuits established schools and universities to indoctrinate their charges. The manning of these educational facilities has caused the Jesuit Order to grow into the largest Roman Catholic order.

Jesuit schools such as Georgetown,[18] St. Louis, and Fordham in the U.S. have been opened. The U.S. is now exchanging ambassadors with the Vatican,[19] and has had a Catholic president.

Missions

Jesuits were used at first to counter Protestant propaganda. Most graduating from their schools learned Dharma and were dependent on the Roman Catholic Church for assurance that their souls would reach heaven. The priests became their gurus. Converts accepting Catholic beliefs entered society as "citizens" of the Roman Church - a country without borders.[20]

Almost every act in the life of a Catholic became enmeshed in the ritual of the Church. The Catholic is born into the Catholic Church, christened by a priest, sent to be schooled by

17 **The Creeds Of Christendom**, Vol I, p. 208, Philip Schaff, DD, LLD, Harper & Bros, NY 1877

18 President Bill Clinton is a product of Georgetown.

19 Catholics are taught that their pope is "infallible," God's representative on earth, and that they are expected to obey him in all things. This power allows the Vatican to make such statements as this: "It is quite unlawful to demand, to defend, or to grant unconditional freedom of thought, of speech, of writing, or of worship." Pope Leo XIII, **Encyclical, on Human Liberty**. 1878-1903. (**Time**, 12- 12-94, "Man of the Year")

20 Dharma-conquered peoples are organized into taxable feudal entities called "countries," "states," "provinces," "counties," and "cities."

priests, is married by a priest, does business with other Catholics under direction of the priest, is ruled by Catholics, and when he dies he is buried by a Catholic priest in sacred ground. From the cradle to the grave. There would be little chance for another revolt.

The Purpose Of Foreign Missions

Wolves cannot enter the sheepfold and eat sheep unless they first bribe the watchman to give them a safe conduct pass into the sheepfold. Otherwise the rams would surround the wolf and kill him. Just as Christians are to forbid entry to strangers[21] they are also forbidden to evangelize them.[22]

The big return from trade has always come from successful foreign missions in targeted trade areas preparing the way for the merchant. In the far east these areas had to be secured by the Catholics before the "heretic" Protestants beat them to it. Jesuits soon appeared at the court of the Emperor of China and opened that country to foreign trade. They did the same in India, Japan, and elsewhere.

This is what trade religions do. They have no boundaries - no countries with border guards. Converts are their citizens. Tithes and offerings are their taxes and tribute. The first object of mission teaching is to persuade as many people as possible to become tithe-paying converts so that the missionary effort may become self-sufficient.

Missions turn potential enemies into friends, supporters and servants. The Buddhist considers the alien and the native to be the same. If the convert can be made to believe that both teacher and pupil worship the same god, and that this same god is the god that truly loves good and hates evil - the missionary has accomplished his mission. All that remains to be done is to teach the new convert what the missionary's god considers good and

21 **GOD'S LAW: "They shall not dwell in thy land, lest they make thee sin against me." Ex 23:33**

22 **GOD'S LAW: "Go not unto the way of the Gentiles, and unto any city of the Samaritans enter ye not: But go rather to the lost sheep of the house of Israel." Matt 10:5,6.**

bad. Since the missionary knows and his pupil doesn't, the missionary speaks for god. This is power indeed.

The convert now believes that the missionary's god is the true "good god," and the convert's old god is a false "evil god." Second, he believes that the missionary is a "guru" - the one who knows the way to heaven. Hindus (and Christian-Hindus) actually believe that their "guru" is a living christ. Since he speaks for god they reverence him as a living christ.[23]

This is what Dharma missions and Dharmamatras do. It is why one party sends religious missions to another party. It is why Catholics send missions to Protestants and Protestants to Catholics. It is why trade as well as political and religious interests finance missions to those whom they have targeted for trade or conquest. It is what they have always done. China had dealings with Hindu-Buddhism for centuries. Chinese nationals converted by Tibetan Buddhists were commanded to support Tibetan interests in trade and banking. Chinese, Indian, and Japanese converts to Roman Catholicism supported their co-religionists in the West. They took the part of Catholic Spain and Portugal in later trade wars and political differences. The Jesuits are still at it. Recently Chinese authorities arrested Catholic priests and laymen "who are part of China's 'underground' Catholic Church that remains loyal to the Vatican," according to the Stamford, Connecticut based Kung Foundation.[24] The article continued: "The Chinese government does not allow the Vatican to choose bishops and other leaders for the Catholic Church in China." The Chinese learned from experience.

The French Jesuits went among the American Indians and those who were converted fought for Catholic France in the "French and Indian War." Those Indians converted by Anglican

---

23 "The pope can modify divine law, since his power is not of man but of God. ... The pope is as it were God on earth, sole sovereign of the faithful of Christ, chief king of kings, having plenitude of power, to whom has been entrusted by the omnipotent God direction not only of the earthly but also of the heavenly kingdom." **Prompta Bibliotheca Canonica,** Vol VI, p. 438, 442, Pope. (The **Catholic Encyclopedia** 1913 edition, Vol VI, p. 48, speaks of this book as "a veritable encyclopedia of religious knowledge," and "a precious mine of information."

24 **Christian News,** p. 18, October 2, 1995

missionaries in early Virginia fought for England against the American settlers in the Revolutionary War and the War of 1812. The Blacks in South Africa, converted by Anglican missionaries, took the part of Anglican Britain against the protestant South African Boers.

The most successful foreign mission in the West in the last several hundred years is the Judeo-Christian (J/C) mission. Until its emergence, the International Trade Cartel suffered one defeat after another in America as the League of Nations was voted down, tariffs were put in place to restrict foreign trade, and immigration was reduced to only a trickle. Judeo-Christianity changed all this.

Judeo-Christianity may be described as an ecumenical Christian sect created by the International Trade Cartel (ITC) to dissolve Christian religious objections to the presence of the international merchant. This has been done by giving media-access, and its accompanying riches, to Christian ministers who favor ITC policy.

Successful J/C preachers can become fantastically rich from the offerings of credulous viewers. Their personal wealth is often measured by the tens of millions of dollars.

Here are some of the things they are permitted to do and some things they are not permitted to do. They are permitted to solicit money. They may use Biblical parables, illustrations, and terminology. They must incorporate Dharma. They may NOT refer to the *Laws, statutes, and Judgments* contained in the Scriptures since the *Commandments* represent a different God from the one followed by the owners of the media (ie. they may not say that the penalty for murder, kidnaping and homosexuality is "death.") They are also required to refer to the Khazar-Turk merchants living in their midst as being "Israel." This gives wolves free passes into the Saxon sheepfold. They also teach a fairly recent belief called "rapture." This belief states that God will, before "the tribulation," take his people away from the earth. In earlier years when Christendom has seen an approaching storm they prepared for it. This "rapture" theory causes them to sit and wait, believing that God will save them at the last moment. In the meantime they make no effort to defend themselves, their family, or their country. A most ingenious theory.

To continue using the media, J/C ministers are required to take their followers on annual pilgrimages to Palestine, refrain from attacking other religions and peoples, promote ecumenism, and when instructed - advocate whatever project or opinion that the ITC wishes to promote.

Most J/C organizations were organized in the presbyterian manner. However, they are considered episcopal because of their required obedience to ITC guidelines.

This new cult, costing nothing more than allowing certain preachers to profit from the media, has persuaded tens of millions of Christians from opposing the International Trade Cartel. As a result, the Christian West has crumbled into a nation having many gods. Such a thing has not been seen since the time of the Dharma-conquered Greek world, the more recent Buddhist conquest of China, and the still more recent Catholic conquest of Japan.

The missionary represents a special interest. He is usually a recruiting agent for an episcopal ruler. Those he is able to recruit become servants of the missionaries' religious Order, who, as history reveals, may act as agents in peace and soldiers in war. The work of the missionary cannot be underestimated or undervalued. First comes the missionary, next comes a king to rule, and at the last comes the merchant- trader who had sent the other two to prepare his way. His customers will now accept him and the king and his soldiers stand ready to protect his gleanings.

Christian missionaries to strangers justify their missionary efforts by using one particular quote from the King James Bible and ignoring others. The quote they use most frequently is:

> *"Go ye into all the world, and preach the gospel to every creature. He that believeth and is baptized shall be saved; but he that believeth not shall be damned." Mark 16:15-16*

This quote, if not interpreted by other quotes of Jesus, creates an oxymoron because it makes Jesus say one thing one time and another thing at another time:

> *"Jesus .... commanded them saying, Go ye not into the way of the gentiles, and into any city of the Samaritans enter ye not; But go rather to the lost sheep of the house of Israel." Matt 10:5-6.*

> *"O children of Israel .... You only have I known of all the families of the earth." Deut 7:6*

> *"I pray not for the world, but for them which thou hast given me, for they are thine." John 17:9*

> *"Give not that which is holy unto the dogs, neither cast ye your pearls before swine, lest they trample them under their feet, and turn again and rend you." Matt. 7:6*

To keep harmony in the scripture, Mark 15:24 must be interpreted in the following manner:

> *"Go ye into all the world (Israel was scattered into all the world), and preach the gospel to every creature ("I am sent but to the lost sheep of the house of Israel." Matt: 15:24) Mark 16:15*

By going into all the world and preaching the gospel "*to every creature*" of Israel - harmony is maintained. The following also helps:

> *"And ye my flock, the flock of my pasture, are men (Heb: "adam" - those that blush rosy), and I am your God." Ezek 34:30-31*

In essence - the Word was God and:

> *"God said let us make man in our image. So God created man in his own image." Gen 1:26-27*

The man that God made in his image was called in the Hebrew - "Adam." The word Adam in the Hebrew means MAN:

Heb: Adam - "to show blood(in the face), ie: to flush or turn rosy: - be (dyed, made) red(ruddy). *Strong's Concordance*

In the beginning God created one in his own image who blushed red. Out of Adam-man whom he created - He then selected "Israel." It was into this Israel he implanted His Word:

> *"He showed his word .... his statutes and his Judgments unto Israel. He hath not delt so with any nation .... they have not known thee." Ps 147:19-20*

And unto these people God said:

> *"Thou art a holy people unto the Lord thy God: The Lord thy God hath chosen thee to be a special people unto himself, above all people that are upon the face of the earth." Deut 7:6; "I will dwell among the children of Israel, and will be their God. Ex 29:45*

Others are not made in God's image. They are not sheep - they are wolves. If they would like to attempt to follow God the WORD and receive the blessing that comes from doing so - fine. BUT, do it somewhere else lest Israel be harmed:

> *"They .... were mingled among the heathen and learned their works." Ps 160:35-36.*

Missions to kinsmen are commanded and commended. Missions to strangers are forbidden. John Calvin recognized this and made little effort to persuade others, because according to the scriptures:

> *"My sheep hear my voice, and I know them, and they follow me." John 10:25-27*

We obey God the WORD and exclude strangers. We do what we do because:

> *"For thou didst separate them from all the people of the world to be thine inheritance." 1 Ki 8:53*

Presbyterian Christendom

The entire Reformation period was brief. The enslaved people of the West tried to regain their land and freedoms from an alien feudal system. They fought against both the Protestant state- church and the Roman Catholic international trade cartel. Their opposition won - their victory bloody. But, the WORD brought by Jesus Christ was pried loose from the clutches of the Catholic Church and is now loose in the land.

Chapter 18

THE GREAT WARS

Bismarck

Bismarck united Germany - both Protestant and Catholic states were brought into one united whole. Lutheranism became a state religion and obediently refrained from teaching the forbidden 71% of the Bible dealing with government and the peoples' rights. The attempt was made to make Roman Catholicism the same - a German Catholic Church state religion with its ecclesiastics being approved by the state like the Lutherans.

In 1870, Catholic France declared war on Germany. At the same time Roman Catholic priests promoted rebellion in Catholic Poland - forcing Germany to fight France in the front and deal with Polish rebellion in the rear.[1] In July 1870, the Pope declared the dogma of papal infallibility. Thus, by his own decree, the Pope's words became divine. They were from God and must be obeyed by the faithful. It's a tricky thing dealing with God's representative on earth - one who is infallible.[2]

The matter quickly came to a head. Bismarck had ordered the German schools to teach certain subjects. The Catholic archbishop of Cologne forbade the students at Bonn to attend these lectures. Enraged that a foreign potentate would interfere in the internal matters of the state, Bismarck expunged from the constitution the paragraphs protecting the Catholic Church; banished the Jesuits and kindred Orders from the empire; made

1 **Bismarck**, Emil Ludwig, p. 416, Little, Brown & Co, Boston, 1927

2 "All dogmatic decrees of the Pope, made with or without his general council, are infallible ... Once made, no pope or council can reverse them ... This is the Catholic principle, that the Church cannot err in faith." **The Catholic World**, June 1871, p. 422-423.

civil marriage compulsory; etc. The Pope retaliated and forbade the German Catholics to obey the new laws. This was the public beginning of the "Kulturkampf" - the war between two states - Germany and the Roman Vatican.[3] Which would rule Germany?

Bismarck declared the Pope's pronouncement invalid. He declared that Rome was the rallying ground of all the foes of the empire. Papal supporters organized the "Center Party" to work against Bismarck in government. All this took place while the Franco- Prussian War was in progress and Germany's survival hung in the balance. The Catholic Church acquired the stigma of troublemaker and traitor. The matter was further confused when some Catholic theologians at the German universities, including Cardinal Hohenlohe, opposed the Pope's dogma of infallibility. Even the powerful Catholic king of Bavaria was against it.

Bismarck's greatest dread was beginning to be realized - the formation of a Catholic league against the young German empire.[4] The unspoken bone of contention was the possession by German Protestant Princes of lands and businesses formerly held by the Catholic Church which were seized during the Thirty Years' War.

The Revolts Of 1848

The establishment knows the grievances of the people. These grievances are the same as they have always been:

(1) The kings must give up their land so that it can again be divided,
(2) Monopolies must be banned,
(3) Taxes must be abolished,
(4) The people must rule their own lands as kings and priests,
(5) We must be separated.

3 Bismark, p. 417
4 Ibid, p. 415

The WORD requires that its people have these things. The faithful want them. These are the very things the establishment has captured and intends to keep for itself - by deception if possible - by force if necessary.[5]

The people of Europe were resentful over the oppressive feudal system. The widespread revolts of 1848 were explosions of pent-up anger aggravated by Jesuit revolutionary activities among the Catholics in Poland and elsewhere against Protestant kings, the tyranny of both Protestant and Catholic absentee landlords, and sweatshop slave labor employed by both.

The West has one peculiarity. Westerners usually claim to be either "Christian" or nothing. Working with this choice - the cartel logically chose "nothing." That is - "nothing" plus Dharma. The result was called "communism." Dharma was the cement. Dharma required communists to accept each other without regard to "race, creed, or color." In this way "no-religion" communism plus Dharma can jump border, religious, and race barriers without coming into conflict with local religions - as would have happened if communism were to have embraced Catholicism. If it had done that it would have alienated the Protestants. If it embraced the Protestants it would have alienated the Catholics. If it had embraced eastern Orthodox or Judaism it would alienate everyone. The communism proclaimed by the establishment embraced NO religion - it was atheism plus Dharma.

---

5 Pope Pius IX anathematized "all such as maintain that the church may not employ force." Pope Pius IX, Encyclical Letter of Dec 8, 1864

There was another factor. The earlier division of Poland between Prussia, Russia, and Austria furnished Germany with a large population of Turk-Jewish revolutionaries whose advance guard was already present in the form of usury bankers to the Catholic Church. Bismarck had given his power of attorney to one of them - a major Jewish Banker named Bleichroder. He caused Bismarck's wealth to multiply greatly.[6] At the same time the same thing was happening with the German Emperor's own affairs: they prospered in the hands of another Jewish banker.[7] Bismarck was impressed. He gave the Jews the same privileges given to other Germans and smiled benignly as they spread over Germany. He offered Karl Marx a position on his staff, an offer that was refused, [8] and "advocated marriages between the nobility and the Jews."[9]

Except to German rulers and nobility who utilized Jewish banking services, Khazar-Turks were a curiosity. Most Germans had never seen a "Jewish-Turk" before. But, while Germans knew little of Turks - the Turks knew about Westerners, and they

---

6 The Southern Confederacy, the South African Republics, and Germany are the three modern holdout states from the International Trade Cartel. All three fell. All three had Turks associated with their leaders (Deu 17:15; I Ki 4:21-24). Judah P. Benjamin was the first Jew in the modern world to be elected by Christians and the first Jew to serve in an American cabinet. He was a protegé of Catholic New Orleans' Slidel machine and met with Salomon de Rothschild before the war. President Jefferson Davis was born Baptist and educated Catholic. Judah P. Benjamin was his Sec. War & Sec. State. Mysteriously, he burned his private papers after the war. The Jewish millionaire, Sammy Marks was Paul Kruger's famous protegé. He advised surrender. Alfred Beit and Julius Wernher, millionaire owners of the largest gold mining firm of Wernher-Beit, furnished Sir Alfred Milner, the British High Commissioner, intelligence on the Boers which kept the war going. All media elected governments are ITC contaminated. All Law violations are punished in time.

7 Bismark, p. 436

8 **Ibid**, p. 245

9 **Ibid**, p. 320

took their prejudices against Western Christendom with them as they moved over Germany.[10]

When it became evident that the nobility of Prussia and the rest of Europe were on a collision course with their own people, and that another "peasants' revolt" was inevitable, well-financed Turk revolutionaries jumped in. Their long experience fighting the rule of Poles and Russians helped them spread their brand of revolution like wildfire over Europe and helped guide its direction. Even the Pope had to flee the Vatican for his life.[11]

Khazar secret societies provided the basic framework for the revolt, provided much of the leadership, and took a prominent part in the revolutions. The failure of the "Revolution of 1848" forced a great many of these revolutionaries to migrate elsewhere to escape prison or worse. A great many came to America and their radical views did much to shape the actions of the Union Army against Southern civilians.[12] It is noteworthy that while the princes of Europe went after "the communists" with a vengeance, the Catholic Church took no punitive action against them. The Jewish banks which financed the revolts remained untouched.

The Communist Manifesto was hastily written so that the Communist Party could claim responsibility and leadership recognition in what was mostly a natural occurrence. Karl Marx, its author and the grandson of a rabbi, had long enjoyed the hospitality of the King of England and the tolerance of England's Anglican Catholic Church. He rushed to complete

10 The West has forgotten the excesses committed against the Turks during the Crusades against the Holy Land. They are treated as a matter of no consequence that happened long ago. But the Turks remember. The Turks fight among themselves because that is their way, but a blow by an outsider against one of their number will, sooner or later, be avenged by the Turk who is able.

11 This does not mean that the Catholic confessional system had broken down and that the Vatican knew nothing of the approaching storm. It means only that the Vatican chose not to interfere for its own reasons. There is almost nothing that happens in this world that is not known by the Catholic Church; every secret treaty, every alliance, every trade pact, every drug operation, and virtually every private indiscretion.

12 "Socialist revolutionaries from the 1848 debacle in Europe flocked to join the Union army as the War For Southern Independence got under way. Lincoln had the verbal support of Marx and Engels as well as that of the Russian revolutionary Bakunin." **President Abraham Lincoln,** VITW, Sept 1995, Box 1883, Arlington Heights, Illinois 60006

his *Communist Manifesto* in time for the revolutions. He was late by a few months. The revolution had started without him.

The Communist Manifesto arrived when Europe was in a religious vacuum. Episcopal Churches (top down Protestant and Catholic) ruled supreme and represented the rulers. The presbyterian church (rule from bottom up) was crushed and offered no rallying place for Europe's oppressed peoples. The Manifesto was written as a shopping list for the unrepresented worker. The Manifesto's "10 planks" were supposedly written to reform the feudal system, but, in fact, only pretended to reform the system while actually retaining the old system, and giving it a new name. Its greatest change was in seeming to introduce new management.

The Communist Manifesto

This is what the Manifesto demanded:

(1) "Abolition of property (rights) in land and application of all rents (taxes) to public purposes."

Communism nationalized property of the nobility and church which was to be managed and used by self-appointed communist commissars. The peasants gained nothing.

(2) "A heavy progressive or graduated income tax."

The peasants continued to pay taxes - Kings and Princes were added to the tax rolls when they were replaced by new rulers.

(3) "Abolition of all right of inheritance."

The houses and land of the peasants belonged to the church and the nobles. Plank #3 merely switched their landlords to the communist party.

(4) "Confiscation of the property of all emigrants (fleeing the system) and rebels."

The plank announced the replacement of old landlords with new ones. It was not directed against "the people" since they had owned nothing of substance for centuries. The communist party stated that, henceforth, new administrators would replace those who had held the land en fief.

(5) "Centralization of credit in the hands of the State, by means of a national bank with state capital an exclusive monopoly."

Europe's banks were private banks managed by the international trade cartel. Number 5 announced a central bank under existing control.

(6) "Centralization of the means of communication and transport in the hands of the State."

ITC government controlled and licensed transportation. Plank #6 announced the continuation of the same policy.

(7) "Extension of factories and instruments of production owned by the state."

Plank #7 announces the arrival of a new tenant - the communist party. Individuals who had earlier refused to sell businesses to ITC bank agents would have their property confiscated and later "privatized." Those who were unable to buy land in the first place would now be able to.

(8) "Equal liability of all to labor."

This keeps alive the ITC ideal of community service.

(9) "Combination of agriculture with manufacturing industries."

The church and state since the days of Charlemagne had owned and managed both agriculture and manufacturing. Platform #9 pre- empted feudal land holdings to prevent the return of the ancient self-sufficient farm system which produced its own cottage industry.

(10) "Free education for all children in public schools."

Dharmamatras educate children to produce compliant "citizens." It is a necessary part of feudalism. Those who educate the children are the rulers.[13] The "free" education promised by the new communist government had a very long string attached. Nothing was changed for the people.

The *Communist Manifesto* gave people nothing they did not already have. Old ideas and concepts were put into a new package, given new titles and names, and sold as something new. It was the act of a new manager who wished to step into the shoes of the old. It was establishment controlled opposition to an existing system.

The manifesto said that the new rulers would be a "dictatorship of the proletariat!" The workers themselves would rule - they would rule themselves. However, until the time was right for the workers to take over government, the self-appointed leaders of the communist party were to rule. It all sounded "syrupy" sweet, but it was the best offer the people had had.

The planks of the *Communist Manifesto*, sold as "freedom" for the workers, actually continued the Feudal System - this time run by Turk converts instead of by the Protestant State or the Catholic Church. It claimed to be "atheist" which made it "middle-of-the-road" where the only other choices were Catholic, Protestant, Eastern Orthodox, and Jewish. Religious opinions polarized political opinions. The oppressed workers were ready for change - any change. Since presbyterianism, the enemy of feudalism, had been crushed, presbyterianism could offer no alternative to the existing government episcopacy. And since the episcopal communists were a change to the well known evils of the episcopacy of the Protestant kings and the Roman Catholic Church - the great masses of Europeans supported "change" - any change.

The revolts of 1848 were suppressed, but they pointed to a red tomorrow.

---

13 GOD'S LAW: "Fear ...God ...teach your children letters, that they may have understanding .... reading unceasingly the law of God." Book of Levi 4:1-2

World War I

A crusade was organized against Protestant Germany and her allies, Austria-Hungary and Turkey.

America's President Wilson offered peace based on his Fourteen Points, one of which was that there was to be no territorial losses or gains by the participants in the war.

The well-financed German Communist Party commenced a revolt. The red flag of revolution was run up over the German High Seas Fleet - which was cowered into passiveness when German submarines loyal to the German Empire pointed their bows at the capital ships threatening to loose torpedoes.

The underground red press began a campaign of vituperation against the Kaiser and his feudal system. The wrongs of centuries were rehashed. Hundreds of thousands joined a general strike. Germany gradually ground to a halt. With conditions on the homefront in this state, the German generals advised negotiations. Germany surrendered based on Wilson's Fourteen Points, meaning - "no territorial losses or gains."

In spite of Western assurances, Germany was dismembered. Former Catholic lands in Eastern Germany were stripped from Protestant Germany and given to Catholic Poland. The German Danzig Corridor, the city of Danzig, Protestant Pomarania, and West Prussia were given to Poland. Alsace-Lorraine, inhabited by Germans, seized by France from the Germans in the 17th century while they were fighting the Islamic invasion of Europe, returned after the French were defeated in the Franco-Prussian War in 1870, was given to Catholic France without the consent of the inhabitants. The German Tyrol was given to Italy, and the extensive German colonies in Africa and the Pacific were divided among the victors.

Britain had signed the Balfour Agreement with world Jewry which gave them Palestine in return for bringing the United States into the war on the side of Britain. To deliver on her promise, Britain sent her armies to take Palestine from the Turks. This is how the most popular shrine of Western Christendom was taken from Islam and given to the Khazar Turks of Russia and the United States.

Most notable - the great Austrian-Hungarian Empire was dismembered. Austria became about a tenth its former size. Slavic Yugoslavia, Hungary (largely Slavic), Czechoslovakia, and Rumania were given their independence as payment for the Russian Pan Slavic alliance joining the revolt against the Russian Feudal System.[14]

Russia Becomes A Prize

The Slavic-Turk takeover of Russia mended the ancient Catholic- Orthodox Church schism. While ritual and other differences remained, the basic reunion had been accomplished.

The traditional religious structure in Russia was similar to that in the West. The Tzar (King) was head of both church and state. His nobles held their land in fief to him. The one who stepped into the Tzar's shoes owned Russia. That someone was standing by.

The Mongols invaded Russia earlier and ruled it for centuries. A Turkic tribe allied to the Mongols was the Khazars. This tribe had earlier converted to Judaism. The Mongols used them for their tax collectors. This caused them to be hated by the captive Slavs. The Slavs under Russ leadership won their freedom and conquered in turn. One of the peoples they conquered in Southern Russia were the former Khazar tax collectors. They knew these people and they treated them as roughly as they themselves had been treated.[15]

In Europe, the Khazars had long been used as tax collectors and usurers by church-appointed kings. Napoleon came to power and picked a fight with the Catholic Church. He disbanded the Vatican's Holy Roman Empire after refusing to allow the Pope to crown him. He refused to act as an agent for the Catholic Church; he was acting for himself. He took over

14 Slavic intellectuals had long envisioned a Slavic unity in which all Slavic peoples ruled themselves and acted in unison for political or economic reasons. Any appeal to this Slavic ideal brings an enthusiastic response.

15 **War Cycles / Peace Cycles**, PO Box 997, Virginia Publishing Co., Lynchburg, Virginia 24505, $12/copy

the government apparatus which included the Jews, intending to use them the way the Catholic Church had used them. To gain their personal loyalty he gave them the rights of native Europeans, and relied on their influence with their brother Khazar-Jews in Russia to help him with his invasion of that vast country.

Neither Europe's Jews nor Russia's Khazar-Jews had any long-term commercial relationship with Napoleon. They did have such a relationship with the Catholic Church. Their help was not forthcoming and Napoleon lost an army deep in the heart of Russia.

In 1917, the Russian Khazar-Jews made common cause with the Russian Slavs and exterminated the Nordic Russ rulers of Russia. On orders from Lenin the royal family was shot.[16]

"Among Radzinsky's discoveries: Discoveries: Despite official denials for decades, it was Lenin who ordered the murders. ... And as a historian, he believes it is vital for the Russian people to realize that the Lenin-ordered murder of the Romanovs foreshadowed the murder of millions more under Stalin. 'Stalin,' Radzinsky says, 'was Lenin's best disciple.'" *The Last Tsar: The Life and Death of Nicholas II.* (Doubleday, $25, Translated by Marian Schwartz), reviewed in *USA Today,* D19, July 30, 1992.

"Socialism received an enormous impetus when Germany gave Lenin & Co., long-time members of the Socialist Insternationale, 50 million gold marks to forment discontent behind the lines in Czarist Russia. In true Socialist fashion Lenin first bought 46 newspapers, then changed the name of this Party from Socialist to Bolshevik, and then to Communist (a name used first by volunteer Russian peasant groups). *Compass*, Otto Scott, October 1, 1992 Vol 3, Issue 26, p. 3. The Communist Party sat on the Tsar's throne. They owned Russia. But the

---

16 "After two generations of denial and accusers being branded 'anti-semitic', the **Jerusalem Post** recently casually admitted that Lenin was Jewish." Leningrad **Literator** (No.38), Sep 12, 1990, **A Ticket To History,** M.S. Shaginyan, 1938, **The Ulyanov Family,** M.S. Shaginyan 1957, **A Jew? - Why, Lenin, of Course!** Michael Checinski, **The Jerusalem Post International Edition.** 1-26-92.

Communist Party was a Khazar party, traditional allies of the Roman Catholic Church.

The allied victors of WWI, to make certain the Communist revolt in Russia succeeded, occupied Russian seaports so that aid could not reach the Tzar's white armies. The world of "separateness" was fast becoming a world of "oneness."

World War II

World War II was fought to keep Germany from breaking away from the repressive conditions imposed on her after her defeat in World War I.

Under the leadership of an upstart commoner, Adolph Hitler, Germany had gradually broken war-imposed ITC restrictions. It had taken over its own currency exchange, stabilized the mark, substituted German national banking in competition to the international banks, had instituted an international trade-barter system by-passing the international banks altogether, and, had stopped WWI reparations. With this load lifted, Germany quickly arose from the great depression of the 1930s while the rest of the world continued mired deep. Germany was an example that could not be allowed to continue.

As a result of these triumphs, Hitler's Germany had more enemies than any political leader has ever had. First, the party of the deposed Kaiser's wished a return of an imperial Germany to ensure old special privileges. The nobles wished to return to the safety of the old regime to guarantee title to land-holdings that had once belonged to the people. Foreign competitors wished to see Germany dismembered and made helpless to ensure competitive trade advantage. Jealous national rivals wanted to keep the economic chains imposed by WWI - the reparations that drained Germany and kept her weak. The Jews were up in arms over Germany's affirmative action. They were being replaced by native Germans and the new government tended to favor native Germans in business dealings. Last - the Roman Catholic Church insisted on preferential treatment, protection of their German assets, and continued government tribute. Hitler had to try to make peace with each of these parties without alienating the rest and throwing the nation into revolution.

Church Interests & WWII

Adolf Hitler was a Catholic. Acting as leader of the German state, he signed a concordant with the Vatican in 1934 in which it was agreed that he would restore Church privileges and protect Church assets in Germany in return for Roman Catholic political endorsement and support.

This treaty gave the Catholics of Austria, and of other German states, permission to wholeheartedly support a Protestant-Catholic Germany.

While Hitler and practically all top echelon National Socialists were Catholic, Catholics are expendable if they stand in the way of "the greater good." Through the ages, many Catholics have followed the way of Joan of Arc and the Templars. Hitler was head of a government ruling a Protestant-Catholic nation that was mostly Protestant. His first obligations were to the German people - both Protestant and Catholic. In his writings he announced his intent to retake Gothic lands in Russia from whence Gothic-Germanic peoples had been driven by the Communist Revolution of 1917 and settle Germans there. This included the Protestant Germans. This is something the ITC could not allow. The ancient schism between the eastern Orthodox and western Catholic churches had recently taken a new turn with the Jewish 1917 takeover of Russia. Europe's Church-owned banks were deeply involved. Russia was a pie in the process of being sliced. German interest in Russia was not welcome.

There was still another thing. During the Reformation, the Grand Master of the Catholic military Order of Teutonic Knights deserted the Papacy and adopted Protestant state-Lutheranism. He and his knights took as their own the lands that they had formerly only held en fief from the Catholic Church.

They retained the old feudal system. The income from the properties that had formerly gone to the papacy went to the nobles. This act took both East and West Prussia out of the Holy Roman Empire. The Catholic Church had long awaited an opportunity to regain these lands as it had regained Alsace-Lorraine, West Prussia, Pomerania, and Czechoslovakia after World War I.

There were interests inside of Germany that wished a change of government. There were foreign interests who looked on Germany as one would a fat goose that still had meat on its bones. It would require a war to separate Germany from her bounty. Germany must be forced into a military confrontation.

Tracing complicity is easy when the answer to the question, "who benefits", is found. The question of "who benefits" is easy to find in the case of defeated Germany. Following the defeat of Germany in 1945, every institution in that country was turned upside down and inside out except one; the Catholic Church. The Catholic Church is the one single German institution that profited from WWII. It regained almost all that had been lost during the Reformation.

The Continuing Episcopal Threat

Religious presbyteries distrust religious episcopacies. They have got good reason. Their experience has been that when it suits episcopal leaders to by-pass the WORD and claim the right to dictate God's will - they will. It results in mayhem and murder - so be it! This has resulted in the Roman Catholic massacre of the Albegensions, the French Huguenots and the Irish Presbyterians. The record of the episcopal state-protestants is as bad; Cromwell massacred both Irish Catholics and Scottish and English Presbyterians, and his steps were followed by Charles II, the Anglican protestant churches' representative of God on earth. The episcopal Lutheran princes massacred their own presbyterian protestant peasants. If the state-protestant toll of killings has not reached the levels of the Catholic Church, it is only because they have not been in business as long. This proves the never-ending danger that episcopacies present to those who wish to follow the WORD.

Episcopacies have the ability to change peace into war in an instant. Are such things still possible? Will people, to save their souls from damnation or to win merit, suddenly seize the weapons at hand and rush out to destroy an enemy pointed out to them by their leaders? Will lightning strike again and again at the same place? Events of the last hundred years in Central and South America point to the danger as being with us still.

Rules Of War

Christian Law teaches its people that Christians are not permitted to raise their hands against their kinsmen.[17] Even if one calling himself Christian attacks a brother for violating the Law he must first send an emissary to tell him to stop the evil he is doing.[18]

Starting Wars

The American South was forced to fire the first shots because Lincoln sent a fleet to join forces with Fort Sumpter to close Charleston Harbor.

Britain made voting demands on the Boers, and then refused to accept their agreement to these demands. The British armies were on the high seas enroute toward South Africa. Whatever the Boer republics did had to be done before the massive British armies landed. The Boers were forced to set a time limit for British agreement. The British merely sat on their hands until the time limit expired and war was declared, thus, the Boer republics received the odium of first declaring war.

Germany was maneuvered into aggressive action by even more skillful means.

17 **GOD'S LAW: "Ye shall not go up, nor fight against your brethren the children of Israel." I Kings 12:24**

18 **"It being part of their law, that they should not bring an army .... without sending an emissary first, and trying whereby whether they will repent or not." Antiquities 5,3,9**

Starting WWII

At the Versailles Treaty in 1919, then Prime Minister Lloyd George of Britain pointing to the dismembered territories on the map exclaimed: "This will be the cause of the next war!"

Fifty-three days after Hitler assumed power in Germany, on March 24, 1933, a meeting of international Jewry declared war on Germany by instituting a boycott. This alerted the ITC media as to new anti-German policy. It was in 1933 that stories of German death camps began being circulated. Also in this year, America's Roosevelt threw off pretenses and recognized the USSR and gave it full diplomatic recognition. Germany signed the Concord with the Catholic Church which supposedly notified Catholics everywhere that Germany had the blessing of the Catholic Church, and were to recognize this Concord and give Germany help if they could.

Americans have little understanding of the deep racial antipathy that exists between the various races of Europe. The Germans who had been handed over to be ruled by Polish Slavs were roughly treated.[19] It started with the Poles closing German schools and the prohibition to open new ones, prohibition to speak German, decrees changing agrarian laws to the detriment of German farmers, revoking German working permits, curtailing church services in German, the singing of German songs, and other sorts of harassment.

Hitler tried diplomatic means to convince the Polish Head of State, Marshal Pilsudski (1867-1935), to intervene in the matter. Marshal Pilsudski agreed to try, but said: "I strongly believe the sincere intentions of your Fuhrer, but please tell him he may not overlook the ancient hatred of my people against all that is German is bottomless."[20]

Between the years 1936-1939 matters went from bad to worse. England and France executed a pact of mutual assistance in case Poland should be invaded. On "Bloody Sunday" in Brom-

19 **GOD'S LAW: "Thou mayest not set a stranger over thee, which is not thy brother." Deu 17:15.**

20 **Facts & Comments**, #1, Col A. Erlanger, KBE, 1989

berg, on September 3-4, 1939, a Polish mob attacked the Germans of the city, shooting men, women, and children. The dead were estimated at 4,537 in Bromberg alone. These sort of conditions existed throughout German lands now occupied by Poland from May to September 1939 and began to suggest a repeat of "1572" and "1641".[21] Adolph Hitler began to come under attack from his own people for his reluctance to protect Germans who had been given to the Poles to rule.

The incident that forced German overt reaction was the attack on the German radio station at the border town of Gleiwitz. Germany invaded Poland and England and France declared war on Germany on September 3, 1939. German soldiers riding into Polish towns record seeing dead German civilians. The torch had been lit. It all could have been avoided by a simple command from the Pope - had he wanted to.

Two weeks later the communist Soviet Union also invaded Catholic Poland. England and France DID NOT declare war on the USSR in spite of their violation of the treaty with Poland. The cartel had selected its enemy. It was Germany.

Germany defeated France and tried to make peace with England. David Irving, Britain's noted historian said:

> "Adolf Hitler's peace offer (to the British) was generous. .... I've seen it in the German, Swedish, Swiss and American archives .... The offer was this: Hitler declared that he was prepared to pull his armies out of France, Holland, Belgium, Norway, Denmark, Poland, and Czechoslovakia - out of all these territories except of course for the regions which had been German before and which he had fought the war over. Now that he had the territories like Alsace and Lorraine back, he was not going to let them go."[22]

Hitler's effort to make peace with Britain was rebuffed, and the USSR waited for the German invasion of Britain to start. They planned to strike while the German army was astride the English channel. German Intelligence informed Hitler that a

21 Pope Pius IX anathematized "all such as maintain that the church may not employ force." Pope Pius IX, Encyclical Letter of Dec 8, 1864

22 **David Irving, in his Speech to the Clarendon Club, 1990.** Printed with permission.

Soviet attack was imminent, so Germany turned and attacked the USSR two weeks before the Russian attack was due to be launched:

> "The German historian Werner Maser .... proves that Hitler was provoked into the War by Moscow. Referring to files and records of talks between Hitler and Stalin's Foreign Minister Molotov in Berlin during 1940, Maser maintains that Hitler must have realized, at least by that stage, that Germany and Europe had only two options: to fight or to submit to the Soviet Union. As confirmed by the Russian general Victor Suvorov in his book '*The Icebreaker* - Hitler in Stalin's View', Hitler's march into the Soviet Union came a mere 14 days before Stalin's troops would have overrun Europe and enslaved it under communism."[23]

General Paulis' German army went all the way to Stalingrad, where it was surrounded. More than 90,000 Germans surrendered. Most were North German Protestants. Only five thousand survived captivity.

German cities were carpet-bombed. Dresden, devoid of military manufacturing and with no defenses, was fire-bombed. One-third of a million women and children died in that single raid.[24] Most were German Protestant refugees from East Germany. The German bombing of England has been used as an excuse for the Allied bombing of German civilians. All the bombs dropped on England during WWII would not equal the total dropped on the city of Frankfurt in one day.

The Crusade alliance of 52 nations invaded Germany. Eisenhower stopped the allied armies before they reached Berlin to give America's Soviet allies a chance to occupy east and middle Germany. The Soviets forced German Protestants from their ancestral homes. Three million died on their forced march to the West. Their homes and lands were given to Polish Slavs.

---

23 **Insider** PO Box 17200, Groenkloof, Pretoria 0027, RSA, 1 Feb 1995, copied from **Gothic Ripples,** Colin Jordan, Thorgarth, Greenhow Hill, Harrogate, HG3 5JQ, ENGLAND, Jan 1995, £6.50/yr

24 ITC anti-German propaganda has capped the Dresden deaths at 25,000 in Germany and 35,000 elsewhere.

Catholic Poland, already in possession of West Prussia from WWI, was given East Prussia, Pomerania, and other German lands - German Protestant lands. The land taken from the Papacy by the Teutonic knights had now been recovered. The Counter-Reformation rolls on. Plots within plots - wars within wars.

Germany was defeated. Her leaders were gathered together, tortured to exact confessions, executed, and their bodies burned. Some say that the sensitive information that they could have revealed would have impacted world politics. It wasn't that the Jews were leaders in world communism - that was already general knowledge. The information that Rudolf Hess possessed was so sensitive that it caused the British to hold him in solitary confinement for almost half a century, and then murder him, it is said, just before he was to be released. It may have been that Rudolf Hess and the other German leaders had seen a figure beyond the Jews. That could explain why they were put to death.

Chapter 19

CORPORATIONS AND THE FEUDAL SYSTEM

Hide The Prey

Once the International Trade Cartel takes a prey - it must be hidden if it is not to fall into the hands of other predators.

For centuries the King and the Church have quarreled over possession of prey taken from the people. By trial and error, twisting the Law to conceal the trail, and working through surrogates, they have learned to hide what is taken.

Corporation City

The Shepherd ordained the self-sufficient Biblical homestead for his sheep. Ideally, one should be able to live on his own homestead with the homestead providing every basic need. It is the sheep's kingdom.[1] The "King-of-Kings" who rules the sheepfold is the Shepherd.

Sheep, free of corporate-domination, live within a sheep-fold and rule their own farm-kingdoms. Wolves live tightly packed together in corporation-cities. This is where they gather captive sheep who have been driven from the protection of their sheepfolds. The leader of the sheepfold is the Shepherd. The leader of the wolf-den is the Alpha-wolf prince. The sheepfold lives by the unchanging "Law of the Shepherd." The wolf-den lives under the constantly-changing "policy of the Alpha-wolf." Sheepfolds are a presbytery - ruled by Law from the bottom up

1 **GOD'S LAW: "The land shall be divided for an inheritance .... To many thou shalt give the more .... to few thou shalt give the less .... the land shall be divided by lot: according to .... their fathers they shall inherit." Num 26:53- 55**

with every man a king. Corporate wolf-dens are ruled by the alpha-wolf's policy from the top down in a stair-step hierarchy - an episcopacy. The sheepfold is composed of "sole owners" and "partnerships." The wolf-den is "corporate" in structure and operates under the "general policy" outlined in the 10 planks of the 1848 Communist Manifesto.[2]

The corporation rule in dealing with sheep is; "*A sheep does not bite the wolf who feeds him.*" Sheep who do are shot in the back of the head and burned.[3]

Corporation - Royal Monopoly

In Britain in the 17th century, corporations were a royal monopoly. The right was jealously guarded. It used to require an act of parliament for anyone other than the King to incorporate. Incorporation limits liability and conceals ownership. The king had much land and many businesses whose title-of-ownership needed to be concealed from the critical view of the people. The king was the head of the Anglican Church which was supposed to preach that monopoly was forbidden by Law.[4] Concealment was better than constant confrontation with the faithful. This issue was also of particular importance to the controlling stockholder since sheep-law stated that not only was monopoly forbidden, but that sheep are not permitted to transact business with wolves,[5] and that wolves are forbidden to rule over sheep.[6]

Modern corporations are much different from sheep-partnerships and sole ownerships. Standing between the controlling-stockholder and the workers is "management" who the controlling-stockholder hired to carry out his wishes. They act as enforcers.

2 This standard "feudal-policy" was known for centuries before Karl Marx gave it the name of "The Communist Manifesto."

3 In Germany, they were tried by Nuremburg statutes made for the occasion, hanged, burned, and their ashes thrown into rivers or flushed down toilets.

4 **GOD'S LAW: "Woe unto them that join house to house, that lay field to field, till there be no place, and they may be placed alone in the midst of the earth." Isaiah 5:8**

5 II Cor 6:15- 17, Judges 2:2, Deut 7:2, Pr 6;1,2, Amos 3:3.

6 **GOD'S LAW: "Thou mayest not set a stranger (Heb: nokriy - racial alien) over thee, which is not thy brother." Deu 17:15**

Corporate Military

A feudal army is organized corporate-style with the corporation providing weapons and pay. Handsome uniforms, honor guards, rituals and medals are given in lieu of paying anything of real value for their services. Its members are corporation employees who serve under "officers and gentlemen" appointed by the chairman-of-the-board - or his representative.

A sheep-army is a militia. They pick their own officers. In Virginia in the 1600s, news of an Indian raid triggered the gathering of "well-armed householders" - all were volunteers. Eight thousand men armed with firearms, swords, clothing, blankets, and mounted on their own horses gathered under command of their own elected officers. They were well- trained, having voluntarily gathered to perfect their military skills each month. Since their lives depended on their weapons, they were the best money could buy - state of the art. Virginia had not invested a shilling. The militia WERE the people of Virginia. This was a militia army - organized from the bottom up. The private was a king along with the commanding officer. The verbal contract was the private's obedience to the commander for the time of the emergency only - and then only in military matters.

Anyone who wore a red coat and whose weapons and equipment were paid for by the Royal Governor was immediately suspect. He was a hireling. He represented the interest of the corporation. Nothing's changed. Today's corporate representatives carry corporation-bought guns and drive corporation-bought cars. Some supplement their pay by running drugs from Colombia and guns to occupied Palestine.

After Virginia's militia thoroughly trounced the Royal Governor's hirelings during Bacon's Rebellion, the attempt was made to replace the militia with regulars and confiscate the militia's guns. That effort was abandoned after a time because there was too much danger from too many Indians and not enough money to pay for King's soldiers to keep both sheep and red-Indians pacified at the same time.[7]

Militia armies raised by the Continental Congress could seldom stand before precision corporation-type armies of the king fighting in open country of their own choosing. The attempt to force militias to do so almost lost the war.

Britain's magnificent Maj. Ferguson and his top-notch light-infantry, trained in irregular warfare and armed with breechloaders, was shot to pieces by frontier militiamen fighting in the woods at King's Mountain. Militia fighting their own way and refusing to fight corporation-style can be a formidable force. The massive U.S. army in Vietnam never did learn to cope with primitive native tunnel-warfare. The corporate army of the U.S. never were able to deal with Confederate ranger-warfare, sharpshooter battalions, expert engineers, and a "tally" money-system that allowed the South's militias to fight four long years against overwhelming odds.[8] They almost always beat the hirelings of the massive corporate Union armies - organized from the top down - armies which considered a soldier's life worth little. This scare caused volunteer militias to be banned in the post-war South, and the attempt is now being made to confiscate the guns of the "unorganized militia" so they won't be able to come together into organized militias and present a stumbling block to future corporate plans.[9]

Feudal Politics

Sheep are made kings and priests by their Shepherd. They cannot elect a king to rule them because the King-of-kings is

7 Nevertheless, many who fought with Bacon were hanged and almost all had their estates confiscated (4th Plank - Communist Manifesto). The Hoskins' estate was confiscated at this time and they joined the "little house" Virginians who were opposed by the "big house" Virginians who had been awarded their confiscated estates.

8 See "Tallies," **War Cycles / Peace Cycles**, Hoskins, Va Pub Co., PO Box 997, Lynchburg, VA 24505, $12/copy.

9 **GOD'S LAW: (1) "When a strong man armed keepeth his palace, his goods are in peace." Luke 11:18, (2) "How can one enter into a strong man's house, and spoil his goods, except he first bind the strong man, and then he will spoil his house." Matt 12:29**; "He said unto them ... he that hath no sword, let him sell his garment and buy one." Luke22:36.

the KING. He gave them Saul as an example of what would happen if they did have a king as other nations did. Men who are made kings and priests by the King-of-kings, are to rule themselves. So, for joint-action they elect "project managers." Viking sheep-kings elected a captain for a voyage - but for the voyage only. At voyage end, the captain reverted to being a sheep-king like everyone else. Sheep-kings elect a manager to build a bridge or to govern - but only for a set term - or a set project. He then becomes like other sheep. A George Washington finishes the job he was called on to do and goes home to his farm. An Oliver Cromwell seizes the throne, confiscates his friends and neighbors, and destroys the Reformation. Then, if the sheep fail to enforce the Law, "King Sauls" may rule for another 400 years until the people's misery compel the sheep to enforce the Law of the Shepherd.[10]

Tens And Hundreds

The old Saxon system of rule was "Tens" and "Hundreds." Hundreds existed in old England and in early Virginia. There was Bermuda Hundred, Carter's Hundred, Beverley's Hundred, etc. Each ten families chose one of their members as spokesman (bottom up - presbyterian system). Each ten spokesmen chose a "representative of 100." He might represent from 750 to 1375 people. This representative of 100 went to Williamburg as a Burgess. The Royal Governor didn't like this and tried to appoint his own leaders of 100 (top down - episcopacy system) - but this didn't work. One man can really know ten people - but no more. If he has to choose between more than 10 he will have to take another's recommendation. Yesterday, one elected his own spokesman for 10. Today the establishment's media says that this man is good and that one bad. The media says it works for us when in reality it works for those who own the media. As a result - today's system is an episcopacy that selects our leaders for us - and we are its slaves.

10 **GOD'S LAW: "Thine own wickedness shall correct thee ...thou hast forsaken the Lord." Jer 2:19**

The sheep-system run according to Law did not allow monopolies. This condition lasted until the ITC found a way around the prohibition. They paid surrogate sheep to authorize "corporations." These corporations bought newspapers. The sheep didn't know that the new owners were using the media to change the nation into a feudal- monopoly.[11] They did not know that their old familiar newspaper "The Daily Sheep-talk," with new owners, had been turned into the "Daily Wolf-howl."

With a media-monopoly, only those who supported the corporations were given the publicity needed to be elected to public office. Only "soviet-style" elections were offered: two candidates, both corporate-chosen by media owners in the background. "Heads I win - tails you lose." The corporation- media selected their own hand picked representatives who became rulers of the sheepfold and Feudalism was quietly established.

The Corporate "Loyal Opposition"

Once a feudal system has been established, malcontents cannot be allowed to run around and form a party that may destroy the system. If a party of malcontents should come to power, it might throw out the corporate king and the unprotected establishment could lose everything it had gained during the last hundred years.

To avoid such a catastrophe, corporate opposition is created by the system itself. Members of the opposition are screened, financed, and its demands are kept before the public. Other malcontents who are certain to arise can only gravitate to the opposition that exists - or form their own third party which is almost certain to fail.

With the opposition thus selected by the system, if it comes to power - nothing is changed. The feudal system operates as it has always done. Only the faces of the rulers are new. All else is as it was. The deposed king now pretends to be the "loyal"

11 Not until the 2nd Bank of the U.S. failed was it learned that the majority of the stock was owned in Britain. This is the bank that furnished most of the money that allowed unknown stockholders to buy up American newspapers. This was the act which so infuriated Andrew Jackson. The sheep never discovered the names of the owners of the newspaper chains.

opposition. In time, malcontents become discouraged and retire from the political field, or they operate outside the law and risk being burned alive as heretics.

In this way we have the Republicans fighting the Democrats. If the Republicans are elected - then the Democrats fight the Republicans. Nothing is ever changed. The Senate is known as the millionaires club and most legislators are lawyers who are trained in feudal law. As lawyers they are also trained to pass statutes to bend the Law of the WORD without causing the sheep to revolt.

If by chance a left-wing liberal named George Wallace should pose as a conservative and form a third party that to everyone's surprise develops overnight into a true opposition party, and if unexpectedly that party captures the peoples' imagination and snowballs into a revolutionary juggernaut that could seize power and destroy the establishment - Wallace is shot. The party disintergrates, and all is as it was before - Democrat vs. Republican.

Opposition Parties

The Christian religion declares absolutes. It cannot yield lest its God be found a liar.

For a thousand years the Catholic Church ruled. It treated its own pronouncements as God-given. Malcontents were burned. To prevent a Martin Luther or John Calvin from appearing, it tolerated Paulicans, and even encouraged them at times. Paulicans are the most ineffective people in the world. Attempting to disprove The WORD carries within itself - lawlessness. If there is no Law, then, what is Lawful? Paulicans in time learn to satisfy their every desire and in so doing degenerate into sleaziness and self-destruct. The handful who become a threat are eliminated by crusades.

The absence of a proper opposition to contain discontent caused the Reformation. The lesson was learned. Today's opposition parties are creations of the establishment and are created in such a way that no true reformation can recur.

Feudalism In The Plant

As a young man I was a management trainee in a large plant in Richmond. I was given "orientation training" and then shown my job. I knew the plant manager by sight, but not the shadowy "big-brass" who lived in N.Y. Once a year they sent a representative to inspect. A group of smiling foremen and plant managers escorted the VIP in a dark business suit through the plant.

My job was to supervise a line of machines and keep them running at maximum output. One worker had a definite attitude. He was personally dirty like "Pigpen" in the Peanuts comic-strip and spread it around. He started work on a clean machine and left it unbelievably filthy. Workers from other shifts who took over from him complained. He just stood there smirking - daring me to do something about it. Foolishly, I tried.

I told him to wipe off oil he had dropped on the machine. He knew corporation policy, I didn't. He started wiping, but while wiping he signaled someone. Soon, a puffing, red-faced union representative rushed up wearing his official union face. He raised his arm as a signal and all machines on the whole floor shut down.

Standing in a vacuum of silence, we waited until the shift supervisor could be summoned. When he arrived, the union representative read me, the shift-supervisor, and everyone in hearing the riot act. He related what management had agreed to do. He told the shift manager what the policy was. He told me what I could do and couldn't do. One thing I definitely could not do was to endanger the life and limb of a worker by having him clean a machine while it was running. The shift manager agreed that I had sinned. I agreed that I had sinned. The workers snickered.

I was properly humbled, contrite, and promised never to do it again. The union then gave the OK and the machines started up and the plant came to life once more. Policy. I had violated policy. They were right and I was wrong. It was that simple. The entire floor had been shut down for 15 minutes. I was responsible for the down-time of every machine on that floor. Machines that ran day and night and never shut down except for mechanical trouble had been brought to a standstill - for 15 whole minutes - and I was responsible. The production figures that went to New York at the end of that day showed a noticeable drop in production for that shift. The phone calls wanted to know "why"? whose fault was it? It was the fault of a young management-trainee named Richard Kelly Hoskins, foreman of the 2nd shift plug-making machines.

I asked my superior for a copy of the plant policy that I was supposed to obey. He informed that no such copy existed. It had never existed. It didn't exist! How could someone obey policy if he didn't know what the policy was? I was quietly informed that "everything is policy." There was little in union-management agreements in writing. Then I learned that at all times everyone is violating some policy. The trick was just not to violate the policy being enforced at the moment. The old-timers laughed and patted me on the shoulder and advised me to never make a decision, keep a low profile, and get an OK for everything I did. I should also try to discover what management wanted, and never ever get involved with anyone who had been called on the carpet.

America's corporate plant is the feudal system from India in miniature - from the top down. It is ruled by policy, ever-changing policy, a lawless cruel world, as America is now discovering. A world in which political-reliability is more important than talent and genius. Everything is whim, everything is negotiable. By sheep-standards, there is no loyalty, no honor, no protection. Workers scheme to get another's job. Anyone can be fired at age 55 for no reason. Maximum output is demanded for the lowest cost. People who work for corporate-America develop the defense mechanism of never having an opinion on anything that might be controversial - and therefore dangerous. The only thing they will express an opinion on is the weather, sports, or agreement with the TV announcer. The Corporation demands a slave mentality - a feudal system. Life in the corporate wolf-den reduces men to wage-slaves - the lowest caste.

Most readers of this book are first, second, and third generation removed from farms. They have been told of a time when people worked hard. Then, women were virtuous and men brave and honorable. It is hard for them to comprehend that in many parts of Europe this very same memory is so old that it has almost been forgotten. The feudal system, now called a corporation, does that to its victims.

Chapter 20

THE U.N. WAR AGAINST THE SAXON NATION

The Imperium

If one wishes to rule others he must establish an episcopacy. The mere existence of an episcopacy is a declaration of hostility against the presbytery and proof that there are those who would rule others.

The presbytery, who rules from the bottom up, seeks less and less regulation: the episcopacy seeks more and more regulation. At some point the presbytery will be forced to fight to maintain its freedom. In time the episcopacy will force its restrictions and demands on presbyteries and will fight to crush their resistance to its rule.

The imperium of the presbytery is individual freedom. The imperium of the episcopacy is to oppress others. Neither will be satisfied with anything less than victory.

Forming The ITC

In the past, the stronger episcopacies of the world struggled with weaker episcopacies for supremacy and trade advantages. When not fighting each other, they collaborated to suppress existing presbytery states such as the American South and South Africa and crush states that tried to break away - such as National Socialist Germany. They cooperated closely to oppress the people they ruled.

The hydrogen bomb changed this. For the first time the possibility exists for the world's rulers to be vaporized along with others in one of the wolf-pack's ongoing quarrels. No longer can the pups of the wolf-pack be allowed to fight over a piece of meat or a new place on the prestige ladder as they had in the past. The weapons have become too powerful and the danger to the others too great.

From now on, every member of the pack must toe a strict line. This is the reason the international trade cartel (ITC) has come together to show a common front. GATT and other such trade treaties supposedly remove irritating trade barriers of the sort that in the past have caused wars. The armed might of captive Western nations is being merged to form a single UN armed force - replacing national armies that have proved troublesome upon occasion in the past. It is the UN's job to enforce the International Trade Cartel's episcopacy on the entire world.

The Saxon race has been the race of whom God demands a presbytery - with every man being a king and a priest - ruling under the Law of the King of Kings. The Saxon race has been the greatest obstacle to the world rule of the ITC. The Saxon race must be subdued once and for all if the New World Order is to become a reality.

Dharma makes the use of force unnecessary. Therefore, Dharma is being utilized as never before. All efforts are being made to force Dharma-toleration. The Dharmamatras of the UN have defined "hate." "Hate" is to criticize any other race, religion or nationality. If the Saxon race can be persuaded to accept others, resistance to alien gods, customs and trade - collapse.

The U.S. Constitution states that both the Constitution of the United States AND treaties are the law of the land. The US Government ratified the UN charter giving both the UN charter and UN proclamations the power of international treaties - and thus of law. The United Nations is the ITC's Dharmamatra.

The following is a proclamation of the UN, having the power of treaty and thus of law. It is of special interest to Christians since it reveals what their own government representatives have contracted for them to do. It selects the parts of their religion which are most offensive to the Hindu - parts that must be suppressed. The UN proclamation on race published by the U.N. Office of Public Information, OPI151-63-27884, in January 1964, outlines these points in detail:

U.N. Proclamations

"*Considering that* .... all human beings are .... entitled to all the rights .... without distinction .... as to race, color or national origin.

"*Considering that* .... all are equal before the law ..... .

"*Considering* .... the U.N. has condemned .... segregation and discrimination ...

"*Considering that* any doctrine of racial differentiation .... is scientifically false, morally condemnable, socially unjust and dangerous, and that there is no justification for racial discrimination either in theory or in practice.[1]

"*Taking into account* the other resolutions .... of discrimination.

"*Taking into account* .... discrimination based on race .... continues to give cause for serious concern.

"*Alarmed by the manifestations* of racial discrimination .... in the form of .... separation .... as well as by .... dissemination of doctrines of racial superiority ..... .

"*Convinced that* .... policies based on the prejudice of .... racial hatred .... jeopardizes .... international peace and security.

"*Convinced* .... that racial discrimination harms .... those who practice it.

"*Convinced further* that the building of a world society free from .... racial segregation .... is one of the fundamental objectives of the U.N..[2]

1 Overwhelming evidence from scientific experiments proves the contrary. There is visual, quantitative, and measurable racial differences. History shows that no Saxon nation and the civilization it has produced has survived integration with a non-Saxon nation.

2 NOTE: Every religion in the world, except Christianity, promotes integration and proselytizing other races.

"1. Solemnly affirms .... speedily eliminating racial discrimination throughout the world ...

"2. Solemnly affirms the necessity of adopting national and international measures to that end ....

"3. Proclaims this Declaration:

Article 1

"Discrimination .... on the grounds of race .... shall be condemned .... as an obstacle to .... peaceful relations .... and as a fact capable of disturbing peace and security among peoples.

Article 2

"1. No State .... group or individual shall make any discrimination whatsoever .... on the grounds of race ...

"2. No State shall .... lend its support, through police action .... to any discrimination based on race ...[3]

"3. Special concrete measures shall be taken in appropriate circumstances .... to secure .... rights for different racial groups.[4]

Article 3

"1. Particular efforts shall be made to prevent discrimination based on race .... in the fields of .... religion[5] .... .

"2. Everyone shall have equal access to any place .... without distinction as to race ....[6]

3 "The Word," the "Word made flesh" and "Israel," are indivisible to Christians and their God. This article requires toleration of "evil." Israel's God has said he will destroy his people for tolerating evil.

4 "Affirmative action," anti-Saxon legislation, anti-Saxon media propaganda, Fort Smith Sedition Trials, anti-separation measures; ie, Ruby Ridge's Weaver assassinations, Waco killings, aid to Black anti-Saxon S. Africa, etc.

5 Of all the world's religions, God "The WORD" of the Christians is the God that forbids racial integration. **Gen 24:3,4, Deut 7:3, Joshua 23:12-13, Hosea 5:7, Neh 13:3, Neh 9:2, Ex 33:16, Lev 20:24, Ezra 10:3, Ex 23:28,33, Deu 28:43, Jubilees 30:6-13**, etc. This article is aimed solely against the world's Saxons.

6 **GOD'S LAW: "When the tabernacle is to be pitched .... the stranger (Heb: zûwr -racial alien) that cometh nigh shall be put to death." Numbers 1:51.**

Article 4

"All States shall take effective measures .... to rescind laws and regulations which have the effect of .... perpetuating racial discrimination .... [7]

Article 5

"An end shall be put without delay to .... policies of *apartheid*[8]

Article 6

"No discrimination by reason of race .... shall be admitted in the enjoyment .... of .... citizenship rights .... [9]

Article 7

"1. Everyone has the right .... to protection by the State ....

"2. Everyone shall have the right to .... protection against any discrimination ....[10]

---

7 This edict is the reason for the Canadian, Swedish, French, British, Australian, and German "anti-Saxon - anti-hate" laws. The governments of these nations are ITC agents and do the will of their masters.

8 These articles express the Hindu ideal to perfection and could have been written in the time of Asoka The Great.

9 **GOD'S LAW: "A bastard (Heb: mamzêr - mixed breed, mongrel) shall not enter into the congregation of Israel." Deut 23:2** (Margin note by the reformers in Geneva Bible 1599). "This was to cause them to live chastely, that their posterity might not be rejected."

10 **GOD'S LAW: "Thou mayest not set a stranger (Heb: nokriy - racial alien) over thee, which is not thy brother." Deut 17:15; "Their nobles shall be of themselves, and their governor shall precede from the midst of them.. Jer 30:21; "Thou shalt reign over many nations, but they shall not reign over thee." Deut 15:6**

Article 8

"All effective steps shall be taken immediately in the fields of teaching, education and information, with a view to eliminating racial discrimination ....[11]

Article 9

"1. All propaganda and organizations .... promoting racial discrimination .... shall be severely condemned.[12]

"2. All incitement to or acts .... against any race .... shall be .... punishable under law.[13]

"3. .... all states shall take immediate and .... legislative and other measures to .... outlaw organizations which promote .... racial discrimination ....[14]

Article 10

"The U.N. .... shall .... by combining legal and other practical measures, will make possible the abolition of all forms of racial discrimination .... [15]

Article 11

"Every State shall promote .... fundamental freedoms in accordance with the Charter of the United Nations."[16]

---

11 This is the compelling reason for court rulings against the WORD in the classroom. **"Read this law before all Israel .... men and women, and children and thy stranger (Heb: gêr - visiting racial kinsman) .... that they may .... do all the words of this law." Deut 31:11-12**

12 This article is the reason for the censorship oppression now taking place in most Saxon nations.

13 **GOD'S LAW: "We must obey God rather than men." Acts 5:29; "If ye love me keep my commandments." John 14:15; "Not everyone shall enter into the kingdom of heaven but he that doeth the will of my Father which is in heaven." Matt 7:21.** Reading the Word must be banned to comply with this statute.

14 Christian gatherings obeying The WORD must be banned to comply with this statute.

15 The "policing map" of the U.S. and other lands by troops foreign to them has already been published and is available from patriotic groups.

16 Only the nations of the West are required to comply. An alien world which hates Christ now sits in judgment over His people. The Saxon ideal is that in time ALL episcopacies - religious, political and economic will cease to exist; Their place taken by private ownership, partnerships, and joint ventures - tens and hundreds - and barter.

Chapter 21

THE BALAK PLAN

Plot To Destroy A Nation

Intermarriage was the single most talked about subject between the years 1865 and 1940 since it lies at the heart of Christianity. Most states followed the public discussion and preempted the work of the Phineas Priesthood (Numbers 25)[1] with laws prohibiting interracial marriages.[2]

After WW II, the media banned public discussion of the subject. The single viewpoint permitted was the one favorable to racial intermarriage. Propaganda, state-religion, judicial and political pressure joined to promote the dubious practice. All done in the absence of public debate.

The question asked was WHY? The answer is that racial integration is Dharma. It is the plan to permanently annex the Western trading areas to the International Trading Cartel in a manner so that its stiff-necked peoples will never be able to expel the international merchant because he is obviously different. This technique has been used before. Josephas related the story of how it almost destroyed Israel 2,000 years ago.

---

1 **"One of the children of Israel came and brought ... a Midianitish woman ... and when Phineas ... saw it, he rose up from among the congregation and took a javelin in his hand ... and thrust both of them through ... And the Lord spake ... saying Phineas ... hath turned my wrath away from the children of Israel ... Behold I give unto him my covenant of peace: ... and his seed after him, even the covenant of an everlasting priesthood: because he was zealous for his God." Num 25:6-13; Ps 106:30; Antiquities 4:6:12-13; Antiquities 4:7:1; Jasher 85:61-63, 86:6; Enoch 46:23-24; Ecclesiasticus 45: 22-24**

2 **Vigilantes Of Christendom**, Hoskins, The Story Of the Phineas Priesthood

Balak's Plot To Destroy Man[3]

The story is as follows: Balak hated the Israelites and wanted to destroy them. He went to the wise man Balaam for advice on how this was to be most easily accomplished. Balaam advised Balak, the ruler of the Moabites, that he must do the following in order to destroy the Israelites:

> "If you... gain a victory over them (the Israelites, then do thusly)
>
> "Set out the handsomest ... of your daughters ... then ... send them to be near the Israelites ... and when they are enamored of them ... persuade them to leave off their obedience to their own laws and the word of that God who established them ... for by this means God will be angry at them. ... when Balaam had suggested this counsel to them, he went his way." Antiquities 4:6:6

The point made is twofold. First, the offspring of an Israelite and a stranger is a *mamzér*. Mixed offspring are rejected by God the WORD.[4] He is rejected by God and will NOT be accepted into the Saxon nation of Israel.

Second: Strangers, unable to destroy the Israelites openly, tempted them to violate God's Law against intermarriage in order to bring them into conflict with their God. If they could be made to violate their God's law, it would anger their God who had promised that he would destroy his own people if they ever intermarried with any other people. A remarkable plan, one diabolical in its simplicity. The plot was activated by merely bringing Israel into contact with strangers and letting nature do the rest.

The integration and destruction of the Saxon nations living in the following nations have been met with complete success; India, Egypt, Syria, Palestine, Egypt, Greece, North Africa, Spain, Southern Italy, Southern France, Bohemia, Hungary,

3 **Strong's Concordance**, MAN - Heb: "Adam," to blush red

4 **GOD'S LAW: "A bastard (Heb: mamzér - mixed breed, mongrel) shall not enter into the congregation of the Lord." Deut 23:2**

Poland, Mexico, and most of South America. The Balak Plan works!

The ITC is once again using the Balak Plan against the remaining Saxon nations of the world: Europe, North America, South Africa, Australia and New Zealand. The Western nations are all being flooded with strangers to accomplish this purpose.

This is why the UN passed integration statutes directed against Saxons. This is why censorship laws are being passed. This is why media propaganda is pro-integration. This is why the media-elected Western governments have passed anti-Christian laws. The Balak Plan is the International Trade Cartel's plan to crush the Saxon once and for all. And, once again the Balak Plan will fail, perhaps for the same reason it failed before. This part of the Balak Plan is told in *Vigilantes of Christendom*, "The story of the Phineas Priesthood."[5]

5 **Vigilantes Of Christendom**, Virginia Publishing Company, PO Box 997, Lynchburg, Virginia 24505. $22/copy.

Chapter 22

THE PROMISED LAND

The Farm

God's promised kingdom on earth is THE FARM.

The self-sufficient farm is ruled by the farmer who is its king, defender, and judge. The farm is the mother of "cottage industry," the mill to help fabricate, and the country store to distribute its products.

Kings Are Forbidden

The WORD which is God[1] specifies exactly how the sheepfold is to be constructed and maintained. God The *WORD* is to rule as *"King of Kings"* - and no one else. The *WORD* created "man" in the beginning.[2] He created him in God's image. He named his sheep "Israel," which means in Hebrew - "to have God's power of attorney." Again, God appointed each of us a king and a priest.[3] Our assignment: to rule the earth in His name. We are to be severely punished if we don't.[4] There is to be no king to rule us except Jesus. God warns against other kings. God says that the nation that chooses a king rejects *Him:*

> *"The elders of Israel ... came to Samuel ... make us a king to judge us like all the nations. ... And the Lord said ... the people ... they have not rejected thee, but they have rejected me, that I should not reign over them. ...*

1 **GOD' LAW:"In the beginning was the WORD, and the word was with God, and the WORD was God." John 1:1, and "The WORD was made flesh, and dwelt among us." John 1:14**

2 "Man." Heb: Adam. "He who blushes red." **Strong's Concordance.**

3 GOD'S LAW: **"Jesus Christ ... hath made us kings and priests." Rev 1:5,6**

4 **GOD'S LAW: "O children of Israel... You only have I known of all the families of the earth: therefore I will punish you for all your iniquities." Am 3:1- 2**

> *"This will be the manner of the king that shall reign over you: He will take your sons, and appoint them for himself, for his chariots, and to be his horsemen; ... And he will take your daughters ... And he will take your fields, and your vineyards, and your oliveyards, even the best of them, and give them to his servants. And he will take the tenth of your seed, and of your vineyards, and give to his officers, and to his servants. ... He shall take the tenth of your sheep: and ye shall be his servants. And ye shall cry out in the day because of your king which ye shall have chosen you; and the Lord will not hear you in that day." I Sam 8:11-18*

Christians recognize no king but Jesus "*The WORD made flesh.*" Each of us has been appointed "king and priest" by him, and he delegated us our authority when he named us Israel.

Wolfpacks are the opposite. A wolfpack cannot exist without a leader - an alpha wolf - a king. The rest of the pack stairsteps down from him in authority. Each wolf, even when living apart, must belong to a pack somewhere. It's the wolf's nature. The sheep know this and consequently look upon any group organized like a wolfpack (from the top down) as being a wolfpack or surrogates of the wolf.

The Sheepfold

An intact sheepfold is like a circle of wagons our forefathers used to defend against attack. This circle protects in all directions. It is called "*The whole armor of God.*" The master of the sheepfold is the WORD - the trusted gatekeeper is the watchman.

It is no profit to the international merchant to go to a far country to trade and not be able to trade because the god of that country will not let its people trade with strangers.[5] Neither is

5 GOD's LAW: (1) "Thou shall make no covenant with them ... For they will turn away thy son from following me, that they may serve other gods." Deut 7:2,4; (2) "If thou hast stricken thy hand with a stranger (Heb: zûwr - racial alien), thou are snared...deliver thyself as a roe from the hand of the hunter." Pr 6:1,2

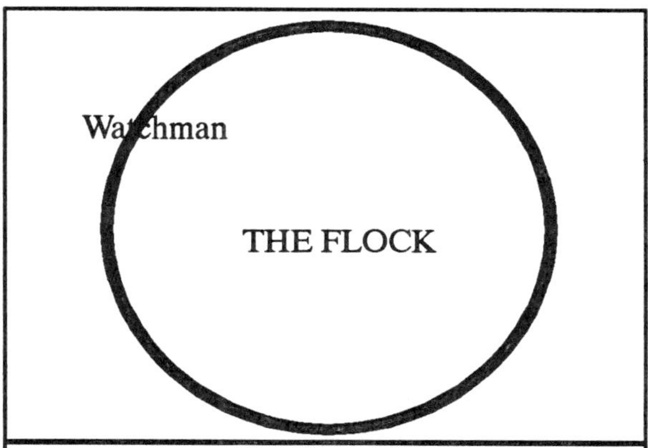

The Sheepfold

The sheepfold looks like a circled wagon train. The land within is divided among the sheep. Each sheep rules his portion as king and priest under God the WORD. There is no king but God the WORD. The watchman warns of approaching danger. The kings and priests live on self-sufficient farms. The trading village is the largest habitation. Large cities and prisons are unknown in a sheepfold.

there profit in entering the sheepfold only to be killed by sheep aroused by the watchman.[6]

To do business in a sheepfold the wolf must first bribe the watchman to allow him to enter. Once in the sheepfold he must find a ram who will act as his agent, who will stand between him and irate rams demanding the return of stolen goods. In payment for protecting the wolf the surrogate-ram is given a generous portion of the slaughtered sheep. Wolves seldom deal with sheep directly; they find it safer to leave this to their surrogates which their wealth has made into kings - well-paid "kings."

Making A King

Wolf-gold, wolf-media, and wolf-strategy can make ordinary sheep into a forbidden "king" - a la "King Saul." It is wolf-money that hires a king's army, and buys media, courts, judges, and lawyers used to conquer neighboring sheep and seize their

6 GOD's LAW: "When the tabernacle is to be pitched ... the stranger (Heb: zûwr - racial alien) that cometh nigh shall be put to death." Numbers 1:51.

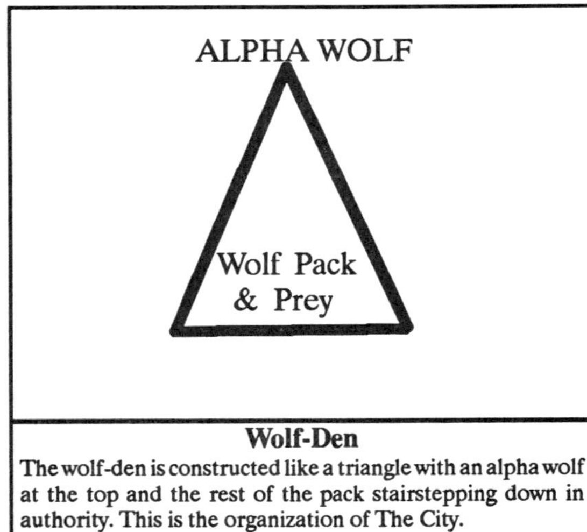

Wolf-Den

The wolf-den is constructed like a triangle with an alpha wolf at the top and the rest of the pack stairstepping down in authority. This is the organization of The City.

lands. If the "watchman" remains dumb while wolves pass by - this is notice to the sheep that the watchman is also in the pay of the wolf.[7]

Bribing A Watchman

Once a watchman has been bribed to pass wolves into the sheepfold, he must remain on the payroll to calm the sheep and see to it that they are not alerted to the wolf's transgressions. Corrupt watchmen refuse to see a stranger even when seating them in their choirs.[8] The wolf's capital crimes of usury, murder, and kidnaping are unseen, unreported, and concealed with silence.[9]

False watchmen earn their tax-exemption by no longer reading, teaching, obeying, or following the *WORD*. They follow the

7 **(1) "Cursed be he that doeth the work of the Lord deceitfully, and cursed be he that keepeth back his sword from blood." Jer 48:10; (2) "Think not that I am come to send peace on earth: I came not to send peace, but a sword." Matt 10:34; (3) "And the Lord said ... Slay utterly ... and begin at my sanctuary. Then they began at the ancient men (important, elders) which were before the house." Ezec (9:1-6)**

8 **"The stranger (Heb: zûwr - racial alien) that cometh nigh (the tabernacle) shall be put to death." No 18:7**

9 **GODS's LAW: (1) "If a false witness rise up ... Then shall ye do unto him, as he had thought to have done unto his brother." Deu 19:16-19; (2) "Not everyone that saith unto me, Lord, Lord, shall enter into the kingdom of heaven; but he that doeth the will of my Father which is in heaven." Matt 7:21**

ecumenical Hindu world force whom they rename - "Jesus." This is the very god the Hindus call Brahma - the god of love. These Christian-Hindus tell their followers that Brahma is "Jesus." But to these hirelings - all gods are one. The only god who accepts all gods is Brahma. To these hired representatives of the wolf - the *WORD* and the *WORD made flesh,* and all His followers who remain steadfast - are a curse.

The Sheepfold

The hard nut to crack is the sheep's Biblical citadel within the sheepfold - the self-sufficient farm.[10] Each "priest and king" rules his own God-mandated kingdom by *the WORD*. This kingdom is self-sufficient and produces practically everything it needs. It raises its own food, weaves clothing from wool taken from its own sheep, blacksmiths, makes shoes, and trades its surplus for those things it does not make. The sheep do not waste time building homes, they live in homes built generations ago on land which The WORD forbids the sheep to sell.[11]

Thomas Jefferson had a clear understanding of the sheepfold and in a letter to Dr. Currie (ii, p.219, 1787, *The Jeffersonian Cyclopedia,* John P. Foley, Funk & Wagnalls, NY 1900), described the Virginia farmer in the following manner:

> "I know no condition happier than that of a Virginia farmer ... His estate supplies a good table, clothes himself and his family with their ordinary apparel, furnishes a small surplus to buy salt, sugar, coffee, and a little finery for his wife and daughters, enables him to receive and to visit his friends and furnishes him pleasing and healthy occupation. To secure all this, he needs the one act of self-denial, to put off buying anything till he has the money to pay for it."

In a letter to William Duane, Ibid, v, 576. Ford Ed., ix, 312, Jefferson said:

10 **GOD's LAW: (1) "The land shall be divided for an inheritance ... To many thou shalt give the more ... to few thou shalt give the less ... the land shall be divided by lot: according to ... their fathers they shall inherit ..." Num 26:53-55.**

11 **GOD's LAW: "The land shall not be sold for ever: for the land is mine." Lev 25:13-28**

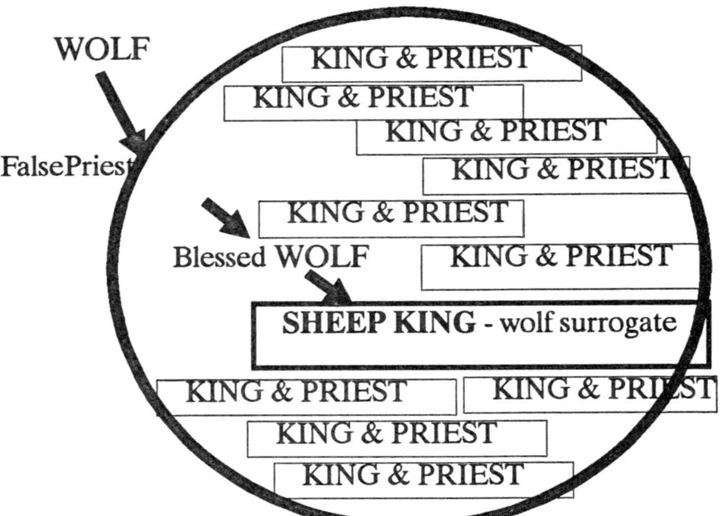

Forcing Entry Into The Sheepfold

The wolf bribes the faithless watchman to bless the one that God has cursed so that he can enter the sheepfold. Once in the sheepfold the wolf hires a king to protect the wolf while he kills sheep. The wolf must bribe both priest and king to safely kill sheep.

> "The truth is that farmers, as we all are, have no command of money. Our necessaries are all supplied, either from our farms, or a neighboring store. Our produce, at the end of the year, is delivered to the merchant, and thus the business of the year is done by barter, without the intervention of scarcely a dollar; and, thus, also, we live with a plenty of everything except money."

Jefferson had a neighbor who bought and sold $20,000 worth of merchandise in a single year, and at the end of the year balanced his books by receiving just thirty-five dollars. Twenty thousand dollars in the early 1800s was a great deal of money. A clipper ship and cargo were valued at $20,000. The interesting thing is that no actual money exchanged hands except at the very end of the year when $35 was received to balance his books. He might as well have received an equal amount of horse shoes or wheat. In other words, money is not necessary to do business in

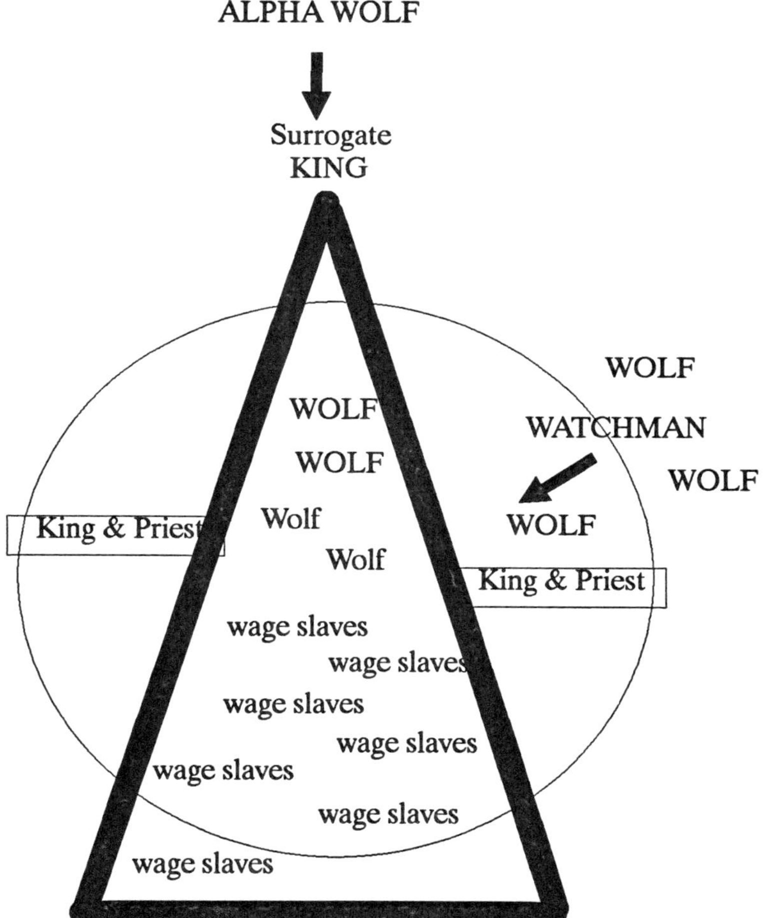

WOLF-DEN CITY ABSORBS SHEEPFOLD

The false priest-watchman blesses the wolf and issues him a safe conduct pass. The wolf freely enters the sheepfold and finances a surrogate sheep to become a powerful king. A powerful king is able to protect the wolf and suppress revolt. The wolf rules through his surrogates - the priest and the king. Since the wolf is Hindu - the priests become Christian-Hindu.The wolf is ferocious - his surrogate-king becomes like his master. If the sheep do not drive the wolf away - they will all be devoured. If the wolf is driven away - the city will die and the self-sufficient farm will again flourish.

a sheepfold. I remember when farmers coming to Lynchburg on Saturday would give their children "twists" of tobacco in trade for candy. Merchants sold the "twists" as chewing tobacco. Farm boys with tobacco twists to trade had more candy than city boys with coins. I know.

Years ago I spent much time in the mountains of Virginia. Near the Priest and the Three Sisters in Nelson County I stumbled on an intact settlement which had been spared the rigors of war. Many of the inhabitants had not traveled the long twisting dirt road down the mountain to Lynchburg town in thirty years. They had no need nor desire to. Their hundred or so acres on top of the mountains provided everything they needed; a horse, a cow or two, sheep, and a garden. They could have planted more wheat or corn than they did - but they couldn't use it. Their usual crop was sufficient to last the winter with enough left over to trade with neighbors. Each family specialized in something different from his neighbors. Some quilted, others were house builders, furniture makers, blacksmiths, gunsmiths, mechanics, wagon makers, teachers and tutors, homeopathic doctors, and shoemakers. Some had gone to town to work and had returned when the city lost its charm. The children were mostly home schooled or had a tutor. I was told that since it was so far away from town no one bothered them with taxes. That was years ago.

There were no police, no preacher, and no jail. There was no crime. The *WORD* of God was enforced by the people themselves who took their jobs seriously. They took turns holding Sunday meetings in each other's houses. A house that burned accidentally was replaced by the whole community within a week. Most dwellings in these remote mountains were log cabins - but you should have seen the cabins! A few were hastily thrown up and were rough, but others were plastered, had shaped roof shingles, chair rails, ornate mantels, banister rails, Chippendale furniture, and good china.[12] The local tutor could teach Latin if you cared to learn it. Everyone seemed to know

12 In Tidewater, many of the old houses in the 17th and 18th centuries were made of brick manufactured on the farm, or clapboard from trees grown on the place. The studding was all heart pine - one stud from one tree. Ask your builder friend about that!

something different from his neighbor. Close kinsmen used first names. Others used the titles "Mister" and "Mrs." as befitted responsible "kings and priests" who ruled kingdoms. They were entitled to that mark of respect. I have never heard of a divorce in a farm family - either in mountain or lowland farms. Divorce was a city thing.

The Country Store

My great grandfather, Maj. William Hoskins, late surgeon 59th Virginia, returned home and practiced medicine in King and Queen County. There was no money (Except two gold coins. That story is told in *War Cycles/Peace Cycles*).[13] People paid him in kind. In time Dr. William accumulated 62 pairs of shoes, 96 hoes, 4 muskrat traps, 416 pounds of tobacco, and a number of other things, so he opened a country store to dispose of them. In time, local cottage industries brought their products to his store to be displayed and sold. His store received one in ten of whatever it sold as payment. He later built Hoskins Mill at the Essex Mill Pond near Dunnsville to grind grain for neighbors; one bushel for each 10 bushels ground. The economy of the Virginia county was based on agriculture, and cottage industries were its by-products. Besides country stores, there were all sorts of water mills - grist, saw, pounding, etc. - There were also iron furnaces and shot towers. The farms within the sheep-fold produced an abundance of cottage industries as men found specialties which filled needs.

The Wife

The family spoke as one. Important business matters were entered into by either party - after prior agreement between the man and wife. The man was the legal head of the house, but the farm wife had a full say. Whatever affected the farm affected the future of her man, herself, their children, and their inheritance.

When the man was away at war, hunting, or dealing with matters concerning his cottage industry, the wife managed the

13 **War Cycles / Peace Cycles**, Va Pub Co, PO Box 997, Lynchburg, VA 24505, $12.

farm - the whole thing. If her man was gone for a month - she managed. If he was gone to the wars for two years - she managed. When Southern men were away for four long years - she managed.

My ancestor, Capt. John Hoskins, son of Bartholomew the immigrant who landed at Jamestown in 1615, owned widely scattered land-grants that he had gotten in exchange for transporting colonists to Virginia. He also owned five or six ships used to transport these colonists. He maintained offices both at Jamestown and in Fleet Street in London. He spent half his time in Virginia and half in London. His affairs were tangled and involved. He managed the London part and his wife managed his Virginia operations. She knew more about them than he did. His son Thomas took part in Bacon's Rebellion against the Royal Governor. While Thomas was away on active duty his wife ran the plantation. Unfortunately, Bacon's Rebellion failed and Thomas was confiscated.[14] The family was forced to live on the charity of kinsmen. Our women stuck with their men through good times and bad. I don't know about the women in the reader's part of the country, but our Virginia women are absolutely magnificent!

The Militia

The old brick cottage with three dormers, "Woodville" near Miller's Tavern, was the manse of the Episcopal priest sent over by his Royal Majesty who was also head of the Church of England and God's representative on earth.

The preacher was paid and "Woodville" was maintained by Essex County and so the place was treated like public land. It was where one cavalry company of the Essex and the King and Queen militia met to drill. The spring down the hill in front of the house is where they watered their horses. The same big oaks a little beyond furnished the shade where they rested from their

14 Confiscating rebels' property violates God's command that landed property be "**never sold.**" However, confiscation is natural when the alpha-wolf claims everything for himself and his subjects only own land "en fief." "Confiscation of rebels" is the 4th plank of the Communist Manifesto, the code which ruled the wolf-den long before Karl Marx.

military exercises in the hot Virginia sun. Before the war Dr. Hoskins acted as surgeon for this company and tended their cuts and broken bones that came mostly from overzealous horseplay as neighbors met to practice the ancient peacetime social event called "soldiering."

This cavalry company was more than 200 years old by 1860. They had fought countless battles in numerous wars in Virginia's past, and their names weren't even listed on the the rolls in Richmond. There were no rolls. Virginia could only guess how many soldiers she had. The militia was volunteer and every man equipped himself at his own expense - uniform (if any), sword, rifle, pistol, tent, blankets, food, and horse. The youngster who aspired to be elected an officer went to the Virginia Military Institute for additional training - at his own expense. (Of course, this was much later. VMI only opened in 1845.)

People tend to forget, but in the 17th century the threat of an Indian raid could field eight thousand well mounted militia virtually overnight. The royal governor in Williamsburg only had 300 paid regulars, and the king back in England had just 10,000 professionals. Little Virginia had almost that many and they were volunteers that cost the colony nothing. The Indians who arrived in Virginia on foot from across the Blue Ridge mountains were lucky to leave Virginia alive. Every mountain pass was quickly sealed, and when located, the Indians war parties were chased down by mounted men trained to their work. They fought Indian style - no prisoners - except to take hostages to trade for captives in Indian hands. Every able bodied Virginian from the age of 16 to 60 was expected to participate in Virginia's defense.

Law Enforcement

Most Virginia settlers were descended from persecuted Scottish Presbyterians, English Puritans, and French Huguenots who had refugeed to Virginia. Their forebears had died for their God, and they had learned their religion from the Geneva Bible whose margin notes by John Calvin and John Knox condemned the King and his wolf-den.

The question then as now is - who enforces the Law? The King and his representatives answered - "the king." Virginia next asked - "who is the king?" The Royal Governor said "Charles!" But it was the king who gave away the Northern Neck to his favorites in fulfillment of the prophecy in *I Sam 8:11-18.* God did not give him the right to do that! The king said that his insistence that black slaves be sold into the colony was his "divine right!" The Royal governor appointed by the king forbade Virginians to protect themselves from marauding Indians because he did not wish to disturb his fur trade with them. The scalps of Virginia's women and children were of less value than profits from Indian fur pelts.[15] If the king and his representative refused to honor God's Law - what then were the people to do?

Virginians knew. They had been brought up on the writings of Calvin listed earlier, but which bear reading once again:

> "Obedience to man must not become disobedience to God. But in that obedience which we have shown to be due the authority of rulers, we are always to make this exception, indeed, to observe it as primary, that such obedience is never to lead us away from obedience to him, to whose will the desires of all kings ought to be subject, to whose decrees all their commands ought to yield, to whose majesty their scepters ought to be submitted. ... How absurd would it be that in satisfying men you should incur the displeasure of him for whose sake you obey men themselves! The Lord, therefore, is the King of Kings, who, when he has opened his sacred mouth, must alone be heard, before all and above all men; next to him we are subject to those men who are in authority over us, but only in him. If they command any thing against him, let it go un-esteemed. ... "[16]

15 **GOD's LAW: (1) "Thou shalt make no covenant with them." Ex 23:31; (2) "Thou hast abandoned Thy people, the house of Jacob, Because ... they strike bargains with the children of foreigners." Isaiah 2:6 (New American); (3) "If thou hast stricken thy hand with a stranger (2114 zûwr), thou are snared." Pr 6:1**

16 **"Institutes of the Christian Religion"** John Calvin, Westminster Press, Philadelphia. 1960, Book 4: Chapter 20: Paragraph 32:

"I know with what great and present peril this constancy is menaced, because kings bear defiance with the greatest displeasure, whose "*wrath is a messenger of death*" *Prov 16:14*, says Solomon. But since this edict has been proclaimed by the heavenly herald, Peter - "*We must obey God rather than men,*" *Acts 5:29* - let us comfort ourselves with the thought that we are rendering that obedience which the Lord requires when we suffer anything rather than turn aside from piety. (Book 4: ch 20, PP 1)

"Earthly princes lay aside their power when they rise up against God, and are unworthy to be reckoned among the number of mankind. We ought, rather, utterly to defy them than to obey them."[17]

John Knox backed this opinion by quoting *The Magdeburg Statement* which says that one has the duty of armed resistance to a ruler who violates the law of God.[18]

Without the lawless suffocating hand of the king and his wolf-den minions to distort and destroy - Virginians spread out over America taking with them the Calvin-Knox dream of Christian freedom in a Christian land. The wolves they left behind dared not follow into the wilderness and those in front were pushed aside. The commands of God were enforced. When Lawlessness appeared - it was judged and capital crimes were punished scriptually:

"The hands of the witnesses shall be first upon him to put him to death, and afterward the hands of all the people." Deut 17:5-7

"If thy brother ... entice thee ... saying, let us go and serve other gods ... thou shall surely kill him; thine hand shall be

17 **Commentaries on Daniel**, (1561, Lecture 30, on Dan. 6:22. (GR 41.25)

18 **History of the Reformation,** John Knox debate w/Lethington 1564 (contained in 4 ch20 v31 FN p. 1519.)

first upon him to put him to death, and afterwards the hand of all the people." Deut. 13:6-11

The enforcement of God's Law produced peace and abundance. Biblical self-sufficient farms were established and protected by those who feared to let evil go unpunished.[19]

War Creates Demand

The King of England first demanded that native wolves be converted into sheep and accepted into the sheepfold. This resulted in a massacre. After this debacle, he demanded that slave wolves be taken into the sheepfold. Next, the Dutch King demanded that trade wolves be allowed to land in New York. The wolf found there was almost nothing that he could offer that was needed or wanted by the American farms and especially the self-sufficient Virginia farms. These farms themselves produced everything the wolf had for sale. What to the sheep was Camelot, was to the wolf a wasteland. To them, farms and farming are beneath contempt.[20] Before farmers and their farms can be converted into profitable consumer and land developments - they must first be separated from each other. This can not be done as long as the *WORD* rules. The *WORD* says that land may not be taxed, sold, or even leased for more than 50 years.

In the North the farm system was destroyed by taxes and usury loans. Farmers borrowed to pay the tax. Wolf-usury lent the money and took the farms. The North and the North Central states were converted into wolf-dens. Former self-sufficient farms now raised livestock or were "developed." Towns became cities. Unused farmland was so plentiful that houses were built in the middle of lots rather than on the front edge to save every square foot in back for gardens. Sweat- shops replaced cottage-industries. Giant power grids replaced water mills. Rolling mills and steel foundries replaced the water mill. Railroads

19 GOD'S LAW: **"Because thou hast let go out of thy hand a man whom I appointed to utter destruction, therefore thy life shall go for his life, and thy people for his people. I Ki 20:42**

20 TALMUD: "No occupation is inferior to that of agricultural labor." Yeb 63a., Exh 161

transported thousands of tons of cheap manufactured goods and dumped them in giant stores - destroying millions of cottage industries.

Before the war the North produced almost nothing that the South needed. After Northern armies destroyed Southern farms the destitute refugees needed everything that they had produced for themselves before the war. Their conquerors moved south and built stores to distribute sweat shop goods manufactured by northern wage-slaves. Destroying the Southern farm created Southern demand and made the South valuable to the new king who now ruled both North and South.

Sherman burned the farms of Georgia, South Carolina, and North Carolina when there was no military reason to do so. Sheridan burned the farms of the Valley of Virginia. Missouri farms were put to the torch by Union Armies. It was no accident that the Union army seldom lost an opportunity to burn mills and farm buildings. President Lincoln stopped all prisoner exchange that would have saved the lives of thousands of farmer-soldiers - both Northern and Southern. The Southland, the land with almost no cities and few needs, once destroyed, experienced massive urban growth as burned out refugees arrived from ruined farms and begged to work for wolf corporations as wage-slaves in newly constructed textile and steel mills. The Southland was converted into a wolfden like the land of their brothers in the North.

SOUTH AFRICA: South Africa's farms were burned to the ground. From that time on practically everything the Boer produced before the war he now had to buy from the international merchant.

RUSSIA: The wolves stormed the Russian sheepfold in 1917 and immediately starved four million Ukrainian farmers to death and combined their independent farms into farm collectives. Survivors had to buy from the wolf things they earlier produced for themselves.

GERMANY: German farms in East Germany were given to the wolves to organize into collectives. The German farmers were driven from the land.

Taxes

Taxes imposed by kings have destroyed more farms than any other single thing.[21]

Cottage-Industries Destroyed By Dumping

Wolf corporations made wage-slaves out of dispossessed farmers and used their sweat shops to mass-produce wares. Train loads of these wares were sent to Richmond and sold for 1/4 the price that Virginia's cottage industry could make and sell them. Virginia's cottage textile industry was destroyed. Sweat-shop shoe companies dumped tens of thousands of shoes which were sold in the same manner. Once cottage-industries had been destroyed, the conquerors built textile mills and shoe factories in Southern towns to use the now unemployed cottage-industry textile and shoe makers. One by one Virginia's cottage industries died.

Separated from the protection of his farm - the farmer became valuable prey - a productive asset for the wolf. His farm is now incorporated into a collective, or sits idle awaiting development. In time, the company he works for as a wage-slave will be forced to close because cheap foreign imports are dumped here. Dispossessed, unemployed, with his family in want - the Saxon faces the greatest opportunity he has had in 2000 years.

To The Death!

The wolf-city is big - the self-sufficient farm is small. Wolf-city needs fleets of 18 wheelers to feed itself and supply its warehouses and supermarkets. The farm needs inexpensive work and transportation machinery.

21 GOD's LAW: "Of whom do the kings of the earth take custom or tribute? of their own children, or of strangers? Peter saith unto him, Of strangers." (Gr: allotrios - foreign, not akin.) ... Then are the children free." Matt 17:25-26.

The wolf-city's power needs are enormous - electric power-grids, gas pipelines, trainloads of coal, million ton oil tankers, and atomic energy. The farm needs a simple windmill or solar cell. Its cottage-industry can produce all the ethanol it needs.

Wolf-city demands over 40% of ones income in taxes. The farm needs no taxes. Even its Burgesses paid their own way to Williamsburg.

Wolf-city requires giant 747s and thousands of acres of macadam runways. The farm requires ultra-lites or small 4- seaters with an unused pasture to land in.

Wolf-city has crime, pollution, unemployment, race-problems, and moral degenerates. These problems do not exist for the farm.

Wolf-city needs expensive mercenaries to enforce wolf-policy. The farm furnishes its own volunteer militia to enforce the *WORD*.

Wolf-cities' "prison industry" requires billions of dollars to house its millions of inmates. The farm has no prisoners or prison industry. It exercises Biblical "restitution." If one commits a crime such as murder or rape for which there can be no restitution - the offender is put to death. Simple - and cheap.

Wolf-city uses mass media and telecommunication systems to rule the sheep through "monopoly of communication" and "false- witness." In time the sheep will recognize what is being done to them, and when they return to obedience to the *WORD* the Law will be enforced and the sheep will be free. One day the sheep will be supplied with a "still to be invented" handheld phone that can dial any place in the world. The "county news" will once again reappear. Monopoly media will disappear.

The Wolf-city requires that all property be corporate property. The sheep will demand at first that all corporations be turned into partnerships with the workers being the partners. At the last they will demand that corporate property taken by fraudulent usury and war be taken and divided so that new farms can be formed.

Conclusion

God created man in his own image. He gave them The WORD which is God. He made them "kings and priests," and gave them his "power-of-attorney." He warned against "kings" and "levites" who would mislead them.[22] He commanded that the land be divided so that each man would have his own kingdom, and that kingdom was never ever to be sold. He commanded that there be no monopoly. He told them not to allow strangers in their midst *"lest ye learn their ways."*

Man tolerated false-watchmen and surrogate kings. As a consequence our sheepfold has been stormed by the enemy. Worldwide, watchmen and kings stand shoulder to shoulder with the wolf. The individual kingdoms given us by God have been stripped from us and as wage-slaves we have been driven to cities and stockpiled there until needed. The wealth which took four centuries to accumulate has been taken and is being consumed in a feeding frenzy by strangers. Now, even the sweatshops in which we labor are being closed one by one and we are to be left to starve.

22 **GOD'S LAW: "Moses commanded the Levites ... saying, Take this ... law and put it in the side of the ark ... that it may be there for a witness against thee. For I know thy rebellion ... behold, while I am yet alive ... ye have been rebellious against the Lord; and how much more after my death? ... For I know that after my death ye will ... turn aside from the way which I have commanded you." Deut 31: 24-29**

Unless we wish to die we now have no option but to obey our God - The WORD.[23] The factories of today's wolfden cities are being disassembled and taken to alien lands. The cities are dying. Already entire sections lie abandoned and store fronts are boarded up. The unneeded sheep-workers will soon have no food, no safety, no work, no shelter. They will either wander around complaining until they fall dead - or they will again look across the Jordan at the promised land and begin to act like kings and priests and go to work to gain their self-sufficient farm-kingdoms where they can live as kings and priests are supposed to live.

One day the 18-wheelers, the trains, the 747's and the great smokestacks will all stand still in a dead wolfden that has been eaten out. Grass will grow on the great interstates and cattle will graze on deserted air-terminals. The circle of self-sufficient farms will close and the wolf will be excluded to howl outside and plot to re-enter still again. Once more, the farms of the West will sound to the laughter of children and wives will sing as they go about their work. Cottage industries will hum to the sound of industry and country stores will spring up to handle the overflow. The McCormicks will again invent their reapers and the Wright Brothers their flying machines.

The inventions with which God faithfully rewards his obedient children will send the younger sons to new kingdoms among the stars.[24]

23 **GOD's LAW: (1) "Do ye not know that the saints shall judge the world?" 1 Cor 6:2; (2) "Take heed what ye do; for ye judge not for man, but for the Lord, who is with you in the judgment." II Cron 19:6**

24 GOD'S LAW: **(1) "The Lord(s) (wisdom) possessed me in the beginning." Prov 8:22 (2) "I (God's wisdom) find out knowledge of witty inventions." Pr 8:12. (3) "Cast not your pearls before swine, lest they ... turn again and rend you." Matt 7:6**

Index